Suicide Information for Teens

TEEN
HEALTH
SERIES

First Edition

Suicide Information for Teens

Health Tips about Suicide Causes and Prevention

Including Facts about Depression, Risk Factors, Getting Help, Survivor Support, and More

Edited by Joyce Brennfleck Shannon

Omnigraphics

615 Griswold Street • Detroit, MI 48226

Bibliographic Note

Because this page cannot legibly accommodate all the copyright notices, the Bibliographic Note portion of the Preface constitutes an extension of the copyright notice.

Edited by Joyce Brennfleck Shannon

Teen Health Series

Karen Bellenir, *Managing Editor*
David A. Cooke, M.D., *Medical Consultant*
Elizabeth Barbour, *Permissions Associate*
Dawn Matthews, *Verification Assistant*
Laura Pleva Nielsen, *Index Editor*
Laurie Hillstrom, *Indexer*

* * *

Omnigraphics, Inc.

Matthew P. Barbour, *Senior Vice President*
Kay Gill, *Vice President—Directories*
Kevin Hayes, *Operations Manager*
Leif Gruenberg, *Development Manager*
David P. Bianco, *Marketing Consultant*

* * *

Peter E. Ruffner, *Publisher*

Frederick G. Ruffner, Jr., *Chairman*

Copyright © 2005 Omnigraphics, Inc.

ISBN 0-7808-0737-5

Library of Congress Cataloging-in-Publication Data

Suicide information for teens : health tips about suicide causes and
prevention including facts about depression, risk factors, getting help,
survivor support, and more / edited by Joyce Brennfleck Shannon.
    p. cm. -- (Teen health series)
Includes index.
ISBN 0-7808-0737-5 (hardcover : alk. paper)
1. Teenagers--Suicidal behavior--Juvenile literature. 2. Suicidal
behavior--Juvenile literature. 3. Suicide--Prevention--Juvenile literature.
I. Shannon, Joyce Brennfleck. II. Series.
HV6546.S8345 2004
362.28'0835--dc22
                                                                    2004019972

The information in this publication was compiled from the sources cited and from other sources considered reliable. While every possible effort has been made to ensure reliability, the publisher will not assume liability for damages caused by inaccuracies in the data, and makes no warranty, express or implied, on the accuracy of the information contained herein.

This book is printed on acid-free paper meeting the ANSI Z39.48 Standard. The infinity symbol that appears above indicates that the paper in this book meets that standard.

Printed in the United States

Table of Contents

Part I: Basic Information About Suicide

Part II: Mental Health Disorders And Life-Threatening Behaviors That Increase Suicide Risk

Part III: Treatment Options For A Person Thinking Of Suicide

Part IV: Preventing Suicide

Part V: When Someone You Know Dies From Suicide

Part VI: If You Need More Information

Preface

About This Book

Suicide is the third leading cause of death among teens in the United States. According to the U.S. Surgeon General's Office, the incidence of suicide attempts reaches a peak during mid-adolescence, and death from suicide increases steadily through the teen years. Although suicide itself is not defined as a mental disorder, the evidence is strong that more than 90 percent of children and adolescents who commit suicide have an identifiable mental illness. To help prevent suicide, teens need to know how, where, and when to seek support or assistance for themselves or their friends.

Suicide Information For Teens describes suicide risks, causes, and prevention. It provides information about mental health problems and life-threatening behaviors that increase the risk of teen suicide, including depression, bipolar disorder, schizophrenia, post-traumatic stress disorder, self-injury, and alcohol and other drug use. Treatment options, such as counseling, outpatient therapy, and medications, are discussed. Suggestions for coping after a suicide loss are included, and directories of resources, crisis hotlines, and support groups are provided for readers who need more information.

How To Use This Book

This book is divided into parts and chapters. Parts focus on broad areas of interest; chapters are devoted to single topics within a part.

Part I: Basic Information About Suicide discusses why teens consider suicide, the seriousness of suicide threats, and the warning signs and risk factors for teen suicide. Facts, fables, and statistics about suicide in the United States are also presented.

Part II: Mental Health Disorders And Life-Threatening Behaviors That Increase Suicide Risk describes the connection between suicide and depression, bipolar disorder, post-traumatic stress disorder, and schizophrenia. It also includes facts about dangerous behaviors—such as alcohol and drug abuse, eating disorders, and self-injury—and their relationship to suicide risk.

Part III: Treatment For A Person Thinking Of Suicide presents facts about different types of psychotherapy and medications that may be used in the treatment of depression and other mental health disorders.

Par IV: Preventing Suicide discusses ways teens can be involved in saving lives. Topics include responding to friends who are suicidal, tips for coping with stress and anger, and peer education programs.

Part V: When Someone You Know Dies From Suicide offers encouragement for people whose lives have been touched by a suicide loss. It provides information about coping with grief, helping friends, strengthening family relationships, and understanding the risk of post-traumatic stress disorder.

Part VI: If You Need More Information includes directories of national organizations able to provide information about suicide, hotlines for crisis intervention, and support group contacts.

Bibliographic Note

This volume contains documents and excerpts from publications issued by the following government agencies: Centers for Disease Control and Prevention (CDC); National Center for Health Statistics (NCHS); National Center for Post-Traumatic Stress Disorder; National Institute of Mental Health (NIMH); National Institute on Alcohol Abuse and Alcoholism (NIAAA); National Strategy for Suicide Prevention; National Women's Health Information Center; National Youth Violence Prevention Resource Center; Substance Abuse and Mental Health Services Administration (SAMHSA); and the U.S. Food and Drug Administration (FDA).

In addition, this volume contains copyrighted documents and articles produced by the following organizations: American Academy of Child and Adolescent Psychiatry; American Academy of Family Physicians; American Association of Suicidology; American Hospice Foundation; American Psychiatric Association; American Psychiatric Publishing, Inc.; American Psychological Association; CrisisLink; Depression and Bipolar Support Alliance; Do It Now Foundation; Handgun-Free America, Inc.; iEmily.com; *International Herald Tribune/New York Times*; Mental Illness Research, Education, and Clinical Center of the VA Desert Pacific Healthcare Network; Minnesota Prevention Resource Center; National Mental Health Association; Nemours Foundation; Ohio State Research Communications; Screening for Mental Health, Inc.; TeenGrowth.com; United Learning; WebMD Corporation; World Fellowship for Schizophrenia and Allied Disorders; Yellow Ribbon Suicide Prevention Program®; Young Minds; and Katherine Dorn Zotovich.

Full citation information is provided on the first page of each chapter. Every effort has been made to secure all necessary rights to reprint the copyrighted material. If any omissions have been made, please contact Omnigraphics to make corrections for future editions.

Acknowledgements

In addition to the organizations listed above, special thanks are due to permissions associate Elizabeth Barbour and to managing editor Karen Bellenir.

About the *Teen Health Series*

At the request of librarians serving today's young adults, the *Teen Health Series* was developed as a specially focused set of volumes within Omnigraphics' *Health Reference Series*. Each volume deals comprehensively with a topic selected according to the needs and interests of people in middle school and high school.

Teens seeking preventive guidance, information about disease warning signs, medical statistics, and risk factors for health problems will find answers to their questions in the *Teen Health Series*. The *Series*, however, is not intended to serve as a tool for diagnosing illness, in prescribing treatments, or as a substitute for the physician/patient relationship. All people concerned about medical symptoms or the possibility of disease are encouraged to seek professional care from an appropriate health care provider.

If there is a topic you would like to see addressed in a future volume of the *Teen Health Series*, please write to:

Editor
Teen Health Series
Omnigraphics, Inc.
615 Griswold Street
Detroit, MI 48226

Locating Information within the *Teen Health Series*

The *Teen Health Series* contains a wealth of information about a wide variety of medical topics. As the *Series* continues to grow in size and scope, locating the precise information needed by a specific student may become more challenging. To address this concern, information about books within the *Teen Health Series* is included in *A Contents Guide to the Health Reference Series*. The *Contents Guide* presents an extensive list of more than 10,000 diseases, treatments, and other topics of general interest compiled from the Tables of Contents and major index headings from the books of the *Teen Health Series* and *Health Reference Series*. To access *A Contents Guide to the Health Reference Series*, visit www.healthreferenceseries.com.

Our Advisory Board

We would like to thank the following advisory board members for providing guidance to the development of this *Series*:

Dr. Lynda Baker, Associate Professor of Library and Information Science, Wayne State University, Detroit, MI

Nancy Bulgarelli, William Beaumont Hospital Library, Royal Oak, MI

Karen Imarisio, Bloomfield Township Public Library, Bloomfield Township, MI

Karen Morgan, Mardigian Library, University of Michigan-Dearborn, Dearborn, MI

Rosemary Orlando, St. Clair Shores Public Library, St. Clair Shores, MI

Medical Consultant

Medical consultation services are provided to the Teen Health Series editors by David A. Cooke, M.D. Dr. Cooke is a graduate of Brandeis University, and he received his M.D. degree from the University of Michigan. He completed residency training at the University of Wisconsin Hospital and Clinics. He is board-certified in internal medicine. Dr. Cooke currently works as part of the University of Michigan Health System and practices in Brighton, MI. In his free time, he enjoys writing, science fiction, and spending time with his family.

Part One

Basic Information About Suicide

Chapter 1

If You Are Thinking About Suicide...Read This First

What Is Suicide?

Ever had one of those horrible, rotten, terrible, no-good days? It happens to all of us at one time or another. Sometimes when life is hard, it can be tempting to give up. That's a normal feeling, but actively thinking about killing yourself—that is something very different.

Unfortunately, many young people try to kill themselves—and many succeed. Every year, more than 2,000 teenagers commit suicide. That makes suicide the third-leading cause of death among teenagers. What's worse is that the number of suicides among young people is going up.

You may know someone (or of someone) who has tried committing suicide, or even someone who has killed herself. You may have wondered: Why did she do it? What was she thinking that made her want to stop living forever? Why couldn't she see how lucky she was, and how much she had going for her?

These are difficult questions, and they don't have easy answers. But here's an important fact that you should know: Most people who try to kill themselves don't really want to die. That may be hard to believe, but it's true. They do want to live; they just don't want to feel pain anymore.

♣ It's A Fact!!

Help, I Want To Commit Suicide

You feel depressed. The things you used to enjoy doing don't interest you anymore. It seems as though your friends have distanced themselves from you. You get the impression your parents are no longer proud of you because you've made a few mistakes. You've reached the point where you believe you can't take it anymore. You're at the end of your rope and you don't know what to do. You want all the pain to go away and you start to think about suicide.

Stop! You Are Wrong.

Suicide Is Never The Answer!

Suicide is the eighth leading cause of death in the U.S., and the second leading cause of death among young people age 15–19 (after traffic accidents). In addition, for every teenage suicide, there are more than 100 unsuccessful attempts, and copycat suicides spread the tragedy even further.

I'm going through a lot of mood swings and I don't like who I am. Sometimes I think about committing suicide. Why is this happening?

Many adolescents experience mood swings and depression. This is partly related to the biological, developmental, and emotional changes associated with puberty. However, if you are beginning to dislike yourself and feel unworthy of other people's attention, it is time to seek counseling services. Counselors who work with teens are trained to treat exactly the symptoms that you are describing. With help, you will be able to value yourself as the unique person you are, just as your family does.

What kind of pain is so terrible that it would make you want to commit suicide?

Most of the people who want to kill themselves are very sick with depression. Depression is an illness, just like the chicken pox or the flu or asthma. It

I don't want to tell my parents what I'm thinking about. Where do I turn for help?

The first step is realizing you need help. Unfortunately, you're not alone in not wanting to talk to your parents about your emotions. When you're feeling badly about yourself, it can be really hard to let someone else know. But you deserve to get some help. Talk to your doctor, the guidance counselor at school, the school nurse, a teacher you trust, a neighbor, or a religious leader. If it's just too hard to start talking to someone, you could even write a short note, hand it to the person, and wait while he or she reads it.

Calling a hot line would also be beneficial. This gives you the opportunity to talk to someone confidentially while still getting the help you need. The people who answer the calls received through the hot line are trained experts who will listen to your problems. Many times, they will also refer you to local resources, such as a counseling service, that will be able to help you further.

No one will care if I commit suicide. Why shouldn't I do it?

By committing suicide, you don't only hurt yourself; you hurt everyone who loves and cares for you. They are left behind with the question of "why." Why did my daughter kill herself? Why didn't my son talk to me? People do care about you, but they may not be expressing it enough for you to recognize it. That's why it is important to talk to someone about your feelings. When you keep things bottled up, it makes it difficult to see what actually may be happening. You continue to focus on what's bothering you, and before long what may have started as a minor problem has become something painful and intolerable.

You're worth it—talk to someone today.

Source: This information is reprinted with permission from www.Teen Growth.com. © 2004. All rights reserved.

makes you feel sad or angry or blue every day for a couple of weeks or longer. A person who is depressed doesn't think like a typical person who is feeling good.

Sometimes, people who are very depressed remember only their bad times and their disappointments. Imagine how hard it would be to think about all of the things that have gone wrong at school and at home—and nothing else. Imagine if you couldn't remember any of the good times—if you suddenly forgot all your happy memories. That would be very hard. That's what it's like for some people who have serious depression.

But not all people who are suicidal are depressed. Sometimes they have other mood disorders. That's something only a health professional will be able to tell.

Are there any special problems that may put people in danger?

There are a few special problems that could make people who are troubled want to die.

- Teens who have anorexia nervosa or bulimia nervosa are more in danger of killing themselves.

- Teens who have problems with drugs and alcohol are also more in danger of killing themselves. When you drink a lot or take drugs, you often do things that are more dangerous, like drink and drive.

- Some teens who want to kill themselves suffer from psychotic illness. People with this illness often hear voices inside their head that tell them to hurt themselves.

- Teens who have already tried to kill themselves once are much more likely to try it again.

Are there any special situations that may put people in danger?

If one of your parents or another close relative has tried to commit suicide, you may be in more danger of doing the same thing. That could be for a couple of reasons. First, you will have all kinds of powerful feelings—like anger and guilt—when this happens, and it can be hard to deal with those feelings. Second, depression sometimes runs in families, meaning that you could have inherited certain problems that have to do with the chemicals in your brain. If you do have this problem, the suicide of someone you love could make those problems worse.

> ✔ Quick Tip
> # National Suicide Prevention Hot lines
>
> Calling for help is the first step toward feeling better.
>
> **National Adolescent Suicide Hot line**
> Toll-Free: 800-621-4000
>
> **National Suicide Hot line**
> Toll-Free: 888-248-2587
>
> **Hope Line Network**
> Toll-Free: 800-SUICIDE (800-784-2433)
>
> **Access Line**
> Toll-Free: 888-7-we-help (888-793-4357)

If someone you love has died, or if your parents have just gotten separated or divorced, you may feel rejected, worthless, or lonely. If you are already feeling depressed or troubled, an important loss could make you feel as if your life is falling apart. It's not falling apart, but you will need some extra support right now.

If your whole sense of self-worth is based on one thing (like being good at sports) and something goes wrong (like not making the team), at that moment, life may seem not worth living.

Teens who have been abused by their parents or by other people have learned that the world is a scary and unsafe place. It doesn't matter if it's physical, emotional, or sexual abuse. If they already feel like a victim, they may not think it's so bad to hurt themselves, but it would be a terrible thing.

If a teen keeps failing in school, she may suffer from poor self-esteem. She may start thinking, "I'm just too dumb," and stop trying altogether.

Sometimes people who feel that they don't fit in at school or who don't have a lot of friends may be more at risk for suicide. It's hard enough being a teenager, and it's much harder if you don't have good friends to support you through the tough times.

Parents fighting a lot with each other can make someone who is depressed become suicidal. That's because fighting is very stressful, and it usually means that people are not really solving their problems. They're just making them worse. It's hard to learn how to work through your own problems if your parents don't set a good example. You may think the only way out is death. That's not true, of course, but it can sure feel that way if there's a lot of yelling and screaming going on around you, or if nobody is talking at all.

Remember!!

If you are feeling suicidal right now, it's important that you get help right away. Call one of the listed national suicide hot lines. If it feels too difficult for you to call a hot line right now, just call 911 and ask the operator for help.

Sometimes, people who know someone who has committed suicide may be more tempted to try it themselves. So right after you hear about the suicide of a classmate, a neighbor, a friend, or even a celebrity, it's good to pay close attention to your friends who may already be troubled.

Do gay, lesbian, and bisexual teens try to kill themselves more often than heterosexuals?

Some studies have shown that gay, lesbian, and bisexual teens are up to three times more likely to try suicide. This is not because they are gay, of course. It probably is because they have to worry about how the kids in school and our society treat people who are gay. Add that to the usual changes that any teenager goes through, and you have double trouble. So some gay, lesbian, and bisexual teens may try to hide who they are. That's not an easy thing to do if you're around people all day long. It can make you feel ashamed, confused, and like a social outcast. That can be very hard on your self-esteem, which makes it harder to battle things like depression.

Additional Information

iEmily.com
Website: http://www.iemily.com

iEmily.com is a health website that provides teens with respectful, in-depth information about physical health and emotional well-being. The site includes articles reviewed by physicians, psychologists, and educators on nutrition, physical fitness, sexual health, emotional and psychological concerns, and other topics. iEmily.com also offers links to websites for additional information, as well as a list of hot lines for immediate help.

TeenGrowth.com
Website: http://www.TeenGrowth.com

TeenGrowth is a website tailored toward the health interests and general well-being of the teenage population. It offers health care information on topics such as alcohol, drugs, emotions, health, family, friends, school, sex, and sports.

Chapter 2

Suicide Threats: When Are They Serious?

Every year there are tragedies in which teens shoot and kill individuals after making threats. When this occurs, everyone asks themselves, "How could this happen?" and "Why didn't we take the threat seriously?"

Most threats made by children or adolescents are not carried out. Many such threats are the teen's way of talking big or tough, or getting attention. Sometimes these threats are a reaction to a perceived hurt, rejection, or attack.

What threats should be taken seriously?

Examples of potentially dangerous or emergency situations with a child or adolescent include:

- threats or warnings about hurting or killing someone
- threats or warnings about hurting or killing oneself
- threats to run away from home
- threats to damage or destroy property

Child and adolescent psychiatrists and other mental health professionals agree that it is very difficult to predict a person's future behavior with complete accuracy. A person's past behavior, however, is still one of the best predictors of future behavior. For example, a teen with a history of violent or assaultive behavior is more likely to carry out his/her threats and be violent.

When is there more risk associated with threats from children and adolescents?

The presence of one or more of the following increases the risk of violent or dangerous behavior:

- past violent or aggressive behavior (including uncontrollable angry outbursts)

- access to guns or other weapons

- bringing a weapon to school

- past suicide attempts or threats

- family history of violent behavior or suicide attempts

- blaming others and/or unwilling to accept responsibility for one's own actions

- recent experience of humiliation, shame, loss, or rejection

> ✔ **Quick Tip**
>
> **Should all suicide threats be taken seriously?**
>
> Yes. Because so many young people are impulsive, threats of suicide should always be taken seriously. Suicide is one case where it's better to guess wrong about someone's intentions than to stay silent.
>
> It's a myth that people who talk about suicide don't do it. They do. And you won't plant a seed in the person's mind that they wouldn't have planted themselves. Suicidal people are stressed and depressed, not stupid. They're capable of thinking of suicide all by themselves. So don't worry about putting ideas into their heads. If the ideas are there, they need to be talked about and dealt with. If they're not there, they won't take root simply because you mention them.
>
> Source: Excerpted with permission from "Teen & Young Adult Suicide, Light & Shadows," by Nancy Merritt. © 2002 Do It Now Foundation. All rights reserved. The mission of the Do It Now Foundation is to distribute accurate, creative, and realistic information about drugs, alcohol, sexuality, and other behavioral health topics to youth. For additional information, visit the Do It Now Foundation website at http://www.doitnow.org.

- bullying or intimidating peers or younger children

- a pattern of threats

- being a victim of abuse or neglect (physical, sexual, or emotional)

- witnessing abuse or violence in the home

- themes of death or depression repeatedly evident in conversation, written expressions, reading selections, or artwork

✎ **Weird Word**

Psychiatrist: A medical doctor with five years of additional training who specializes in the diagnosis and treatment of mental disorders.

- preoccupation with themes and acts of violence in TV shows, movies, music, magazines, comics, books, video games, and Internet sites

- mental illness, such as depression, mania, psychosis, or bipolar disorder

- use of alcohol or illicit drugs

- disciplinary problems at school or in the community (delinquent behavior)

- past destruction of property or vandalism

- cruelty to animals

- fire-setting behavior

- poor peer relationships and/or social isolation

- involvement with cults or gangs

- little or no supervision or support from parents or other caring adult

What should be done if parents or others are concerned?

When an adolescent makes a serious threat it should not be dismissed as just idle talk. Parents, teachers, or other adults should immediately talk with the teen. If it is determined that the teen is at risk and the teen refuses to talk, is argumentative, responds defensively, or continues to express violent or dangerous thoughts or plans, arrangements should be made for an immediate evaluation by a mental health professional with experience evaluating children and adolescents. Evaluation of any serious threat must be done in the context of the individual teen's past behavior, personality, and current stressors. In an emergency situation or if the teen or family refuses help, it may be necessary to contact local police for assistance or take the adolescent to the nearest emergency room for evaluation. Teens who have made serious threats must be carefully supervised while awaiting professional intervention. Immediate evaluation and appropriate ongoing treatment of adolescents who make serious threats can help the troubled teen and reduce the risk of tragedy.

 Remember!!

Any threats that mention hurting, killing, or committing suicide must always be taken seriously.

Chapter 3

In Harm's Way: Suicide In America

Suicide is a tragic and potentially preventable public health problem. In 2000, suicide was the 11th leading cause of death in the U.S.[1] Specifically, 10.6 out of every 100,000 persons died by suicide. The total number of suicides was 29,350 or 1.2 percent of all deaths. Suicide deaths outnumber homicide deaths by five to three. It has been estimated that there may be from eight to 25 attempted suicides per every one suicide death.[2] The alarming numbers of suicide deaths and attempts emphasize the need for carefully designed prevention efforts.

Suicidal behavior is complex. Some risk factors vary with age, gender, and ethnic group and may even change over time. The risk factors for suicide frequently occur in combination. Research has shown that more than 90 percent of people who kill themselves have depression or another diagnosable mental or substance abuse disorder, often in combination with other mental disorders.[2, 3] Also, research indicates that alterations in neurotransmitters such as serotonin are associated with the risk for suicide.[4] Diminished levels of this brain chemical have been found in patients with depression, impulsive disorders, a history of violent suicide attempts, and also in post-mortem brains of suicide victims.

About This Chapter: Text in this chapter is from "In Harm's Way: Suicide in America," National Institute of Mental Health, NIH Publication No. 03-4594, revised April 2003.

♣ It's A Fact!!

Suicide: Cost To The Nation

- Suicide takes the lives of more than 30,000 Americans every year.

- Every 18 minutes another life is lost to suicide.

- Every day 80 Americans take their own lives and over 1,900 Americans visit emergency departments for self-inflicted injury (National Hospital Ambulatory Medical Care Survey, total 706,000).

- Suicide is now the 11th leading cause of death in Americans.

- For every two victims of homicide in the U.S., there are three persons who take their own lives.

- There are now twice as many deaths due to suicide as to HIV/AIDS.

- Between 1952 and 1995, the incidence of suicide among adolescents and young adults nearly tripled.

- In the month prior to their suicide, 75% of elderly persons had visited a physician.

- Over half of all suicides occur in adult men, aged 25–65.

- Many who attempt suicide never seek professional care.

- Males are four times more likely to die from suicide than are females.

- More teenagers and young adults die from suicide than from cancer, heart disease, AIDS, birth defects, stroke, pneumonia and influenza, and chronic lung disease, combined.

Source: National Strategy for Suicide Prevention (NSSP), 2001.

Adverse life events in combination with other risk factors such as depression may lead to suicide. However, suicide and suicidal behavior are not normal responses to stress. Many people have one or more risk factors and are not suicidal. Other risk factors include: prior suicide attempt; family history of mental disorder or substance abuse; family history of suicide; family violence, including physical or sexual abuse; firearms in the home; incarceration; and exposure to the suicidal behavior of others, including family members, peers, or even in the media.[2]

Gender Differences

Suicide was the 8th leading cause of death for males and the 19th leading cause of death for females in 2000.[1] More than four times as many men as women die by suicide,[1] although women report attempting suicide during their lifetime about three times as often as men.[5] Suicide by firearm is the most common method for both men and women, accounting for 57 percent of all suicides in 2000. White men accounted for 73 percent of all suicides and 80 percent of all firearm suicides.

Children, Adolescents, And Young Adults

In 2000, suicide was the 3rd leading cause of death among 15- to 24-year-olds—10.4 of every 100,000 persons in this age group—following unintentional injuries and homicide. Suicide was also the 3rd leading cause of death among children ages 10 to 14, with a rate of 1.5 per 100,000 children in this age group. The suicide rate for adolescents ages 15 to 19 was 8.2 deaths per 100,000 teenagers, including five times as many males as females. Among people 20 to 24 years of age, the suicide rate was 12.8 per 100,000 young adults, with seven times as many deaths among men as among women.[1, 6]

Older Adults

Older adults are disproportionately likely to die by suicide. Comprising only 13 percent of the U.S. population, individuals age 65 and older accounted for 18 percent of all suicide deaths in 2000. Among the highest rates (when categorized by gender and race) were white men age 85 and older with 59 deaths per 100,000 persons, more than five times the national U.S. rate of 10.6 per 100,000.[1, 6]

Attempted Suicides

Overall, there may be between eight and twenty-five attempted suicides for every suicide death; the ratio is higher in women and youth and lower in men and the elderly.[2] Risk factors for attempted suicide in adults include depression,

---

♣ It's A Fact!!

Guns And Suicide

200 million guns are presently in the hands of Americans, which is more than twice the number held in 1969. Contrary to what most people think, the majority of all firearms-related fatalities in the United States are in fact due to suicide and not homicide.[1] In 1998 alone, 30,575 Americans committed suicide.[2] Much of this unbelievably high suicide rate is due to the overwhelming prevalence of firearms—and handguns in particular. Roughly 60% of all suicides are committed using a firearm, and roughly 40% of all suicides are committed using handguns.[3] With so many firearms available, handguns have clearly become the method of choice for suicide. Several studies have found that states with stricter gun control laws have lower total suicide rates, a fact that speaks heavily on the need to reduce the availability of handguns in the U.S.

Did You Know?

- Firearm suicide attempts result in death in approximately 85% of cases.[11]

- Overall, suicide is the eighth leading cause of death for all Americans.

Suicide has had an enormous impact on American society. Every year, tens of thousands of individuals commit suicide using a gun. In 1998, for example, 17,424 people in America committed suicide using a gun.[4] That is almost 50 people every single day! In addition, the number of children who use firearms to commit suicide in America is alarming. In 1998, for example, 1,200 children between 10 and 19 years old committed suicide using a firearm—a whopping one suicide every seven hours.[5] Despite the fact that most gun owners keep

alcohol abuse, cocaine use, and separation or divorce.[7, 8] Risk factors for attempted suicide in youth include depression, alcohol or other drug use disorder, physical or sexual abuse, and disruptive behavior.[8, 9] As with people who die by suicide, many people who make serious suicide attempts have co-occurring mental or substance abuse disorders. The majority of suicide attempts are expressions of extreme distress and not just harmless bids for attention. A suicidal person should not be left alone and needs immediate mental health treatment.

firearms in their home under the pretense of protection and self-defense, amazingly, only 2% of gun related deaths in the home are the result of a homeowner shooting an intruder, while 3% are accidental child shootings, 12% are the result of shootings by a family member or other intimate, and a staggering 83% are the result of a suicide.

Suicide has also become an enormous problem among the elderly. According to the CDC, one older adult commits suicide every 90 minutes.[6] Of all firearm-related injuries involving people 65 or older, 78% are intentionally self-inflicted gunshot wounds.[7] White males aged 85 and older account for the highest rate of suicide by firearms (49 per 100,000).[8]

Suicide is a very impulsive act, and the easier it is to do, the more it will be done. The easy access to firearms—and to handguns in particular—means that the rate of fatal suicide attempts in the United States is extremely high. In fact, it often takes less than 5 minutes from the time a person considers committing suicide until the time they attempt suicide. If they are able to access a gun within this 5 minute period, the chances of a fatal suicide attempt will be significantly higher. According to recent data, suicide attempts by drug overdose have a 20% chance of being fatal, while suicide attempts with a gun have a fatality rate of more than 90%.

While waiting periods for firearm purchases have reduced the ease of obtaining a weapon for the purposes of committing suicide, these laws cannot do anything to prevent people who already have access to firearms from committing

continued

Prevention

Preventive efforts to reduce suicide should be based on research that shows which risk and protective factors can be modified, as well as which groups of people are appropriate for the intervention. In addition, prevention programs must be carefully tested to determine if they are safe, truly effective, and worth the considerable cost and effort needed to implement and sustain them.[10]

---

continued from previous page

suicide. In roughly 90% of cases of suicide involving a firearm, the firearm used was one that was already owned or available to the individual. Only 10% of all firearms used in suicides were purchased specifically for the purpose of committing suicide.[9] In fact, simply having access to a firearm increases your chances of committing suicide. A person who lives in a home with a gun is five times more likely to commit suicide than a person who lives in a home without a gun.[10]

What Can We Do?

If we are going to successfully decrease the rate of suicide in the United States, one of the most effective steps we can take is to decrease the overall access to firearms by prohibiting private ownership of handguns.

References

1. Hoyert, DL, Kochanek, KD, et al. *Deaths: Final Data for 1997*. National Vital Statistics Report. 1999.

2. National Center for Injury Prevention and Control. *Injury Fact Book 2001–2002*. Atlanta, GA: Centers for Disease Control and Prevention; 2001.

3. CDC National Center for Injury Prevention and Control Fact Sheet. "Suicide in the United States," and, Wintemute, GJ, Teret, SP, et al. "The Choice of Weapons in Firearm Suicides." *American Journal of Public Health*. Vol. 78, No. 7. 1988. PP. 824-826.

4. Centers for Disease Control and Prevention. National Center for Health Statistics.

Many interventions designed to reduce suicide also include the treatment of mental and substance abuse disorders. Because older adults, as well as women who die by suicide, are likely to have seen a primary care provider in the year prior to their suicide, improving the recognition and treatment of mental disorders and other suicide risk factors in primary care settings may be one avenue to prevent suicides among these groups.[11] Improving outreach to men at risk for suicide is a major challenge in need of investigation.

5. Centers for Disease Control and Prevention. National Center for Health Statistics.

6. National Center for Injury Prevention and Control. *Injury Fact Book 2001–2002*. Atlanta, GA: Centers for Disease Control and Prevention; 2001.

7. "Surveillance for Fatal and Nonfatal Firearm-Related Injuries—United States, 1993-1998." *Morbidity and Mortality Weekly Report*. Centers for Disease Control and Prevention. CDC Surveillance Summaries. Vol. 50, No. SS-2. April 13, 2001.

8. *CDC: National Vital Statistics Report*, Vol. 47, No. 9, 1998; p.68.

9. Myron Boor. "Methods of Suicide and Implications for Suicide Prevention." *Journal of Clinical Psychology*. Vol. 37, January 1981. PP. 70-75.

10. Kellerman, AL, Rivera, FP, et al. "Suicide in the Home in Relation to Gun Ownership." *New England Journal of Medicine*. Vol. 314, No. 24. 1986. PP. 1557-1560.

11. National Institute of Justice. Research in Brief, May 1997, Washington, D.C.; U.S. Department of Justice.

Recently, the manufacturer of the medication clozapine received the first ever Food and Drug Administration indication for effectiveness in preventing suicide attempts among persons with schizophrenia.[12] Additional promising pharmacologic and psychosocial treatments for suicidal individuals are currently being tested.

References

1. Miniño AM, Arias E, Kochanek KD, Murphy SL, Smith BL. Deaths: final data for 2000. *National Vital Statistics Reports*, 50(15). Hyattsville, MD: National Center for Health Statistics, 2002.

2. Moscicki EK. Epidemiology of completed and attempted suicide: toward a framework for prevention. *Clinical Neuroscience Research*, 2001; 1: 310-23.

3. Conwell Y, Brent D. Suicide and aging. I: patterns of psychiatric diagnosis. *International Psychogeriatrics*, 1995; 7(2): 149-64.

4. Mann JJ, Oquendo M, Underwood MD, Arango V. The neurobiology of suicide risk: a review for the clinician. *Journal of Clinical Psychiatry*, 1999; 60(Suppl 2): 7-11; discussion 18-20, 113-6.

5. Weissman MM, Bland RC, Canino GJ, Greenwald S, Hwu HG, Joyce PR, Karam EG, Lee CK, Lellouch J, Lepine JP, Newman SC, Rubio-Stipec M, Wells JE, Wickramaratne PJ, Wittchen HU, Yeh EK. Prevalence of suicide ideation and suicide attempts in nine countries. *Psychological Medicine*, 1999; 29(1): 9-17.

6. Office of Statistics and Programming, NCIPC, CDC. Web-based Injury Statistics Query and Reporting System (WISQARSTM): http://www.cdc.gov/ncipc/wisqars/default.htm.

7. Kessler RC, Borges G, Walters EE. Prevalence of and risk factors for lifetime suicide attempts in the National Comorbidity Survey. *Archives of General Psychiatry*, 1999; 56(7): 617-26.

8. Petronis KR, Samuels JF, Moscicki EK, Anthony JC. An epidemiologic investigation of potential risk factors for suicide attempts. *Social Psychiatry and Psychiatric Epidemiology*, 1990; 25(4): 193-9.

9. Gould MS, Greenberg T, Velting DM, Shaffer D. Youth suicide risk and preventive interventions: a review of the past 10 years. *Journal of the American Academy of Child and Adolescent Psychiatry*, 2003; 42(4): 386-405.

10. U.S. Public Health Service. *National strategy for suicide prevention: goals and objectives for action*. Rockville, MD: USDHHS, 2001.

11. Luoma JB, Pearson JL, Martin CE. Contact with mental health and primary care prior to suicide: a review of the evidence. *American Journal of Psychiatry*, 2002; 159: 909-16.

12. Meltzer HY, Alphs L, Green AI, Altamura AC, Anand R, Bertoldi A, Bourgeois M, Chouinard G, Islam MZ, Kane J, Krishnan R, Lindenmayer JP, Potkin S; International Suicide Prevention Trial Study Group. Clozapine treatment for suicidality in schizophrenia: International Suicide Prevention Trial (InterSePT). *Archives of General Psychiatry*, 2003; 60(1): 82-91.

For More Information

National Institute of Mental Health (NIMH)
6001 Executive Blvd., Rm. 8184, MSC 9663
Bethesda, MD 20892-9663
Toll-Free: 866-615-6464
Phone: 301-443-4513
Fax: 301-443-4279
TTY: 301-443-8431
Website: http://www.nimh.nih.gov
E-mail: nimhinfo@nih.gov

American Association of Suicidology
4201 Connecticut Ave., NW, Suite 408
Washington DC 20008
Phone: 202-237-2280
Website: http://www.suicidology.org
E-mail: info@suicidology.org

National Hopeline Network
Toll-Free 24-hour crisis hot line: 1-800-SUICIDE (1-800-784-2433)
Website: http://suicidehot lines.com

☞   Remember!!

If someone is suicidal, he or
she must not be left alone. Try to get
the person to seek help immediately from
his or her doctor or the nearest hospital emergency room, or call 911. It is also important
to limit the person's access to firearms,
medications, or other lethal
methods for suicide.

Chapter 4

Teen Suicide

Teen suicide is becoming more common every year in the United States. In fact, only car accidents and homicides (murders) kill more people between the ages of 15 and 24, making suicide the third leading cause of death in teens and overall in youths ages 10 to 19 years old.

Read on to learn more about this serious issue—including what causes a person to consider taking their own life, what puts a teen at risk for suicide or self-harm, and warning signs that someone might be considering suicide and how they can get help to find other solutions.

Thinking About Suicide

It's common for teens to think about death to some degree. Teens' thinking capabilities have matured in a way that allows them to think more deeply—about their existence in the world, the meaning of life, and other profound questions and ideas. Unlike kids, teens realize that death is permanent. They may begin to consider spiritual or philosophical questions such as what happens after people die. To some, death, and even suicide, may seem poetic

About This Chapter: This information was provided by TeensHealth, one of the largest resources online for medically reviewed health information written for parents, kids, and teens. For more articles like this one, visit www.TeensHealth.org, or www.KidsHealth.org. © 2002 The Nemours Center for Children's Health Media, a division of The Nemours Foundation.

(consider Romeo and Juliet, for example). To others, death may seem frightening or be a source of worry. For many, death is mysterious and beyond our human experience and understanding.

Thinking about suicide goes beyond normal ideas teens may have about death and life. Wishing to be dead, thinking about suicide, or feeling helpless and hopeless about how to solve life's problems are signs that a teen may be at risk—and in need of help and support. Beyond thoughts of suicide, actually making a plan or carrying out a suicide attempt is even more serious.

What makes some teens begin to think about suicide—and even worse, to plan or do something with the intention of ending their own lives? One of the biggest factors is depression. Suicide attempts are usually made when a person is seriously depressed or upset. A teen who is feeling suicidal may see no other way out of problems, no other escape from emotional pain, or no other way to communicate their desperate unhappiness.

The Link Between Depression And Suicide

The majority of suicide attempts and suicide deaths happen among teens with depression. Consider these statistics about teen suicide and teen depression: about 1% of all teens attempts suicide and about 1% of those suicide attempts results in death (that means about 1 in 10,000 teens dies from suicide). But for adolescents who have depressive illnesses, the rates of suicidal thinking and behavior are much higher. Most teens who have depression think about suicide, and between 15% and 30% of teens with serious depression who think about suicide go on to make a suicide attempt.

Keep in mind that most of the time for most teens depression is a passing mood. The sadness, loneliness, grief, and disappointment we all feel at times are normal reactions to some of the struggles of life. With the right support, some resilience, an inner belief that there will be a brighter day, and decent coping skills, most teens can get through the depressed mood that happens occasionally when life throws them a curve ball.

But sometimes depression doesn't lift after a few hours or a few days. Instead it lasts, and it can seem too heavy to bear. When someone has a depressed or sad mood that is intense and lingers almost all day, almost every day for 2 weeks or more, it may be a sign that the person has developed major depression. Major depression, sometimes called clinical depression, is beyond a passing depressed mood—it is the term mental health professionals use for depression that has become an illness in need of treatment. Another form of serious depression is called bipolar disorder, which includes extreme low moods (major depression) as well as extreme high moods (these are called manic episodes).

Though children can experience depression, too, teens are much more vulnerable to major depression and bipolar illness. Hormones and sleep cycles, which both change dramatically during adolescence, have an effect on mood and may partly explain why teens (especially girls) are particularly prone to depression. Believe it or not, as many as 20% of all teens have had depression that's this severe at some point. The good news is that depression is treatable—most teens get better with the right help.

✔ Quick Tip

Depression is a treatable illness. Most people get well with the right help.

It's not hard to see why serious depression and suicide are connected. Serious depression (with both major depression and bipolar illness) involves a long-lasting sad mood that doesn't let up, and a loss of pleasure in things you once enjoyed. It also involves thoughts about death, negative thoughts about oneself, a sense of worthlessness, a sense of hopelessness that things could get better, low energy, and noticeable changes in appetite or sleep.

Depression also distorts a person's viewpoint, allowing them to focus only on their failures and disappointments and to exaggerate these negative things. Depressed thinking can convince someone there is nothing to live for. The loss of pleasure that is part of depression can seem like further evidence that there's nothing good about the present. The hopelessness can make it seem like there will be nothing good in the future; helplessness can make it seem like there's nothing you can do to change things for the better. And the low energy that is part of depression can make every problem (even small ones) seem like too much to handle.

When major depression lifts because a person gets the proper therapy or treatment, this distorted thinking is cleared and they can find pleasure, energy, and hope again. But while someone is seriously depressed, suicidal thinking is a real concern. When teens are depressed, they often don't realize that the hopelessness they feel can be relieved and that hurt and despair can be healed.

What Else Puts Teens At Risk For Suicide?

In addition to depression, there are other emotional conditions that can put teens at greater risk for suicide—for example, girls and guys with conduct disorder are at higher risk. This may be partly because teens with conduct disorder have problems with aggression and may be more likely than other teens to act in aggressive or impulsive ways to hurt themselves when they are depressed or under great stress. The fact that many teens with conduct disorder also have depression may partly explain this, too. Having both serious depression and conduct disorder increases a teen's risk for suicide.

Substance abuse problems also put teens at risk for suicidal thinking and behavior. Alcohol and some drugs have depressive effects on the brain. Misuse of these substances can bring on serious depression, especially in teens prone to depression because of their biology, family history, or other life stressors.

Besides depressive effects, alcohol and drugs alter a person's judgment. They interfere with the ability to assess risk, make good choices, and think of solutions to problems. Many suicide attempts occur when a teen is under the influence of alcohol or drugs. Teens with substance abuse problems often have serious depression or intense life stresses, too, further increasing their risk.

Life Stress And Suicidal Behavior

Let's face it—being a teen is not easy for anyone. There are many new social, academic, and personal pressures. And for teens who have additional problems to deal with, life can feel even more difficult.

Some teens have been physically or sexually abused, have witnessed one parent abusing another at home, or live with lots of arguing and conflict at home. Others witness violence in their neighborhoods. Many teens have parents who divorce, and others may have a parent with a drug or alcohol addiction. Some teens are struggling with concerns about sexuality and relationships, wondering if their feelings and attractions are normal, if they will be loved and accepted, or if their changing bodies are developing normally. Others struggle with body image and eating problems, finding it impossible to reach a perfect ideal, and therefore having trouble feeling good about themselves. Some teens have learning problems or attention problems that make it hard for them to succeed in school. They may feel disappointed in themselves or feel they are a disappointment to others.

All these things can affect mood and cause some people to feel depressed or to turn to alcohol or drugs for a false sense of soothing. Without the necessary coping skills or support, these social stresses can increase the risk of serious depression, and therefore, of suicidal ideas and behavior. Teens who have had a recent loss or crisis or who had a family member who committed suicide may be especially vulnerable to suicidal thinking and behavior themselves.

Guns And Suicide Risk

Finally, having access to guns is extremely risky for any teen who has any of the other risk factors. Depression, anger, impulsivity, life stress, substance abuse, feelings of alienation or loneliness—all these factors can place a teen at major risk for suicidal thoughts and behavior. Availability of guns along with one or more of these risk factors is a deadly equation. Many teen lives could be saved by making sure those who are at risk don't have access to guns.

Different Types Of Suicidal Behaviors

Teen girls attempt suicide far more often (about nine times more often) than teen guys, but guys are about four times more likely to succeed when they try to kill themselves. This is because teen guys tend to use more deadly methods, like guns or hanging. Girls who try to hurt or kill themselves tend to use overdoses of medications or cutting. More than 60% of teen suicide deaths happen with a gun. But suicide deaths can and do occur with pills and other harmful substances and methods.

Sometimes a depressed person plans a suicide in advance. Many times, though, suicide attempts are not planned in advance, but happen impulsively, in a moment of feeling desperately upset. Sometimes a situation like a breakup, a big fight with a parent, an unintended pregnancy, being harmed by abuse or rape, being outed by someone else, or being victimized in any way can cause a teen to feel desperately upset. In situations such as these, teens may fear humiliation, rejection, social isolation, or some terrible consequence they think they can't handle. If a terrible situation feels too overwhelming, a teen may feel that there is no way out of the bad feeling or the consequences of the situation. Suicide attempts can occur under conditions like this because, in desperation, some teens—at least for the moment—see no other way out and they impulsively act against themselves.

Sometimes teens who feel or act suicidal mean to die and sometimes they don't. Sometimes a suicide attempt is a way to express the deep emotional pain they're feeling in hopes that someone will get the message they are trying to communicate.

Even though a teen who makes a suicide attempt may not actually want or intend to die, it is impossible to know whether an overdose or other harmful action they may take will actually result in death or cause a serious and lasting illness that was never intended. Using a suicide attempt to get someone's attention or love or to punish someone for hurt they've caused is never a good idea. People usually don't really get the message, and it often backfires on the teen. It's better to learn other ways to get what you need and deserve from people. There are always people who will value, respect, and love you—sure, sometimes it takes time to find them—but it is important to value, respect, and love yourself, too.

Unfortunately, teens who attempt suicide as an answer to problems tend to try it more than once. Though some depressed teens may first attempt suicide around age 13 or 14, suicide attempts are highest during middle adolescence. Then by about age 17 or 18, the rate of teen suicide attempts lowers dramatically. This may be because with maturity, teens have learned to tolerate sad or upset moods, have learned how to get support they need and deserve, and have developed better coping skills to deal with disappointment or other difficulties.

Warning Signs—What To Look For

Many times, there are warning signs that someone is seriously depressed and may be thinking about or planning a suicide attempt. Here are some of them:

- pulling away from friends or family and losing desire to go out

- trouble concentrating or thinking clearly

- changes in eating or sleeping habits

- major changes in appearance (for example, if a normally neat person looks very sloppy—as if they're not taking the usual care of themselves)

- talk about feeling hopeless or feeling guilty

- talk about suicide

- talk about death

- talk about "going away"

- self-destructive behavior (drinking alcohol, taking drugs, or driving too fast, for example)

- no desire to take part in favorite things or activities

- the giving away of favorite possessions (like offering to give away a favorite piece of jewelry, for example)

- suddenly very happy and cheerful moods after being depressed or sad for a long time (this may mean that a person has decided to attempt suicide and feels relieved to have found a "solution")

♣ It's A Fact!!
Teen binge drinking episodes frequently precede serious suicide attempts.

Paying attention to and responding to these clues can sometimes save a life and prevent a tragedy. Most of the time, teens who are considering suicide are willing to discuss it if someone asks them out of concern and care. Some people (teens and adults) are reluctant to ask teens if they have been thinking about suicide or hurting themselves for fear that, by asking, they may plant the idea of suicide. This is a myth. It is always a good thing to ask and to initiate the conversation with someone you think may be considering suicide. First, it allows you to get help for the person. Second, just talking about it may help the person to feel less alone, less isolated, more cared about and understood—the opposite of many feelings that may have led to suicidal thinking to begin with. Third, it may give the person an opportunity to consider that there may be another solution.

Sometimes, a specific event, stress, or crisis can trigger suicidal behavior in someone who's at risk. Common triggers are a parent's divorce, a breakup with a boyfriend or girlfriend, or the death of a friend or relative, for example. It's always good to ask a friend who's going through a crisis how they're doing, if they're getting any support, how they're coping, and if they need some more support. There are plenty of adults who can help you or a friend find the support you need. Everyone deserves that support.

Sometimes, teens who make a suicide attempt—or who die as a result of suicide—seem to give no clue beforehand. This can leave loved ones feeling not only grief stricken, but guilty and wondering if they missed something. It is important for family members and friends of those who die by suicide to know that sometimes there is no warning and they should not blame themselves.

Getting Help

If you have been thinking about suicide, get help right away, rather than simply hoping your mood might improve. When a person has been feeling down for so long, it's hard for him to understand that suicide isn't the answer—it's a permanent solution to a temporary problem. Talk to anyone you know as soon as you can—a friend, a coach, a relative, a school counselor, a religious leader, a teacher, or any trusted adult. Call your local emergency number or check in the front pages of your phone book for the number of a local suicide crisis line. These toll-free lines are staffed 24 hours a day, 7 days a week by trained professionals who can help you without ever knowing your name or seeing your face. All calls are confidential—nothing is written down and no one you know will ever find out that you've called. There is also a National Suicide Helpline—1-800-SUICIDE.

If you have a friend or classmate who you think is considering suicide, get help right away rather than waiting to see if he will feel better. Even if your friend or classmate swears you to secrecy, you must get help as soon as possible—your friend's life could depend on it. A person who is seriously thinking about suicide is depressed—and isn't able to see that suicide is never the answer to his problems.

Although it is never your job to single-handedly prevent your friend from attempting suicide, you can help by first reassuring your friend, then going to a trusted adult as soon as possible. If necessary, you can call your local emergency number or the toll-free number of the National Suicide Helpline— 1-800-SUICIDE. However you go about finding assistance for your friend, you must involve an adult—even if you think you can handle your friend on your own, this may not be the case.

After Suicide

Sometimes even if you get help and adults intervene, a friend or class-mate may attempt or commit suicide. When this happens, it's common to have many different emotions. Some teens say they feel guilty—especially if they felt they could have inter-preted their friend's actions and words better. Others say they feel angry with the person who com-mitted or attempted suicide for doing something so selfish. Still others say they feel nothing at all— they are too filled with grief. When someone attempts suicide, the people around him may feel afraid or uncomfortable about talking with him about it. Try to resist this urge; this is a time when a person absolutely needs to feel connected to others.

> 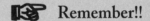 **Remember!!**
>
> Help is available for depression and other problems. Suicide is never the answer to a problem.

When someone commits suicide, the people around him may become very depressed and even think about suicide themselves. It's important to know that you should never blame yourself for someone's death—you could question yourself forever, which will only make you unhappy and won't bring your friend back. It's also good to know that any emotion you feel is appropriate; there is no right or wrong way to feel. Many schools will address the problem of a student's suicide head-on and call in special counselors to talk with students and help them deal with their feelings. If you are having difficulty dealing with a friend or classmate's suicide, it's best to make use of these resources or talk to an adult you trust. Feeling grief after a friend commits suicide is normal; it's when it begins to interfere with your everyday life that you may need to speak with someone about your feelings.

Chapter 5

Frequently Asked Questions About Suicide

What should you do if someone tells you they are thinking about suicide?

If someone tells you they are thinking about suicide, you should take their distress seriously, listen without judging, and help them get to a professional for evaluation and treatment. People consider suicide when they are hopeless and unable to see alternative solutions to problems. Suicidal behavior is most often related to a mental disorder (depression) or to alcohol or other substance abuse. Suicidal behavior is also more likely to occur when people experience stressful events (death, loss of a job, being in jail).

What are the most common methods of suicide?

Firearms are the most commonly used method of suicide for men and women, accounting for 60 percent of all suicides. Nearly 80 percent of all firearm suicides are committed by white males. The second most common method for men is hanging; for women, the second most common method is self-poisoning including drug overdose. The presence of a firearm in the home has been found to be an independent, additional risk factor for suicide. Thus, when a family member or health care provider is faced with an individual at risk for suicide, they should make sure that firearms are removed from the home.

About This Chapter: Text in this chapter is from "Frequently Asked Questions about Suicide," National Institute of Mental Health (NIMH), updated January 2000.

Why do men commit suicide more often than women do?

More than four times as many men as women die by suicide; but women attempt suicide more often during their lives than do men, and women report higher rates of depression. Men and women use different suicide methods. Women in all countries are more likely to ingest poisons than men. In countries where the poisons are highly lethal and/ or where treatment resources scarce, rescue is rare and hence female suicides outnumber males.

> **✔ Quick Tip**
>
> If someone is in danger of harming himself or herself:
>
> • do not leave the person alone,
>
> • get help, call 911 if necessary, and
>
> • limit access to guns or other means of committing suicide.

Who is at highest risk for suicide in the U.S.?

There is a common perception that suicide rates are highest among the young. However, it is the elderly, particularly older white males that have the highest rates. And among white males 65 and older, risk goes up with age. White men 85 and older have a suicide rate that is six times that of the overall national rate. Some older persons are less likely to survive attempts because they are less likely to recuperate. Over 70 percent of older suicide victims have been to their primary care physician within the month of their death, many did not tell their doctors they were depressed nor did the doctor detect it. This has led to research efforts to determine how to best improve physicians' abilities to detect and treat depression in older adults.

Are gay and lesbian youth at high risk for suicide?

With regard to completed suicide, there are no national statistics for suicide rates among gay, lesbian, or bisexual (GLB) persons. Sexual orientation is not a question on the death certificate, and to determine whether rates are higher for GLB persons, we would need to know the proportion of the U.S. population that considers themselves gay, lesbian, or bisexual. Sexual orientation is a personal characteristic that people can, and often do choose to hide, so that in psychological autopsy studies of suicide victims where risk factors are examined, it is difficult to know for certain the victim's sexual orientation. This is particularly a problem when considering GLB youth who may be less certain of their sexual orientation and less open. In the few studies examining risk factors for suicide where sexual orientation was assessed, the risk for gay or lesbian persons did not appear any greater than among heterosexuals, once mental and substance abuse disorders were taken into account.

With regard to suicide attempts, several state and national studies have reported that high school students who report to be homosexually and bisexually active have higher rates of suicide thoughts and attempts in the past year compared to youth with heterosexual experience. Experts have not been in complete agreement about the best way to measure reports of adolescent suicide attempts, or sexual orientation, so the data are subject to question. But they do agree that efforts should focus on how to help GLB youth grow up to be healthy and successful despite the obstacles that they face. Because school based suicide awareness programs have not proven effective for youth in general, and in some cases have caused increased distress in vulnerable youth, they are not likely to be helpful for GLB youth either. Because young people should not be exposed to programs that do not work, and certainly not to programs that increase risk, more research is needed to develop safe and effective programs.

Are African American youth at great risk for suicide?

Historically, African Americans have had much lower rates of suicides compared to white Americans. However, beginning in the 1980s, the rates for African American male youth began to rise at a much faster rate than their white counterparts. The most recent trends suggest a decrease in suicide across all gender and racial groups, but health policy experts remain concerned about the increase in suicide by firearms for all young males. Whether African American male youth are more likely to engage in victim-precipitated homicide by deliberately getting in the line of fire of either gang or law enforcement activity, remains an important research question, as such deaths are not typically classified as suicides.

Is suicide related to impulsiveness?

Impulsiveness is the tendency to act without thinking through a plan or its consequences. It is a symptom of a number of mental disorders, and therefore, it has been linked to suicidal behavior usually through its association with mental disorders and/or substance abuse. The mental disorders with impulsiveness most linked to suicide include borderline personality disorder among young females, conduct disorder among young males, antisocial behavior in adult males, and alcohol and substance abuse among young and middle-aged males. Impulsiveness appears to have a lesser role in older adult suicides. Attention deficit hyperactivity disorder that has impulsiveness as a characteristic is not a strong risk factor for suicide by itself. Impulsiveness has been linked with aggressive and violent behaviors including homicide and suicide. However, impulsiveness without aggression or violence present has also been found to contribute to risk for suicide.

Is there such a thing as rational suicide?

Some right-to-die advocacy groups promote the idea that suicide, including assisted suicide, can be a rational decision. Others have argued that suicide is never a rational decision and that it is the result of depression, anxiety, and fear of being dependent or a burden. Surveys of terminally ill persons indicate that very few consider taking their own life, and when they do, it is in the context of depression. Attitude surveys suggest that assisted suicide is more acceptable by the public and health providers for the old who are ill or disabled, compared to the young who are ill or disabled. At this time, there is limited research on the frequency with which persons with terminal illness have depression and suicidal ideation, whether they would consider assisted suicide, the characteristics of such persons, and the context of their depression and suicidal thoughts, such as family stress, or availability of palliative care. Neither is it yet clear what effect other factors such as the availability of social support, access to care, and pain relief may have on end-of-life preferences. This public debate will be better informed after such research is conducted.

What biological factors increase risk for suicide?

Researchers believe that both depression and suicidal behavior can be linked to decreased serotonin in the brain. Low levels of a serotonin metabolite, 5-HIAA, have been detected in cerebral spinal fluid in persons who have attempted suicide, as well as by postmortem studies examining certain brain regions of suicide victims. One of the goals of understanding the biology of suicidal behavior is to improve treatments. Scientists have learned that serotonin receptors in the brain increase their activity in persons with major depression and suicidal behavior, which explains why medications that desensitize or down-regulate these receptors (such as the serotonin reuptake inhibitors, or SSRIs) have been found effective in treating depression. Currently, studies are underway to examine to what extent medications like SSRIs can reduce suicidal behavior.

✎ Weird Words

Biological Factor: Something in a body (for example, a decrease in a hormone) which brings about a change in a health condition.

Borderline Personality Disorder: A pattern of mood instability, poor self-image, constant mood swings, and bouts of anger which often include suicidal threats.

Conduct Disorder: A pattern of anti-social behavior in children or teens which includes aggression, lying, and impulsive behaviors.

Homicide: Murder, killing someone.

Inheritance: A biological or genetic characteristic or tendency given to a child from their parents.

Rational: Reasoning based on objective or scientific information.

Risk Factor: A behavior or characteristic which increases the chance of death.

Suicide: Killing oneself.

Can the risk for suicide be inherited?

There is growing evidence that familial and genetic factors contribute to the risk for suicidal behavior. Major psychiatric illnesses, including bipolar disorder, major depression, schizophrenia, alcoholism and substance abuse, and certain personality disorders which run in families increase the risk for suicidal behavior. This does not mean that suicidal behavior is inevitable for individuals with this family history; it simply means that such persons may be more vulnerable and should take steps to reduce their risk, such as getting evaluation and treatment at the first sign of mental illness.

Does depression increase the risk for suicide?

Although the majority of people who have depression do not die by suicide, having major depression does increase suicide risk compared to people without depression. The risk of death by suicide may, in part, be related to the severity of the depression. New data on depression that has followed people over long periods of time suggests that about 2% of those people ever treated for depression in an outpatient setting will die by suicide. Among those ever treated for depression in an inpatient hospital setting, the rate of death by suicide is twice as high (4%). Those treated for depression as inpatients following suicide ideation or suicide attempts are about three times as likely to die by suicide (6%) as those who were only treated as outpatients. There are also dramatic gender differences in lifetime risk of suicide in depression. Whereas about 7% of men with a lifetime history of depression will die by suicide, only 1% of women with a lifetime history of depression will die by suicide.

Another way about thinking of suicide risk and depression is to examine the lives of people who have died by suicide and see what proportion of them were depressed. From that perspective, it is estimated that about 60% of people who commit suicide have had a mood disorder (e.g., major depression, bipolar disorder, dysthymia). Younger persons who kill themselves often have a substance abuse disorder in addition to being depressed.

Does alcohol and other drug abuse increase the risk for suicide?

A number of recent national surveys have helped shed light on the relationship between alcohol and other drug use and suicidal behavior. A review of minimum-age drinking laws and suicides among youths age 18 to 20 found that lower minimum-age drinking laws were associated with higher youth suicide rates. In a large study following adults who drink alcohol, suicide ideation was reported among persons with depression. In another survey, persons who reported that they had made a suicide attempt during their lifetime were more likely to have had a depressive disorder, and many also had an alcohol and/or substance abuse disorder. In a study of all nontraffic injury deaths associated with alcohol intoxication, over 20 percent were suicides.

In studies that examine risk factors among people who have completed suicide, substance use and abuse occurs more frequently among youth and adults, compared to older persons. For particular groups at risk, such as American Indians and Alaskan Natives, depression and alcohol use and abuse are the most common risk factors for completed suicide. Alcohol and substance abuse problems contribute to suicidal behavior in several ways. Persons who are dependent on substances often have a number of other risk factors for suicide. In addition to being depressed, they are also likely to have social and financial problems. Substance use and abuse can be common among persons prone to be impulsive, and among persons who engage in many types of high risk behaviors that result in self-harm. Fortunately, there are a number of effective prevention efforts that reduce risk for substance abuse in youth, and there are effective treatments for alcohol and substance use problems. Researchers are currently testing treatments specifically for persons with substance abuse problems who are also suicidal, or have attempted suicide in the past.

What does suicide contagion mean, and what can be done to prevent it?

Suicide contagion is the exposure to suicide or suicidal behaviors within one's family, one's peer group, or through media reports of suicide and can result in an increase in suicide and suicidal behaviors. Direct and indirect exposure to suicidal behavior has been shown to precede an increase in suicidal behavior in persons at risk for suicide, especially in adolescents and young adults.

The risk for suicide contagion as a result of media reporting can be minimized by factual and concise media reports of suicide. Reports of suicide should not be repetitive, as prolonged exposure can increase the likelihood of suicide contagion. Suicide is the result of many complex factors; therefore, media coverage should not report oversimplified explanations such as recent negative life events or acute stressors. Reports should not divulge detailed descriptions of the method used to avoid possible duplication. Reports should not glorify the victim and should not imply that suicide was effective in achieving a personal goal such as gaining media attention. In addition, information such as hot lines or emergency contacts should be provided for those at risk for suicide.

Following exposure to suicide or suicidal behaviors within one's family or peer group, suicide risk can be minimized by having family members, friends, peers, and colleagues of the victim evaluated by a mental health professional. Persons deemed at risk for suicide should then be referred for additional mental health services.

> **☞ Remember!!**
> There is no test or definite way to determine which persons with suicide risk factors will ultimately commit suicide.

Is it possible to predict suicide?

At the current time there is no definitive measure to predict suicide or suicidal behavior. Researchers have identified factors that place individuals at higher risk for suicide, but very few persons with these risk factors will actually commit suicide. Risk factors include mental illness, substance abuse, previous suicide attempts, family history of suicide, history of being sexually abused, and impulsive or aggressive tendencies.

Chapter 6

Suicide Facts, Fables, And Statistics

Suicide Among The Young

- For young people 15–24 years old, suicide is among the three leading causes of death. In 1998, more teenagers and young adults died of suicide than from cancer, heart disease, AIDS, birth defects, stroke, pneumonia and influenza, and chronic lung disease combined.

- Persons under the age of 25 accounted for 4,459 suicides in the U.S. Those aged 20–24 years represented 7% of the population, but 8% of all suicide deaths in 1998. The rate among children aged 10–14 was 1.7/100,000, the rate for children aged 15–19 was 8.9 per 100,000, and the rate for young people aged 20–24 was 13.6/100,000.

- Suicidal behaviors in young people are usually the result of a process that involves multiple social, economic, familial, and individual risk factors with mental health problems playing an important part in its development.

- Identified risk factors for suicide and attempted suicide for young people include the following: mood disorders, substance abuse disorders, certain personality disorders, low socioeconomic status, childhood maltreatment,

About This Chapter: Text in this chapter is from "At a Glance—Suicide Among the Young," National Strategy for Suicide Prevention, 2001; and "Suicide Facts and Statistics," National Institute of Mental Health, updated April 2004.

Myths About Suicide   ♣ It's A Fact!!

Myth: Only adults can get truly depressed.

Fact: Kids as young as 8 or 9 can get severely depressed. Depression is epidemic among teens today.

Myth: Depression is a weakness.

Fact: Depression is a serious but treatable illness that has nothing to do with moral strength or weakness.

Myth: Depression is mostly a white, middle class problem.

Fact: Depression is an equal opportunity illness that can affect anyone, regardless of race or socioeconomic level. Depression and suicide rates among young African-American males and Hispanic teenage girls in particular have dramatically increased in the past 20 years.

Myth: Only depressed kids attempt suicide.

Fact: Kids don't have to be clinically depressed to have suicidal feelings or to attempt suicide. Even feeling extremely bummed out for a relatively short period of time can lead to impulsive suicide attempts. Nevertheless, a person who is clinically depressed for longer periods of time is at higher risk for attempting suicide.

Myth: People who are depressed always feel sad.

Fact: Other symptoms of depression can be irritability, lack of energy, change in appetite, substance abuse, restlessness, racing thoughts, reckless behavior, too much or too little sleep, or otherwise unexplained physical ailments.

Myth: People who talk about suicide don't kill themselves.

Fact: People who are thinking about suicide usually find some way of communicating their pain to others—often by speaking indirectly about their intentions. Most suicidal people will admit to their feelings if questioned directly.

Myth: There's really nothing you can do to help someone who's truly suicidal.

Fact: Most people who are suicidal don't really want their lives to end—they just want the pain to end. The understanding, support, and hope that you offer can be their most important lifeline.

Myth: Discussing suicide may cause someone to consider it or make things worse.

Fact: Asking someone if they're suicidal will never give them an idea that they haven't thought about already. Most suicidal people are truthful and relieved when questioned about their feelings and intentions. Doing so can be the first step in helping them to choose to live.

Myth: Telling someone to cheer up usually helps.

Fact: Trying to cheer someone up might make them feel even more misunderstood and ashamed of their thoughts and feelings. It's important to listen well and take them seriously.

Myth: It's best to keep someone's suicidal feelings a secret.

Fact: Never, ever keep your or someone else's suicidal thoughts and feelings a secret—even if you're asked to do so. Friends never keep deadly secrets!

Myth: If someone promised to seek help, your job is done.

Fact: You need to make sure that any suicidal person stays safe until you can help them connect with a responsible adult.

Source: "Suicide Myths (Youth)," © 2003 CrisisLink. All rights reserved. Reprinted with permission. CrisisLink provides a 24-hour crisis and referral hot line, 1-800-SUICIDE. (1-800-784-2433). Information about CrisisLink is also available on their website, http://www.crisislink.org.

parental separation or divorce, inappropriate access to firearms, and interpersonal conflicts or losses.

- Only a few studies have examined protective factors among youth for suicidal behavior. Both parent-family connectedness and perceived school connectedness have been shown to be protective against suicidal behavior.

- Over the last several decades, the suicide rate in young people has increased dramatically. From 1952–1994, the incidence of suicide among adolescents and young adults nearly tripled, although there has been a general decline in youth suicides since 1994. However, national surveys of high school students during the 1990s have found an increase in those reporting suicide attempts that require medical treatment.

- An international study of suicides for those aged 15–24 years in 34 high and upper middle income nations showed the United States had the 12th leading suicide rate.

- Firearms (60%) and hanging (26%) were the two most common methods of suicide used by persons aged 0–24 years.

- Males under the age of 25 are much more likely to commit suicide than their female counterparts. The 1998 sex ratio for people aged 15–19 was 5:1 (males to females), while among those aged 20–24 it was 6:1.

- Studies examining the relationship between suicidal behavior and sexual orientation have shown there is an increased risk for suicide attempts among youth reporting gay/lesbian/bisexual orientation especially for males. There are currently no empirical data on suicides to support assertions about increased risk for that behavior.

- In 1999, the Youth Risk Behavior Surveillance System, in a nationwide survey of high school students found that in the 12 months preceding the survey, one-fifth had seriously considered suicide and one in thirteen had attempted suicide, the latter represents an estimated 1.3 million students. The survey found that females (10.9%) were significantly more likely than males (5.7%) to have reported a suicide attempt.

- In 1998, in a nationwide survey of students attending alternative high schools, the Youth Risk Behavior Surveillance System, found that in the 12 months preceding the survey, one-fourth had seriously considered suicide and approximately one in six had attempted suicide. Again females (20.0%) were significantly more likely than males (12.1%) to have reported a suicide attempt.

Suicide Facts And Statistics

Suicide Deaths, U.S., 2001*

- Suicide was the 11th leading cause of death in the United States.

- It was the 8th leading cause of death for males, and 19th leading cause of death for females.

- The total number of suicide deaths was 30,622.

- The 2001 age-adjusted rate** was 10.7/100,000 or 0.01%.

  - 1.3% of total deaths were from suicide. By contrast, 29% were from diseases of the heart, 23% were from malignant neoplasms (cancer), and 6.8% were from cerebrovascular disease (stroke)—the three leading causes.

  - Suicides outnumbered homicides (20,308) by 3 to 2.

  - There were twice as many deaths due to suicide than deaths due to HIV/AIDS (14,175).

> 👉 **Remember!!**
>
> Statistics indicate that teens are at a high risk of dying by suicide or attempting suicide. All teens need to learn how to seek help for themselves or their friends when life is painful or overwhelming. Call a suicide hot line or 911 if you are thinking of suicide. Help is available.

- Suicide by firearms was the most common method for both men and women, accounting for 55% of all suicides.

- More men than women die by suicide.

Table 6.1. High School Students Attempting Suicide. Percent of high school students who seriously considered suicide, attempted suicide, or injured themselves attempting suicide; by sex, grade level, and race–United States 1997, 1999, 2001.

Sex, grade level, race	1997	1999	2001
Percent of students who seriously considered suicide[1]			
Total	20.5	19.3	19.0
Male			
Total	15.1	13.7	14.2
9th grade	16.1	11.9	14.7
10th grade	14.5	13.7	13.8
11th grade	16.6	13.7	14.1
12th grade	13.5	15.6	13.7
White (Not Hispanic or Latino)	14.4	12.5	14.9
Black or African American	10.6	11.7	9.2
Female			
Total	27.1	24.9	23.6
9th grade	28.9	24.4	26.2
10th grade	30.0	30.1	24.1
11th grade	26.2	23.0	23.6
12th grade	23.6	21.2	18.9
White (Not Hispanic or Latino)	26.1	23.2	24.2
Black or African American	22.0	18.8	17.2
Hispanic or Latino	30.3	26.1	26.5
Percent of students who attempted suicide [1]			
Total	7.7	8.3	8.8
Male			
Total	4.5	5.7	6.2
9th grade	6.3	6.1	8.2
10th grade	3.8	6.2	6.7
11th grade	4.4	4.8	4.9
12th grade	3.7	5.4	4.4
White (Not Hispanic or Latino)	3.2	4.5	5.3
Black or African American	5.6	7.1	7.5
Hispanic or Latino	7.2	6.6	8.0

Table 6.1. High School Students Attempting Suicide (continued)

Sex, grade level, race	1997	1999	2001
Percent of students who attempted suicide [1] (continued)			
Female			
Total	11.6	10.9	11.2
9th grade	15.1	14.0	13.2
10th grade	14.3	14.8	12.2
11th grade	11.3	7.5	11.5
12th grade	6.2	5.8	6.5
White (Not Hispanic or Latino)	10.3	9.0	10.3
Black or African American	9.0	7.5	9.8
Hispanic or Latino	14.9	18.9	15.9
Percent of students with an injurious suicide attempt [1,2]			
Total	2.6	2.6	.2.6
Male			
Total	2.0	2.1	2.1
9th grade	3.2	2.6	2.6
10th grade	1.4	1.8	2.5
11th grade	2.6	2.1	1.6
12th grade	1.0	1.7	1.5
White (Not Hispanic or Latino)	1.5	1.6	1.7
Black or African American	1.8	3.4	3.6
Hispanic or Latino	2.1	1.4	2.5
Female			
Total	3.3	3.1	3.1
9th grade	5.0	3.8	3.8
10th grade	3.7	4.0	3.6
11th grade	2.8	2.8	2.8
12th grade	2.0	1.3	1.7
White (Not Hispanic or Latino)	2.6	2.3	2.9
Black or African American	3.0	2.4	3.1
Hispanic or Latino	3.8	4.6	4.2

[1] Response is for the 12 months preceding the survey.
[2] A suicide attempt that required medical attention.

Notes: Only youth attending school participated in the survey. Persons of Hispanic origin may be of any race.

Source: Excerpted from Table 58, National Youth Risk Behavior Survey (YRBS), National Center for Chronic Disease Prevention and Health Promotion, Centers for Disease Control and Prevention.

Table 6.2. 2001 Suicide Deaths In U.S. Intentional Self-Harm (Suicide) Deaths By State, 2001.

State	Number of Deaths	State	Number of Deaths
United States	30,622	Missouri	725
Alabama	512	Montana	175
Alaska	102	Nebraska	187
Arizona	767	Nevada	387
Arkansas	382	New Hampshire	167
California	2831	New Jersey	588
Colorado	722	New Mexico	362
Connecticut	283	New York	1253
Delaware	108	North Carolina	997
District of Columbia	40	North Dakota	79
Florida	2314	Ohio	1219
Georgia	935	Oklahoma	515
Hawaii	136	Oregon	505
Idaho	210	Pennsylvania	1276
Illinois	1139	Rhode Island	88
Indiana	715	South Carolina	467
Iowa	304	South Dakota	105
Kansas	293	Tennessee	711
Kentucky	495	Texas	2225
Louisiana	493	Utah	321
Maine	161	Vermont	72
Maryland	454	Virginia	797
Massachusetts	426	Washington	712
Michigan	1051	West Virginia	286
Minnesota	480	Wisconsin	639
Mississippi	328	Wyoming	83

Source: Table 30, *National Vital Statistics Reports*, Vol. 52, No. 3, September 18, 2003, National Center for Health Statistics.

- The gender ratio is 4:1.

- 73% of all suicide deaths are white males.

- 80% of all firearm suicide deaths are white males.

- Among the highest rates (when categorized by gender and race) are suicide deaths for white men over 85, who had a rate of 54/100,000.

- Suicide was the 3rd leading cause of death among young people 15 to 24 years of age, following unintentional injuries and homicide. The rate was 9.9/100,000 or .01%.

  - The suicide rate among children ages 10–14 was 1.3/100,000 or 272 deaths among 20,910,440 children in this age group. The gender ratio for this age group was 3:1 (males: females).

  - The suicide rate among adolescents aged 15–19 was 7.9/100,000 or 1,611 deaths among 20,271,312 adolescents in this age group. The gender ratio for this age group was 5:1 (males: females).

  - Among young people 20 to 24 years of age, the suicide rate was 12/100,000 or 2,360 deaths among 19,711,423 people in this age group. The gender ratio for this age group was 7:1 (males: females).

♣ **It's A Fact!!**
Leading Causes Of Death In U.S. Teens, 2001

Ages 10–14 Years

1. Accidents (unintentional injuries)—1,553

2. Malignant neoplasms (cancer)—515

3. Intentional self-harm (suicide)—272

4. Congenital malformations, deformations, and chromosomal abnormalities (physical problems people are born with)—194

5. Assault (murder)—189

Ages 15–19

1. Accidents (unintentional injuries)—6,646

2. Assault (murder)—1,899

3. Intentional self-harm (suicide)—1,611

4. Malignant neoplasms (cancer)—732

5. Diseases of the heart—347

Source: Table 1, *National Vital Statistics Reports*, Vol. 52, No. 9, November 7, 2003, National Center for Health Statistics.

Attempted Suicides

• No annual national data on all attempted suicides are available.

• Other research indicates that:

  • there are an estimated 8–25 attempted suicides for each suicide death; the ratio is higher in women and youth and lower in men and the elderly.

  • more women than men report a history of attempted suicide, with a gender ratio of 3:1.

* 2001 U.S. mortality data are based on the International Classification of Disease, 10th revision (ICD-10), whereas ICD-9 has been used from 1979–1998. For this reason, comparisons between data from years 1999–2001 and earlier mortality data should be made carefully. For a full explanation of the implications of this change, see http://www.cdc.gov/ncipc/wisqars/fatal/help/datasources.htm#6.3.

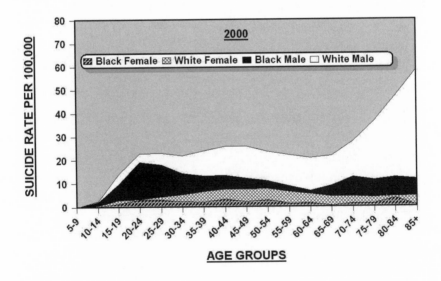

Figure 6.1. U.S. Suicide Rates By Age, Gender, And Racial Group (Source: National Institute of Mental Health Data: Centers for Disease Control And Prevention, National Center For Health Statistics, 2001.)

** Age-adjusted rates refer to weighting rates by a population standard to allow for comparisons across time and among risk groups. The 2001 mortality data are calculated using figures from the 2000 census, whereas previous years have been calculated using 1940 census data. For this reason, comparisons between data from years 2000 to 2001 and earlier mortality data should be made carefully. For a full explanation of the implications of this change, see http://www.cdc.gov/ncipc/wisqars/fatal/help/datasources.htm#6.2.

Chapter 7

Know Suicide Warning Signs And Risk Factors

What types of people are more likely to attempt suicide?

At one time or another, just about everyone thinks of suicide. Still, young people who try to kill themselves usually fall into one of three main groups.

- **Well adjusted, but living with stressful situations.** They may be having difficulty in coping with a sudden crisis—their parents' divorce, for example, or the death of a friend. Failure in school, a romantic break-up, or any other major loss could also serve as a trigger.

- **Depressed or anxious.** People who feel stressed out or emotionally down are at a much higher risk of suicide. And the risk is higher still when emotional problems are coupled with substance abuse or interpersonal loss.

- **Impulsive, aggressive, or self-destructive.** Run-aways and drug and alcohol abusers often fit in this high-risk group. Teen suicide attempts are usually impulsive acts, and they're linked to impulsive kids.

About This Chapter: The information in this chapter is excerpted with permission from "Teen & Young Adult Suicide: Light & Shadows," by Nancy Merritt. © 2002 Do It Now Foundation. All rights reserved. The mission of the Do It Now Foundation is to distribute accurate, creative, and realistic information about drugs, alcohol, sexuality, and other behavioral health topics to youth. For additional information, visit the Do It Now Foundation website at http://www.doitnow.org. In addition, text under the heading "National Institute Of Mental Health Suicide Awareness Information" is excerpted from "Hearing on Suicide Awareness and Prevention," National Institute of Mental Health, February 2002.

✔ Quick Tip

**People With Major Depression
May Have Higher Suicide Risk**

People suffering from major depression and posttraumatic stress disorder (PTSD) are more likely to attempt suicide, and women with both disorders are more likely to have attempted suicide than men with both disorders, according to a new report in the March 2003 *American Journal of Psychiatry*, the monthly scientific journal of the American Psychiatric Association.

The study also found that women, who may be either exposed to more trauma and/or biologically vulnerable to developing PTSD after trauma may be at higher risk for PTSD. In fact, in this study, more women than men reported abuse in childhood and developed PTSD.

"Association of Comorbid Posttraumatic Stress Disorder and Major Depression with Greater Risk for Suicidal Behavior," by Maria A. Oquendo, M.D. et al, p. 580, *American Journal of Psychiatry*, March 2003.

Source: Excerpted with permission from "People with Major Depression May Have Higher Suicide Risk— Study," a news release from the American Psychiatric Association, February 25, 2003. © 2003 American Psychiatric Association.

Other factors also play a role, and some have different impact than you might expect.

Take money, for example. Even though the problem is often portrayed in economic terms, suicide isn't usually a matter of dollars and cents.

Statistics show that rich kids kill themselves as often as poor or middle-income kids.

On the other hand, gender does seem to be an important factor. Many young people who are confused about their sexual identity—or who have experienced sexual guilt or embarrassment—can see suicide as a way to stop their shame or confusion. And even though girls are about twice as likely to attempt suicide, boys are four times more likely to complete the act.

Is there a link between drugs and alcohol and suicide?

Yes, and not just those involving young people. Drugs and alcohol play a major role in suicides of all types. Today, an estimated half of all suicides are committed by problem drinkers, while as many as two-thirds of all suicides involving young people center around drug use.

Drugs and alcohol become particularly lethal when combined with emotional depression and interpersonal loss—a romantic break-up, for example, or the death of a loved one. In fact, studies have shown that rates for suicide and attempted suicide are five to 20 times higher among drug and alcohol abusers than the general population.

Drugs and alcohol can be doubly dangerous since so few chemical abusers realize that depression is often drug-related. They think their feelings are a reflection of the way things really are, which can make them feel even more depressed—and more desperate.

Why do so many young people attempt suicide?

There are a lot of reasons for the current explosion of suicide among the young, but none is more important than the stress that kids go through today. Because the fact is that growing up is more stressful today than it's ever been before.

A lot of factors have been blamed—everything almost from overpopulation and the breakdown of the family to increased pressure to excel and easy access to firearms. Still, we all know that the cumulative weight of life's stresses makes growing up a difficult experience for many young people, one that can seem overwhelming to some.

On top of everything else, there's the romantic image of suicide to contend with. The fact that suicide is only messy and sad—and hardly romantic—doesn't seem to occur to many young people. It just seems a quick, easy way to make a point—or make someone sorry.

Then there's impulsiveness. Young people often act impulsively, and suicide is usually an impulsive act. Impulsiveness becomes a particular problem when someone is drunk or high.

A final reason young people commit suicide can be seen in the rash of copy-cat or cluster suicides that happen from time to time. Still, although they're highly publicized, cluster suicides only account for about 5 percent of all suicides.

♣ It's A Fact!!
Non-Traditional Risk Factors For Suicide Attempts

- Drinking within three hours of the attempt was the most important alcohol-related risk factor for nearly lethal suicide attempts, more important than alcoholism and binge drinking.

- Moving in the past 12 months was associated with an increased risk for a nearly lethal suicide attempt. Frequency of moving, distance moved, recency of move, and difficulty staying in touch were all factors that increased the likelihood of nearly lethal suicide attempts.

- Nearly 1 in 4 of those who made nearly lethal suicide attempts reported that less than 5 minutes passed between their decisions to attempt suicide and their actual attempts, indicating impulsive attempts.

- Young men with medical conditions were more than 4 times more likely to attempt suicide than those without such conditions.

- Nearly-lethal suicide attempters more often sought help from family and friends than from professionals.

Source: National Center for Injury Prevention and Control Press Release, April 3, 2002.

Should all suicide threats be taken seriously?

Yes. Because so many young people are impulsive, threats of suicide should always be taken seriously. Suicide is one case where it's better to guess wrong about someone's intentions than to stay silent.

It's a myth that people who talk about suicide don't do it. They do. And you won't plant a seed in the person's mind that they wouldn't have planted themselves. Suicidal people are stressed and depressed, not stupid. They're capable of thinking of suicide all by themselves. So don't worry about putting ideas into their heads. If the ideas are there, they need to be talked about and dealt with. If they're not there, they won't take root simply because you mention them.

What are the warning signs?

Symptoms that may indicate whether or not a person is suicidal fall into three main groups:

- **Behavioral changes.** Warning signs can include changes in eating or sleeping patterns, withdrawal from friends and family, drinking or drug use, loss of interest in favorite activities, or giving away valued possessions.

- **Personality changes.** Common moods involve anger, anxiety, or depression. Other changes to look for include aggressiveness, hopelessness, hypersensitivity, boredom, difficulty concentrating, or an unexplained decline in school performance.

- **Health problems.** Red flags here could involve any serious or life-threatening illness, and even such minor complaints as frequent headaches, weight loss or gain, nausea, or fatigue.

At this point, we need to point out that the symptoms listed don't necessarily mean someone is considering suicide. Still, they are signs of a problem and need to be considered carefully. Because the fact is that two-thirds of those who commit suicide give some warning first. That means it's up to us—as friends, teachers, parents, or relatives—to recognize the signal and respond, person to person.

♣ **It's A Fact!!**

Suicide Attempts In Adults Influence Suicidal Tendencies In Their Children

Children of parents who have attempted suicide and who also have siblings with a history of suicide attempt are at high risk for a suicide attempt at an early age, according to a study to be published in the August 2003 *American Journal of Psychiatry*, the monthly scientific journal of the American Psychiatric Association.

The study suggests that a strong family history of suicidal behavior was associated with a greater risk of suicidal behavior and earlier age at first suicide attempt in offspring, as well as greater impulsive aggression in both parents and offspring.

The study also suggests that the transmission of impulsive aggression may influence onset of the suicidal acts by increasing the tendency to act on powerful suicidal feelings. These results are consistent with studies of teen suicide attempters, whose parents are 4–6 times more likely to have made a suicide attempt or committed suicide, and strongly support a familial, and perhaps genetic component to suicidal behavior which is related to impulsive aggression.

Source: Excerpted with permission from "Suicide Attempts in Adults Influence Suicidal Tendencies in Their Children—Study" a news release from the American Psychiatric Association. August 1, 2003. © 2003 American Psychiatric Association.

Suicide Solutions

If a person is really determined to die, he or she can usually figure out a way, no matter what anyone does. As painful as that may be, we need to accept it. Still, many young people who consider—or even attempt—suicide aren't that determined to kill themselves. And there are a lot of things we can all do to make suicide more difficult and less likely.

Since about half of all young people who kill themselves do it with guns kept at home, one solution is for parents to keep guns hidden and unloaded, with bullets stored separately.

Researchers say that suicidal impulses usually last only about 15 minutes. Making it past that time may be enough to defuse the situation.

The same rule applies to prescription drugs and alcohol. If you keep them in your home, keep them out of easy reach.

If you're a young person and a friend mentions suicide, talk to a caring adult—a parent, counselor, or someone else you can trust—as soon as you can. This is no time to keep a secret. If you prevent your friend from committing suicide, he or she may be upset for a while. But chances are they won't be upset for long. At least they'll have a lifetime to change their mind.

Pushing Past Panic

Although depression has long been linked with suicide, scientists now think that panic is even more likely to trigger suicidal thinking and behavior. In one recent study, researchers at Columbia University found that people who suffer from panic disorder are much more likely to commit suicide than even the severely depressed.

Panic disorder, which affects an estimated 1.5 percent of the U.S. population, is marked by intense anxiety, rapid heartbeat, and a fear that one is about to die or go crazy. Researchers say the evidence linking panic to suicide is unmistakable. In fact, they say that panic sufferers are more likely than those with any other emotional disorder to report suicidal thoughts or actions.

Still, there is a bright side to the panic problem. For one thing, panic usually passes all by itself, in 90 minutes or so. For another, victims of chronic anxiety or panic are more likely to seek professional help than those reporting other emotional difficulties. Also, panic attacks are increasingly treatable through combinations of short-term drug treatment and psychotherapy.

♣ **It's A Fact!!**

Psychiatric And Family Problems And Teen Suicide Risk

Suicide rates among teens are on the rise in the United States, and suicide is the third leading cause of death among 15- to 24-year-olds, according to the Centers for Disease Control and Prevention. What factors place teens at greater risk for committing suicide?

Danish researchers studied 496 10- to 21-year-olds who committed suicide between 1981 and 1997. Using medical records and family interviews, the researchers determined whether the person had received treatment for mental health problems such as schizophrenia, eating disorders, and other psychiatric problems. Family members also provided information about alcohol use and family relationships. The researchers then compared the suicidal person's information to information provided by control subjects, who were people of similar economic status and age who had not committed suicide.

Males were 3.5 times more likely to commit suicide than females, and people who had been admitted to the hospital for treatment of mental illness were more likely to commit suicide. Other factors associated with an increased risk of suicide included having a parent who had committed suicide, being single or unemployed, being on welfare, having a sibling who was treated for a mental illness, having a mother who died young or left the country, or having a poor or uneducated father.

What This Means to You: The results of this study indicate that teens with a history of mental illness or who have family members with mental illness are more likely to commit suicide. Warning signs in a teen who may be contemplating suicide include withdrawal from friends and family, an inability to concentrate, and a preoccupation with death. If you are concerned that your teen may be at risk for suicide, speak with your child's doctor or seek help immediately from an organization such as the National Suicide Hot line at (800) SUICIDE.

Source: Esben Agerbo; Merete Nordentoft; Preben Bo Mortensen; *British Medical Journal*, July 2002.

This information was provided by KidsHealth, one of the largest resources online for medically reviewed health information written for parents, kids, and teens. For more articles like this one, visit www.KidsHealth.org, or www.Teens Health.org. © 2002 The Nemours Center for Children's Health Media, a division of The Nemours Foundation.

National Institute Of Mental Health Suicide Awareness Information

What We Know About Risk Factors

Despite the 30,000 lives that suicide claims each year, and despite the searing intensity of the act of suicide—for family members and other survivors, as well as for the victim of an attempted or completed suicide—the relative infrequency of suicide in the population at large was long believed to have stymied attempts to identify specific, reliable risk factors. In fact, we know a considerable amount about risk factors for suicide.

- The first and most profoundly important risk factor: From psychological autopsy studies in which a suicide victim's medical, psychological, social history are systematically studied, we have learned that the vast majority—estimated at more than 90 percent—of suicide victims have had a mental and/or substance abuse disorder.

- Follow-up studies of adults with mental or substance abuse disorders reveal the inordinately high risk of suicide associated with these disorders. Some 30 years ago, Guze and Robins documented that patients who had been hospitalized for affective disorders had an alarmingly high rate of suicide and subsequently estimated that persons with depression had a lifetime risk for suicide of 15 percent. Since their work, numerous other studies have followed other patients with depression—including less severely ill patients who had been treated in outpatient as well as inpatient settings—for longer periods of time.

  - Although the revised estimates from this research are less dismal, the lifetime risk for suicide is still 6 times higher for persons with a diagnosable depression than for a person without the illness.

  - Among persons with schizophrenia, over the typically life-long course of this illness, the risk for suicide is between 4- and 6 percent (Inskip et al, 1998; Fenton et al., 1997), but with risk higher earlier in the course of illness (Inskip et al, 1998).

  - Approximately 7 percent of those with alcohol dependence will die by suicide.

- Persons with mental disorders who attempt suicide are at significantly elevated risk—3 to 7 times greater than others with the same illnesses—for eventually completing suicide.

- In the U.S. population at large, an average American, has less than a 1 percent likelihood of dying by suicide.

Clinical risk profiles vary by age and gender. For example,

- Among adolescent male suicide victims, the most common profile is depression, complicated by a pattern of problematic behavior at home and in school, including alcohol or other substance abuse that often leads to isolation and rejection.

- Among adolescent females, a mood disorder is most likely, with conduct problems and substance abuse less likely.

☞ Remember!!

There are a lot of things anyone can—and should—do to help a suicidal person. Besides just being there (which can make a major difference) it can also help to:

- **Listen.** Sometimes it helps just knowing that someone else knows how we feel—and cares.

- **Be honest.** Ask if the person is thinking of suicide. Don't worry about planting an idea that wasn't already there. You won't.

- **Ask if they've considered a method and have plans to carry it out.** The more specific the plans and the more lethal the method, the more serious the threat.

- **Provide emotional strength.** Be positive and supportive. Fall apart later if you need to. But in a crisis, focus on the other person's needs — and give all the compassion and caring you can muster.

Finally, never leave a person alone who is threatening suicide, call a crisis hot line or 911 for help.

Part Two

Mental Health Disorders
And Life-Threatening Behaviors
That Increase Suicide Risk

Chapter 8

What Is Mental Health?

Adolescent Mental Health

Like adults, adolescents can have mental health disorders that interfere with the way they think, feel, and act. When untreated, mental health disorders can lead to school failure, family conflicts, drug abuse, violence, and even suicide. Untreated mental health disorders can be very costly to families, communities, and the health care system.

Mental Health Disorders Are More Common In Young People Than Many Realize

Studies show that at least one in five children and adolescents have a mental health disorder. At least one in 10, or about 6 million people, have a serious emotional disturbance.

About This Chapter: This information is from "Child and Adolescent Mental Health," Substance Abuse and Mental Health Services Administration (SAMHSA), November 2003; and "You and Mental Health," Substance Abuse and Mental Health Services Administration (SAMHSA), reviewed in June 2004 by Dr. David A. Cooke, M.D., Diplomate, American Board of Internal Medicine.

You And Your Mental Health—What's The Big Deal?

What is mental health?

Mental health is how you think, feel, and act in order to face life's situations. It is how you look at yourself, your life, and the people in your life; how you evaluate your options and make choices. Mental health includes things like handling stress, relating to other people, and making decisions. And like many physical aspects of your health, it develops as you get older.

Everyone has mental health. Mental health ranges from good to not so good and even to poor. A person's mental health may move through the range; sometimes a person is healthier than at other times and sometimes he or she needs help to handle problems. Many people experience mental health problems at some time during their lives.

I'm fine. My friends are fine. So why do I need to know about this?

Mental health problems can happen to people of any age, race, or religion or from any kind of family—no matter what kind of job, education, or income level. What you learn now may be useful later for yourself or someone you know. You can help reduce people's fears and lack of understanding by sharing what you've learned—that mental health problems are real and that people with mental health problems can and should get help.

What are mental health problems?

Mental health problems are real. They affect your thoughts, body, feelings, and behavior. Doctors call some of them:

- depression
- bipolar or manic-depressive illness
- attention deficit hyperactivity disorder (ADHD)
- anxiety disorders
- eating disorders
- schizophrenia
- conduct disorder

These disorders are not just a passing phase; they can really interfere with a person's life. Mental health problems can be severe and can lead to school failure, loss of friends, or family problems.

♣ **It's A Fact!!**

Mental health problems affect one in every five young people at any given time. Mental health problems include the range of all diagnosable emotional, behavioral, and mental disorders. They include depression, attention deficit/hyperactivity disorder, and anxiety, conduct, and eating disorders. Serious emotional disturbances for children and adolescents refer to the listed disorders when they severely disrupt daily functioning in home, school, or community. Serious emotional disturbances affect 1 in every 10 young people at any given time.

Source: U.S. Department of Health and Human Services. (1999). *Mental Health: A Report of the Surgeon General,* Rockville, MD: U.S. Department of Health and Human Services.

What causes these problems?

Mental health problems in young people are caused by biology, environment, or a mix of both. If young people are exposed to violence, loss of important people, abuse, or neglect, then they are more likely to be at risk for mental health problems. Other risk factors may include feeling continuous rejection because of race, religion, sexual orientation, or family income.

Schools, families, and communities can probably prevent some mental health problems by protecting young people from these extremely stressful kinds of environmental factors. And when there are problems, seeking help early may prevent them from getting worse.

Mental Illness And Suicide

Although the great majority of people who suffer from a mental illness do not die by suicide, having a mental illness does increase the likelihood of suicide compared to people who do not have one.

• An estimated 2–15% of persons who have been diagnosed with major depression die by suicide. Suicide risk is highest in depressed individuals who feel hopeless about the future, those who have just been discharged from the hospital, those who have a family history of suicide, and those who have made a suicide attempt in the past.

• An estimated 3–20% of persons who have been diagnosed with bipolar disorder die by suicide. Hopelessness, recent hospital discharge, family history, and prior suicide attempts all raise the risk of suicide in these individuals.

• An estimated 6–15% of persons diagnosed with schizophrenia die by suicide. Suicide is the leading cause of premature death in those diagnosed with schizophrenia. Between 75 and 95% of these individuals are male.

• Also at high risk are individuals who suffer from depression at the same time as another mental illness. Specifically, the presence of substance abuse, anxiety disorders, schizophrenia, and bipolar disorder put those with depression at greater risk for suicide.

• People with personality disorders are approximately three times as likely to die by suicide than those without. Between 25 and 50% of these individuals also have a substance abuse disorder or major depressive disorder.

• People who die by suicide are frequently suffering from undiagnosed, under-treated, or untreated depression.

Source: "Suicide–Some Answers," National Strategy for Suicide Prevention (NSSP), available at http://www.mentalhealth.samhsa.gov/suicideprevention/suicidefacts.asp.

Mental health problems are not your fault. They don't mean you are weak or a failure. They don't mean you aren't trying. Whatever the cause, the important thing is to get help.

What are some warning signs of a mental health problem?

There are many different signs that may point to a possible problem. Some of them are included in the following list. Pay attention if you (or your friends) are troubled by feeling:

- Really sad and hopeless without good reason and the feelings won't go away
- Very angry most of the time, cry a lot, or overreact to things
- Worthless or guilty a lot
- Anxious or worried a lot more than other kids
- Unable to get over a loss or death of someone important
- Extremely fearful—you have unexplained fears or more fears than most kids
- Constantly concerned about physical problems or physical appearance
- Like your mind is being controlled or is out of control

Experience big changes in the way you get along; for example you:

- Do much worse in school
- Lose interest in things you usually enjoy
- Have unexplained changes in sleeping or eating
- Avoid friends or family and want to be alone all the time
- Daydream so much you can't get things done
- Feel as if you can't handle life or consider suicide
- Hear voices talking to you or about you that you cannot explain

Find yourself limited by:

- Poor concentration—you can't think straight or make up your mind

- Being unable to sit still or focus your attention

- Worrying about being harmed, hurting others, or about doing something bad

- Feeling like you have to wash, clean things, or perform certain routines hundreds of times a day in order to avoid danger

- Thoughts that race through your head—almost so fast you can't follow them

- Persistent nightmares

Behave in ways that cause you problems, for example:

- Use alcohol or other drugs

- Eat large amounts of food and then make yourself vomit, abuse laxatives or take enemas to avoid weight gain

- Continue to diet and/or exercise obsessively although bone-thin

- Constantly violate the rights of others or break the law without regard for other people

- Do things that can be life threatening

What helps?

Mental health problems are painful. They can hurt as much as (or more than) a serious physical injury. If you have a mental health problem, the sooner you get the right help, the sooner you may feel better.

Some of the things that may help are:

- counseling

- family therapy

- group therapy

- crisis care

- behavior therapy

- special camp programs

- medications

- day treatment
- education programs
- tutoring

The people who help you should understand you and your family situation. They should talk about your strong points as well as your problems. And they should respect you and your feelings.

How can I find help?

Find an adult you trust and talk to. This might be your parent, another relative, friend, neighbor, teacher, coach, member of the clergy, or family doctor. It's okay to ask for help. If one adult doesn't have the answers, find someone who does.

You may also decide to get help from someone trained to support those with mental health problems, such as a:

- family doctor
- psychiatrist
- psychologist
- social worker
- school counselor
- special education teacher
- religious counselor
- nurse

Examples of where these people may work are:

- clinics or private offices
- schools
- social service agencies
- community mental health centers
- health maintenance organizations (HMOs)

Or you can call a local hot line: Call telephone directory assistance to get a local hot line number. Chapter 34 of this book offers a listing of mental health hot lines.

☞ **Remember!!**

Every person's mental health is important. Many teens have mental health problems. These problems are real, painful, and can be severe. Mental health problems can be recognized and treated. Caring families and communities working together can help. Information is available; call 1-800-789-2647.

What should I do if I think a friend has a mental health problem?

Encourage your friend to talk to a trusted adult. If he or she won't, you should talk with an adult you trust. If your friend talks about suicide, talk to an adult immediately. Don't go it alone.

But above all, hang in there. Continue to be a friend. Listening to and being open to another person's feelings are important. Your friend doesn't need blame or shame. He or she needs your friendship.

Chapter 9

Depression: A Key Risk For Suicide

Facts For Teens: Depression

It is entirely normal to feel blue occasionally or to feel down for a while after something bad happens. For teenagers with major depression however, feelings of sadness and hopelessness may last for weeks or months and can eventually dominate their lives. They lose interest in activities they used to enjoy, and relationships with family and friends can begin to suffer.

Depression can lead to poor school attendance and performance, running away, and feelings of worthlessness and hopelessness. Some teens try to make the pain of depression go away by drinking or taking drugs, which only makes the depression worse. Still others contemplate suicide.

Depression is not a sign of weakness—it is a real medical illness. The vast majority of teens with depression can be helped with treatment, which typically includes counseling and/or medication. Unfortunately, most teens with mental health problems do not get the help they need. And when depression isn't treated, it can get worse, last longer, and prevent teens from getting the most out of life. So, it is important to get help immediately if you think you or a friend may be suffering from depression.

About This Chapter: This chapter includes text from "Facts for Teens: Depression," National Youth Violence Prevention Resource Center, 2002; and "Does Depression Increase the Risk for Suicide?" National Strategy for Suicide Prevention, 2001.

How common is depression among teenagers?

Major depression strikes about 1 in 12 adolescents.[1] In any given 6-month period, about 5 percent of 9- to 17-year-olds are estimated to be suffering from major depression.[2]

What are the symptoms of major depression?

All too often, depression is left untreated because people fail to recognize the symptoms and believe that it is just normal sadness, a phase that a teen is going through, or a sign of weakness. This can be a terrible mistake. It is important to know the symptoms, so that you can distinguish depression from occasional normal sadness or moodiness.

Common symptoms of depression include:

• Sad or irritable mood

• Loss of interest in activities that were once enjoyable

• Large changes in appetite or weight

✎ Weird Words

Monoamine Oxidase Inhibitor: A chemical compound that blocks the breakdown of certain monoamine neurotransmitters in the brain, used for the treatment of depression.

Norepinephrine Transport Blocker: Blocks the body's response to stressful challenges which increase heart rate and blood pressure, the "flight or fight" syndrome. Used in the treatment of depression.

Serotonin Transport Blocker: Helps to increase the available supply of serotonin in the brain to improve mood and decrease depression.

Dopamine Transport Blocker: Helps to regulate an overactive dopamine system by inhibiting the uptake of dopamine which may be a factor in depression and helps to restore chemical balance.

Serotonin 5-HT-2A Receptor Blocker: Blocks reception of serotonin 5-HT-2A to restore chemical balance in the brain, used in the treatment of depression.

♣ It's A Fact!!
Be Able To Tell Fact From Fiction

Myths about depression often prevent people from doing the right thing. Some common myths are:

Myth: It's normal for teenagers to be moody; teens don't suffer from real depression.

Fact: Depression is more than just being moody, and it can affect people at any age, including teenagers.

Myth: Telling an adult that a friend might be depressed is betraying a trust. If someone wants help, he or she will get it.

Fact: Depression, which saps energy and self-esteem, interferes with a person's ability or wish to get help. It is an act of true friendship to share your concerns with an adult who can help.

Myth: Talking about depression only makes it worse.

Fact: Talking through feelings with a good friend is often a helpful first step. Friendship, concern, and support can provide the encouragement to talk to a parent or other trusted adult about getting evaluated for depression.

Source: Excerpted from "Let's Talk About Depression," National Institute of Mental Health (NIMH), updated February 6, 2003. The entire document is available at http://www.nimh.nih.gov/publicat/letstalk.cfm.

- Difficulty sleeping, or oversleeping

- Slow or agitated movement

- Loss of energy

- Feelings of worthlessness or guilt

- Difficulty concentrating

- Frequent thoughts of death or suicide[3]

Most teens experience some of these symptoms occasionally. But if a teen has a number of these symptoms for more than a few weeks, he or she is likely to have major depression, and may need professional help.

Teenagers Often Show Depression In Other Ways

Some other signs to watch for in teens include:[4]

- Frequent headaches, muscle aches, stomach aches, or tiredness without a medical cause

- Frequent absences from school or poor performance in school

- Talk of or efforts to run away from home

- Boredom, sulking

- Lack of interest in spending time with friends or family

- Alcohol or substance abuse

- Social isolation, poor communication

- Fear of death

- Extreme sensitivity to rejection or failure

- Increased irritability, anger, hostility, or crying

- Reckless behavior

- Neglect of clothing and appearance

- Difficulty with relationships

- Changes in mood

If you suspect that you or a friend may be suffering from depression, talk to an adult you can trust—and get help.

Depression Can Take Many Forms

Some teens experience only one episode of major depression. Other teens may experience many bouts during their teenage years.

Some teens suffer from dysthymia, a less severe and chronic form of depression that may continue for years, interfering

♣ **It's A Fact!!**

Alcohol Used In Adolescence Is Associated With Depression And Suicide

- Among 12–17 year-olds who were current drinkers, 31 percent exhibited extreme levels of psychological distress and 39 percent exhibited serious behavioral problems.

- Twelve- to sixteen-year-old girls who were current drinkers were four times more likely than their non-drinking peers to suffer depression.

- Twenty-eight percent of suicides by children ages 9–15 could be attributed to alcohol.

- Using a national school sample, a study reported that suicide attempts among heavy-drinking adolescents were three to four times greater than among abstainers.

Source: Excerpted from "Suicide, Depression, and Youth Drinking," *Prevention Alert*, Vol. 5, Number 17, December 13, 2002, Substance Abuse and Mental Health Services Administration (SAMHSA).

with a teen's ability to enjoy and get the most out of life. A teen with dysthymia also may have occasional episodes of major depression.

Other teens suffer from bipolar (or manic-depressive) disorder, which involves severe mood swings from periods of depression to periods of high energy,
overly inflated self-esteem, and agitation, or hyperactivity.[5] Twenty to 40 percent
of adolescents with major depression develop bipolar disorder within 5 years.[6]

Some Teens Are At Greater Risk For Depression

Teenage girls are twice as likely as boys to develop depression,[7] and teens
with a family history of depression are also at greater risk.[8] Other things that
put teens at higher risk include:

- Stress[9]

- Loss of a parent or loved one[10]

- Break-up of a romantic relationship[11]

- Attention, conduct, or
  learning disorder(s)[12]

- Chronic illnesses, such as diabetes[13]

- Abuse or neglect[14]

- Other trauma, including exposure to violence and natural disasters[15]

✔ Quick Tip

If you are suffering from depression, seek help immediately!

Depression And Drug Use

Depression and drugs are a dangerous combination. Depressed teens—
like depressed adults—frequently also have problems with alcohol or other
drugs.[16] Sometimes drug and alcohol use can lead to depression; but more
frequently, teens who are depressed seek out alcohol and other drugs to avoid
dealing with their depression and how it makes them feel.

Depression And Suicide

Suicide can be a deadly outcome of depression. Teens who are depressed
are much more likely than other teens to attempt suicide. Among teens who

develop major depression, as many as 7 percent (or 1 in 14) will commit suicide as young adults.[17] If a teenager thinks or talks about suicide, it is important to take the threat seriously and seek professional help.

What You Can Do

If you think you may be suffering from depression:

Find help. Being depressed can make you feel exhausted, worthless, helpless, and hopeless. It can make you believe that nothing you do will make a difference and that things cannot get better. It is important to realize that these negative views are part of the illness. Effective treatments are available that can help you feel better!

There are many people you can talk to in order to get the help you need:

- psychologist
- a psychiatrist
- your school counselor or nurse
- your parents or a trusted family member

♣ **It's A Fact!!**

The Prevalence Of Major Depression And Mood Disorders In Suicide

A Report of the Surgeon General, states that "major depressive disorders account for about 20 to 35 percent of all deaths by suicide."

- In three psychological autopsy studies of adolescents 41%, 43%, and 32% of adolescent suicides were determined to have had major depression prior to death.

- Three studies of adolescent suicides found prevalence estimates for "mood disorders" or "affective disorders" of 61%, 63%, and 67% respectively.

- The available data suggest that the 20-35% estimate for the prevalence of major depressive disorder in completed suicide is probably somewhat conservative and that a 30-40% prevalence estimate is probably more accurate. This estimate includes both secondary and primary depression.

Source: "Depression and Mood Disorders," National Strategy for Suicide Prevention (NSSP), 2001.

- your family doctor

- your clergy

- a social worker

- a professional at a mental health center

If you think that a friend is depressed:

Talk to your friend. Your friend may not realize that he or she is suffering from depression. Listen to your friend, and make sure your friend knows that you care. Help your friend understand that no matter how overwhelming problems seem, help is available.

Encourage your friend to find help. Remember that you're not a professional therapist and that the most helpful thing you can do is to make sure your friend gets help. Encourage your friend to talk to a professional, such as a school counselor or family doctor, or to a trusted family member.

If your friend doesn't seek help quickly, talk to an adult you trust and respect—especially if your friend mentions death or suicide. Depressed teens may be unmotivated or unable to seek out help on their own because the depression can make them feel that things are hopeless and that nothing they do will make a difference. You can be the most help by referring your friend to someone with the professional skills to provide the help that he or she needs while you continue to offer support. Talk with an adult you trust about your friend's situation so that you aren't carrying the burden by yourself.

Antidepressant Medications

After evaluating a teen experiencing depression, a doctor may prescribe an antidepressant to treat the depression symptoms. Always tell the doctor about all medications you take, both prescription and over-the-counter drugs. Also, follow the directions and tell the doctor of any side effects you experience. Antidepressant drugs take time to work so don't become discouraged. Stay in contact with your healthcare provider as you find the right dosage for you. Table 9.1 lists the different types of antidepressant drugs and how they function.

Types Of Treatment For Depression

Clinical depression is a treatable illness. Clinical depression is one of the most treatable medical illnesses and getting treatment can save lives. The most commonly used treatments are antidepressant medications, psychotherapy, or a combination of the two. The choice of treatment depends on how severe the depressive symptoms are and the history of the illness. When you talk to your doctor and/or other mental health professional, it is important to explore the range of treatment options.

Medication

The symptoms of depression are caused by imbalances in chemicals in the brain and other parts of the body that influence things like mood, sleep, and how much energy we have. Antidepressant medication acts on chemical pathways of the brain. There are many extremely effective antidepressants. The two most common types are selective serotonin reuptake inhibitors (SSRIs) and tricyclic antidepressants (TCAs). Recent research strongly supports the use of medication for the more severe episodes of clinical depression.

Antidepressant medications are not habit-forming. It may take up to eight weeks before you notice an improvement. It is usually recommended that medications be taken for at least four to nine months after the depressive symptoms have improved. Those with chronic depression may need to stay on medication to prevent or lessen further episodes.

As with any medication, side effects may occur. Make sure you are under the supervision of a doctor or other qualified mental health professional to ensure the best treatment with the fewest side effects.

Psychotherapy

Talking with a trained mental health professional can help teach better ways of handling problems. Therapy can be effective in treating clinical depression, especially depression that is less severe. Scientific studies have shown that short-term (10–20 weeks) courses of therapy are often helpful in treating depression.

Cognitive/behavioral therapy helps change negative styles of thinking and behavior that may contribute to clinical depression.

Interpersonal therapy focuses on dealing more effectively with other people, working to change relationships that can cause or worsen clinical depression.

Other Treatments

Electroconvulsive therapy (ECT) may be recommended in the following cases:

- when people cannot take or do not improve with medication,

- when the risk of suicide is high, or

- if someone is debilitated due to another physical illness.

ECT has been improved to make it a safer and more effective form of treatment. It is intended for the more severe depressions and for patients who either cannot tolerate medication because of a medical condition or who are at immediate risk for suicide.

It still remains a controversial treatment for some people who may experience troubling side effects such as memory loss. A thorough discussion between patient and doctor needs to take place when ECT is being considered.

Making The Most Of Your Treatment

Make treatment a partnership. Treatment is a partnership between the person with clinical depression and their health care provider. Be sure to discuss treatment options and voice your concerns with your doctor or therapist. Become informed—ask questions and demand answers.

Take medications wisely. Don't stop taking your antidepressant medication too soon or without your doctor's knowledge. Inform your doctor about any side-effects. Remember, it may take up to eight weeks before you start feeling better. It is usually recommended that you take your medication for four to nine months after you feel better in order to prevent a recurrence of clinical depression. Carefully follow your doctor's instructions to be sure you take a sufficient dose.

Change your treatment or get a second opinion. Treatment changes may be necessary if there is no improvement after six to eight weeks of treatment, or if symptoms worsen. Trying another treatment approach, another medication, or getting a second opinion from another health care professional may be appropriate.

Join a patient support group. In addition to treatment, participation in a patient support group can also be very helpful during the recovery process. Support group members share their experience with the illness, learn coping skills, and exchange information on community resources.

Take care of yourself. Take good care of yourself during treatment for clinical depression. Be sure to get plenty of rest, sunshine, exercise, and eat nutritious, well-balanced meals. Reducing the stress in your life will also help. Share this information with your family and friends and ask for extra support and understanding. Many people also find strength and support through their religious affiliations.

Source: "Types of Treatment," © 2003 National Mental Health Association, reprinted with permission. Copyrighted and published by the National Mental Health Association, no part of this document may be reproduced without consent.

Table 9.1. Classification Of Antidepressant Drugs

Function	Antidepressant
Monoamine oxidase inhibitor	Marplan (isocarboxazid)
	Nardil (phenelzine)
	Parnate (tranylcypromine)
Norepinephrine transport blocker	Asendin (amoxapine)
	Norpramin
	Pertofrane (desipramine)
	Adapin
	Sinequan (doxepin)
	Ludiomil (maprotiline)
	Aventyl
	Pamelor (nortriptyline)
	Vivactil (protriptyline)
Serotonin transport blocker	Elavil (amitriptyline)
	Celexa (citalopram)
	Anafranil (clomipramine)*
	Prozac (fluoxetine)
	Luvox (fluvoxamine)
	Tofranil (imipramine)
	Paxil (paroxetine)
	Zoloft (sertraline)
	Surmontil (trimipramine)
	Effexor (venlafaxine)
Dopamine transport blocker	Wellbutrin (bupropion)
Serotonin 5-HT-2A receptor blocker	Remeron (mirtazapine)
	Serzone (nefazodone)
	Desyrel (trazodone)

*Approved for use in the U.S. only for the treatment of obsessive-compulsive disorder

Source: Mayo Clinic. Reprinted from "The Lowdown on Depression," *FDA Consumer*, Jan/Feb 2003.

Does Depression Increase The Risk For Suicide?

Although the majority of people who have depression do not die by suicide, having major depression does increase suicide risk compared to people without depression. The risk of death by suicide may, in part, be related to the severity of the depression. New data on depression that has followed people over long periods of time suggests that about 2% of those people ever treated for depression in an outpatient setting will die by suicide. Among those ever treated for depression in an inpatient hospital setting, the rate of death by suicide is twice as high (4%). Those treated for depression as inpatients following suicide ideation or suicide attempts are about three times as likely to die by suicide (6%) as those who were only treated as outpatients. There are also dramatic gender differences in lifetime risk of suicide in depression. Whereas about 7% of men with a lifetime history of depression will die by suicide, only 1% of women with a lifetime history of depression will die by suicide.

Another way about thinking of suicide risk and depression is to examine the lives of people who have died by suicide and see what proportion of them were depressed. From that perspective, it is estimated that about 60% of people who commit suicide have had a mood disorder (e.g., major depression, bipolar disorder, dysthymia). Younger persons who kill themselves often have a substance abuse disorder in addition to being depressed.

✔ Quick Tip

FDA Warning About Using Antidepressants

In March 2004, the FDA issued a public health advisory warning doctors, patients, and families to watch for signs of worsening depression or suicidal thoughts at the beginning of anti-depressant therapy or if the dosage of current medication is changed.

Drugs of concern include: Prozac, Paxil, Zoloft, Effexor, Celexa, Remeron, Lexapro, Luvox, Serzone, and Wellbutrin. Most are known to affect the brain chemical serotonin.

🖘 Remember!!

Another way to think of suicide risk and depression is to examine the lives of people who have died by suicide and see what proportion
of them were depressed. From that perspective, it is estimated that about 60%
of people who commit suicide have had a mood disorder (e.g., major depression,
bipolar disorder, dysthymia). Younger persons who kill themselves often have a
substance abuse disorder in addition to being depressed.

If you or someone you know experiences depression, be aware of
suicide risks and warning signs. Always take suicide thoughts,
talk, and threats seriously. Call 911 if you need immediate help.

Internet Links About Depression And Suicide

Centers for Disease Control and Prevention
Website: http://www.cdc.gov

Tips 4 Youth
Website: http://www.cdc.gov/tobacco/tips4youth.htm

Suicide in the United States
Website: http://www.cdc.gov/ncipc/factsheets/suifacts.htm

Center for Mental Health Services
Website: http://www.mentalhealth.org

National Institute of Mental Health
Website: http://www.nimh.nih.gov

National Strategy for Suicide Prevention
Website: http://www.mentalhealth.org/suicideprevention/default.asp

A Teenager's Guide to... Fitting in, Getting involved, Finding yourself
Website: http://www.ncfy.com/expreng.pdf

References

1. Birmaher, B., Ryan, N.D., Williamson, D.E., et al. (1996). Childhood and adolescent depression: a review of the past 10 years. Part 1. *Journal of the American Academy of Child and Adolescent Psychiatry*, 35(11), 1427-39.

2. Schaffer, D., Fisher, P., Dulkan, M.K., et al. (1996). The NIMH Diagnostic Interview Schedule for Children Version 2.3 (DISC-2.3): description, acceptability, prevalence rates and performance in the MECA study. *Journal of the American Academy of Child and Adolescent Psychiatry*, 35(7), 865-77.

3. American Psychiatric Association. (1994). *Diagnostic and Statistical Manual of Mental Disorders. Fourth Edition (DSM IV)*. Washington, DC: American Psychiatric Press.

4. National Institute of Mental Health. *Depression in Children and Adolescents: A Fact Sheet for Physicians*.

5. Lewinsohn, P.M., Klein, D.N., Seely, J.R. (1995). Bipolar disorders in a community sample of older adolescents: prevalence, phenomenology, comorbidity, and course. *Journal of the American Academy of Child and Adolescent Psychiatry*, 34(4), 454-63.

6. Birmaher, B., Ryan, N.D., Williamson, D.E., et al. (1996). Childhood and adolescent depression: a review of the past 10 years. Part 1. *Journal of the American Academy of Child and Adolescent Psychiatry*, 35(11), 1427-39.

7. Birmaher, B., Ryan, N.D., Williamson, D.E., et al. (1996). Childhood and adolescent depression: a review of the past 10 years. Part 1. *Journal of the American Academy of Child and Adolescent Psychiatry*, 35(11), 1427-39.

8. Harrington, R., Rutter, M., Weissman, M.M., et al. (1997). Psychiatric disorders in the relatives of depressed probands. Comparison of prepubertal, adolescent and early adult onset cases. *Journal of Affective Disorders*, 42(1), 9-22.

9. Lewinsohn, P.M., Rohde, P., Seeley, J.R. (1998). Major depressive disorder in older adolescents: prevalence, risk factors, and clinical implications. *Clinical Psychology Review*, 18(7), 765-94.

10. Wells, V.E., Deykin, E.Y., Klerman, G.L. (1985) Risk factors for depression in adolescence. *Psychiatric Development*, 3(1), 83-108.

11. Monroe, S.M., Rohde, P., Seeley, J.R., et al. (1999). Life events and depression in adolescence: relationship loss as a prospective risk factor for first onset of major depressive disorder. *Journal of Abnormal Psychology*, 108(4), 606-14.

12. Spencer, T., Biederman, J., Wilens, T. (1999). Attention-deficit/hyperactivity disorder and comorbidity. *Pediatric Clinics of North America*, 46(5), 915-27.

13. Kovacs, M. (1997). Psychiatric disorders in youths with IDDM: rates and risk factors. *Diabetes Care*, 20(1): 36-44.

14. Brown, J., Cohen, P., Johnson, J.G., et al. (1999). Childhood abuse and neglect: specificity of effects on adolescent and young adult depression and suicidality. *Journal of the American Academy of Child and Adolescent Psychiatry*, 38(12), 1490-6.

15. Krug, E.G., Kresnow, M., Peddicord, J.P., et al. (1998). Suicide after natural disasters. *New England Journal of Medicine*, 338(6), 373-8.

16. Deykin, E.Y., Levy, J.C., Wells, V. (1987). Adolescent depression, alcohol and drug abuse. *American Journal of Public Health*, 76, 178-182.

17. Weissman, M.M., Wolk, S., Goldstein, R.B., et al. (1999). Depressed adolescents grown up. *Journal of the American Medical Association*, 281, 1701-13.

Chapter 10

Bipolar Disorder

Bipolar disorder, also known as manic-depressive illness, is a brain disorder that causes unusual shifts in a person's mood, energy, and ability to function. Different from the normal ups and downs that everyone goes through, the symptoms of bipolar disorder are severe. They can result in damaged relationships, poor job or school performance, and even suicide. But there is good news: bipolar disorder can be treated, and people with this illness can lead full and productive lives.

More than 2 million American adults,[1] or about 1 percent of the population age 18 and older in any given year,[2] have bipolar disorder. Bipolar disorder typically develops in late adolescence or early adulthood. However, some people have their first symptoms during childhood, and some develop them late in life. It is often not recognized as an illness, and people may suffer for years before it is properly diagnosed and treated. Like diabetes or heart disease, bipolar disorder is a long-term illness that must be carefully managed throughout a person's life.

About This Chapter: Text in this chapter is from "Bipolar Disease," National Institute of Mental Health (NIMH), September 2002. For additional information from the National Institute of Mental health, visit http://www.nimh.nih.gov.

What Are The Symptoms Of Bipolar Disorder?

Bipolar disorder causes dramatic mood swings—from overly high and/or irritable to sad and hopeless, and then back again, often with periods of normal mood in between. Severe changes in energy and behavior go along with these changes in mood. The periods of highs and lows are called episodes of mania and depression.

Signs and symptoms of mania (or a manic episode) include:

- Increased energy, activity, and restlessness
- Excessively high, overly good, euphoric mood
- Extreme irritability
- Racing thoughts and talking very fast, jumping from one idea to another
- Distractibility, cannot concentrate well
- Little sleep needed
- Unrealistic beliefs in one's abilities and powers
- Poor judgment
- Spending sprees
- A lasting period of behavior that is different from usual

✎ **Weird Words**

Dysthymia: A long lasting depressed mood which may start at an early age with chronic, but less severe symptoms than those found in clinical depression or bipolar disorder.

Cyclothymia: A disorder which has less severe mood swings from depression to hypomania than in bipolar disorder.

Psychosis: A loss of contact with reality which causes the person to be unable to function in normal life situations.

- Increased sexual drive

- Abuse of drugs, particularly cocaine, alcohol, and sleeping medications

- Provocative, intrusive, or aggressive behavior

- Denial that anything is wrong

A manic episode is diagnosed if elevated mood occurs with three or more of the other symptoms most of the day, nearly every day, for 1 week or longer. If the mood is irritable, four additional symptoms must be present.

Signs and symptoms of depression (or a depressive episode) include:

- Lasting sad, anxious, or empty mood

- Feelings of hopelessness or pessimism

- Feelings of guilt, worthlessness, or helplessness

- Loss of interest or pleasure in activities once enjoyed, including sex

- Decreased energy, a feeling of fatigue or of being slowed down

- Difficulty concentrating, remembering, making decisions

- Restlessness or irritability

- Sleeping too much, or cannot sleep

- Change in appetite and/or unintended weight loss or gain

- Chronic pain or other persistent bodily symptoms that are not caused by physical illness or injury

- Thoughts of death or suicide, or suicide attempts

A depressive episode is diagnosed if five or more of these symptoms last most of the day, nearly every day, for a period of 2 weeks or longer.

- **Hypomania.** A mild to moderate level of mania is called hypomania. Hypomania may feel good to the person who experiences it and may even be associated with good functioning and enhanced productivity. Thus even when family and friends learn to recognize the mood swings as possible bipolar disorder, the person may deny that anything is wrong. Without proper treatment, however, hypomania can become severe mania in some people or can switch into depression.

- **Psychosis.** Sometimes, severe episodes of mania or depression include symptoms of psychosis (or psychotic symptoms). Common psychotic symptoms are hallucinations (hearing, seeing, or otherwise sensing the presence of things not actually there) and delusions (false, strongly held beliefs not influenced by logical reasoning or explained by a person's usual cultural concepts). Psychotic symptoms in bipolar disorder tend to reflect the extreme mood state at the time. For example, delusions of grandiosity, such as believing one is the President or has special powers or wealth, may occur during mania; delusions of guilt or worthlessness, such as believing that one is ruined and penniless or has committed some terrible crime, may appear during depression. People with bipolar disorder who have these symptoms are sometimes incorrectly diagnosed as having schizophrenia, another severe mental illness.

It may be helpful to think of the various mood states in bipolar disorder as a spectrum or continuous range. At one end is severe depression, above which is moderate depression and then mild low mood, which many people call the blues when it is short-lived, but is termed dysthymia when it is chronic. Then there is normal or balanced mood, above which comes hypomania (mild to moderate mania), and then severe mania.

In some people, however, symptoms of mania and depression may occur together in what is called a mixed bipolar state. Symptoms of a mixed state often include agitation, trouble sleeping, significant change in appetite, psychosis, and suicidal thinking. A person may have a very sad, hopeless mood while at the same time feeling extremely energized.

Bipolar disorder may appear to be a problem other than mental illness—for instance, alcohol or drug abuse, poor school or work performance, or strained interpersonal relationships. Such problems in fact may be signs of an underlying mood disorder.

Bipolar Disorder In Youth

Bipolar disorder is difficult to recognize and diagnose in youth, however, because it does not fit precisely the symptom criteria established for adults, and because its symptoms can resemble or co-occur with those of other common childhood-onset mental disorders. In addition, symptoms of bipolar disorder may be initially mistaken for normal emotions and behaviors of children and adolescents. But unlike normal mood changes, bipolar disorder significantly impairs functioning in school, with peers, and at home with family.

Effective treatment depends on appropriate diagnosis of bipolar disorder in children and adolescents. There is some evidence that using antidepressant medication to treat depression in a person who has bipolar disorder may induce manic symptoms if it is taken without a mood stabilizer. In addition, using stimulant medications to treat attention deficit hyperactivity disorder (ADHD) or ADHD-like symptoms in a child with bipolar disorder may worsen manic symptoms. While it can be hard to determine which young patients will become manic, there is a greater likelihood among children and adolescents who have a family history of bipolar disorder. If manic symptoms develop or markedly worsen during antidepressant or stimulant use, a physician should be consulted immediately, and diagnosis and treatment for bipolar disorder should be considered.

Existing evidence indicates that bipolar disorder beginning in childhood or early adolescence may be a different, possibly more severe form of the illness than older adolescent- and adult-onset bipolar disorder.[1, 2] When the illness begins before or soon after puberty, it is often characterized by a continuous, rapid-cycling, irritable, and mixed symptom state that may co-occur with disruptive behavior disorders, particularly attention deficit hyperactivity disorder (ADHD) or conduct disorder (CD), or may have features of these disorders as initial symptoms. In contrast, later adolescent- or adult-onset bipolar disorder tends to begin suddenly, often with a classic manic episode, and to have a more

continued

continued from previous page

episodic pattern with relatively stable periods between episodes. There is also less co-occurring ADHD or CD among those with later onset illness.

A child or adolescent who appears to be depressed and exhibits ADHD-like symptoms that are very severe, with excessive temper outbursts and mood changes, should be evaluated by a psychiatrist or psychologist with experience in bipolar disorder, particularly if there is a family history of the illness. This evaluation is especially important since psychostimulant medications, often prescribed for ADHD, may worsen manic symptoms. There is also limited evidence suggesting that some of the symptoms of ADHD may be a forerunner of full-blown mania.

Findings from an NIMH-supported study suggest that the illness may be at least as common among youth as among adults. In this study, one percent of adolescents ages 14 to 18 were found to have met criteria for bipolar disorder or cyclothymia, a similar but milder illness, in their lifetime.[3] In addition, close to six percent of adolescents in the study had experienced a distinct period of abnormally and persistently elevated, expansive, or irritable mood even though they never met full criteria for bipolar disorder or cyclothymia. Compared to adolescents with a history of major depressive disorder and to a never-mentally-ill group, both the teens with bipolar disorder and those with subclinical symptoms had greater functional impairment and higher rates of co-occurring illnesses (especially anxiety and disruptive behavior disorders), suicide attempts, and mental health services utilization. The study highlights the need for improved recognition, treatment, and prevention of even the milder and subclinical cases of bipolar disorder in adolescence.

Treatment

Once the diagnosis of bipolar disorder is made, the treatment of children and adolescents is based mainly on experience with adults, since as yet there is very limited data on the efficacy and safety of mood stabilizing medications in youth.[4] The essential treatment for this disorder in adults involves the use of appropriate doses of mood stabilizers, most typically lithium and/or valproate, which are often very effective for controlling mania and preventing recurrences of manic and depressive episodes. Research on the effectiveness of these and other medications in children and adolescents with bipolar disorder is ongoing. In addition, studies are investigating various forms of psychotherapy, including cognitive-behavioral therapy, to complement medication treatment for this illness in young people.

Valproate Use

According to studies conducted in Finland in patients with epilepsy, valproate may increase testosterone levels in teenage girls and produce polycystic ovary syndrome in women who began taking the medication before age 20.[5] Increased testosterone can lead to polycystic ovary syndrome with irregular or absent menses, obesity, and abnormal growth of hair. Therefore, young female patients taking valproate should be monitored carefully by a physician.

References

1. Carlson GA, Jensen PS, Nottelmann ED, eds. Special issue: current issues in childhood bipolarity. *Journal of Affective Disorders*, 1998; 51: entire issue.

2. Geller B, Luby J. Child and adolescent bipolar disorder: a review of the past 10 years. *Journal of the American Academy of Child and Adolescent Psychiatry*, 1997; 36(9): 1168-76.

3. Lewinsohn PM, Klein DN, Seely JR. Bipolar disorders in a community sample of older adolescents: prevalence, phenomenology, comorbidity, and course. *Journal of the American Academy of Child and Adolescent Psychiatry*, 1995; 34(4): 454-63.

4. McClellan J, Werry J. Practice parameters for the assessment and treatment of adolescents with bipolar disorder. *Journal of the American Academy of Child and Adolescent Psychiatry*, 1997; 36(Suppl 10): 157S-76S.

5. Vainionpaa LK, Rattya J, Knip M, et al. Valproate-induced hyperandrogenism during pubertal maturation in girls with epilepsy. *Annals of Neurology*, 1999; 45(4): 444-50.

Source: Excerpted from "Child and Adolescent Bipolar Disorder: An Update from the National Institute of Mental Health," National Institute of Mental Health (NIMH), updated April 2003.

Diagnosis Of Bipolar Disorder

Like other mental illnesses, bipolar disorder cannot yet be identified physiologically—for example, through a blood test or a brain scan. Therefore, a diagnosis of bipolar disorder is made on the basis of symptoms, course of illness, and, when available, family history. The diagnostic criteria for bipolar disorder are described in the *Diagnostic and Statistical Manual for Mental Disorders, fourth edition (DSM-IV)*.[3]

Suicide

Some people with bipolar disorder become suicidal. Anyone who is thinking about committing suicide needs immediate attention, preferably from a mental health professional or a physician. Anyone who talks about suicide should be taken seriously. Risk for suicide appears to be higher earlier in the course of the illness. Therefore, recognizing bipolar disorder early and learning how best to manage it may decrease the risk of death by suicide.

Signs and symptoms that may accompany suicidal feelings include:

• talking about feeling suicidal or wanting to die

• feeling hopeless, that nothing will ever change or get better

• feeling helpless, that nothing one does makes any difference

• feeling like a burden to family and friends

• abusing alcohol or drugs

• putting affairs in order (e.g., organizing finances or giving away possessions to prepare for one's death)

• writing a suicide note

• putting oneself in harm's way, or in situations where there is a danger of being killed

If you are feeling suicidal or know someone who is:

• call a doctor, emergency room, or 911 right away to get immediate help

- make sure you, or the suicidal person, are not left alone

- make sure that access is prevented to large amounts of medication, weapons, or other items that could be used for self-harm

While some suicide attempts are carefully planned over time, others are impulsive acts that have not been well thought out; thus, the point of limiting access to large amounts of medication, weapons, or other items that could be used for self-harm may be a valuable long-term strategy for people with bipolar disorder. Either way, it is important to understand that suicidal feelings and actions are symptoms of an illness that can be treated. With proper treatment, suicidal feelings can be overcome.

What Is The Course Of Bipolar Disorder?

Episodes of mania and depression typically recur across the life span. Between episodes, most people with bipolar disorder are free of symptoms, but as many as one-third of people have some residual symptoms. A small percentage of people experience chronic unremitting symptoms despite treatment.[4]

The classic form of the illness, which involves recurrent episodes of mania and depression, is called bipolar I disorder. Some people, however, never develop severe mania, but instead experience milder episodes of hypomania that alternate with depression; this form of the illness is called bipolar II disorder. When four or more episodes of illness occur within a 12-month period, a person is said to have rapid-cycling bipolar disorder. Some people experience multiple episodes within a single week, or even within a single day. Rapid cycling tends to develop later in the course of illness and is more common among women than among men.

People with bipolar disorder can lead healthy and productive lives when the illness is effectively treated. Without treatment, however, the natural course of bipolar disorder tends to worsen. Over time a person may suffer more frequent (more rapid-cycling) and more severe manic and depressive episodes than those experienced when the illness first appeared.[5] But in most cases, proper treatment can help reduce the frequency and severity of episodes and can help people with bipolar disorder maintain good quality of life.

Can Children And Adolescents Have Bipolar Disorder?

Both children and adolescents can develop bipolar disorder. It is more likely to affect the children of parents who have the illness.

Unlike many adults with bipolar disorder, whose episodes tend to be more clearly defined, children and young adolescents with the illness often experience very fast mood swings between depression and mania many times within a day.[6] Children with mania are more likely to be irritable and prone to destructive tantrums than to be overly happy and elated. Mixed symptoms also are common in youths with bipolar disorder. Older adolescents who develop the illness may have more classic, adult-type episodes and symptoms.

Bipolar disorder in children and adolescents can be hard to tell apart from other problems that may occur in these age groups. For example, while irritability and aggressiveness can indicate bipolar disorder, they also can be symptoms of attention deficit hyperactivity disorder, conduct disorder, oppositional defiant disorder, or other types of mental disorders more common among adults such as major depression or schizophrenia. Drug abuse also may lead to such symptoms.

For any illness, however, effective treatment depends on appropriate diagnosis. Children or adolescents with emotional and behavioral symptoms should be carefully evaluated by a mental health professional.

What Causes Bipolar Disorder?

Scientists are learning about the possible causes of bipolar disorder through several kinds of studies. Most scientists now agree that there is no single cause for bipolar disorder—rather, many factors act together to produce the illness.

Because bipolar disorder tends to run in families, researchers have been searching for specific genes—the microscopic building blocks of DNA inside all cells that influence how the body and mind work and grow—passed down through generations that may increase a person's chance of developing the illness. But genes are not the whole story. Studies of identical twins, who share all the same genes, indicate that both genes and other factors play a role in bipolar disorder. If bipolar disorder were caused entirely by genes, then the identical twin of someone with the illness would always develop the illness, and research has shown that this is not the case. But if one twin has bipolar disorder, the other twin is more likely to develop the illness than is another sibling.[7]

In addition, findings from gene research suggest that bipolar disorder, like other mental illnesses, does not occur because of a single gene.[8] It appears likely that many different genes act together, and in combination with other factors of the person or the person's environment, to cause bipolar disorder. Finding these genes, each of which contributes only a small amount toward the vulnerability to bipolar disorder, has been extremely difficult. But scientists expect that the advanced research tools now being used will lead to these discoveries and to new and better treatments for bipolar disorder.

Brain-imaging studies are helping scientists learn what goes wrong in the brain to produce bipolar disorder and other mental illnesses.[9, 10] New brain-imaging techniques allow researchers to take pictures of the living brain at work, to examine its structure and activity, without the need for surgery or other invasive procedures. These techniques include magnetic resonance imaging (MRI), positron emission tomography (PET), and functional magnetic resonance imaging (fMRI). There is evidence from imaging studies that the brains of people with bipolar disorder may differ from the brains of healthy individuals. As the differences are more clearly identified and defined through research, scientists will gain a better understanding of the underlying causes of the illness, and eventually may be able to predict which types of treatment will work most effectively.

How Is Bipolar Disorder Treated?

Most people with bipolar disorder—even those with the most severe forms—can achieve substantial stabilization of their mood swings and related symptoms with proper treatment.[11, 12, 13] Because bipolar disorder is a recurrent illness, long-term preventive treatment is strongly recommended and almost always indicated. A strategy that combines medication and psychosocial treatment is optimal for managing the disorder over time.

In most cases, bipolar disorder is much better controlled if treatment is continuous than if it is on and off. But even when there are no breaks in treatment, mood changes can occur and should be reported immediately to your doctor. The doctor may be able to prevent a full-blown episode by making adjustments to the treatment plan. Working closely with the doctor and communicating openly about treatment concerns and options can make a difference in treatment effectiveness.

In addition, keeping a chart of daily mood symptoms, treatments, sleep patterns, and life events may help people with bipolar disorder and their families to better understand the illness. This information also can help the doctor track and treat the illness most effectively.

Medications

Medications for bipolar disorder are prescribed by psychiatrists—medical doctors (M.D.) with expertise in the diagnosis and treatment of mental disorders. While primary care physicians who do not specialize in psychiatry also may prescribe these medications, it is recommended that people with bipolar disorder see a psychiatrist for treatment.

Medications known as mood stabilizers usually are prescribed to help control bipolar disorder.[11] Several different types of mood stabilizers are available. In general, people with bipolar disorder continue treatment with mood stabilizers for extended periods of time (years). Other medications are added when necessary, typically for shorter periods, to treat episodes of mania or depression that break through despite the mood stabilizer.

✔ Quick Tip
Treatment Of Bipolar Depression

Research has shown that people with bipolar disorder are at risk of switching into mania or hypomania, or of developing rapid cycling, during treatment with antidepressant medication.[16] Therefore, mood-stabilizing medications generally are required, alone or in combination with antidepressants, to protect people with bipolar disorder from this switch. Lithium and valproate are the most commonly used mood-stabilizing drugs today. However, research studies continue to evaluate the potential mood-stabilizing effects of newer medications.

Thyroid Function

People with bipolar disorder often have abnormal thyroid gland function.[5] Because too much or too little thyroid hormone alone can lead to mood and energy changes, it is important that thyroid levels are carefully monitored by a physician.

People with rapid cycling tend to have co-occurring thyroid problems and may need to take thyroid pills in addition to their medications for bipolar disorder. Also, lithium treatment may cause low thyroid levels in some people, resulting in the need for thyroid supplementation.

Medication Side Effects

Before starting a new medication for bipolar disorder, always talk with your psychiatrist and/or pharmacist about possible side effects. Depending on the medication, side effects may include weight gain, nausea, tremor, reduced sexual drive or performance, anxiety, hair loss, movement problems, or dry mouth. Be sure to tell the doctor about all side effects you notice during treatment. He or she may be able to change the dose or offer a different medication to relieve them. Your medication should not be changed or stopped without the psychiatrist's guidance.

Psychosocial Treatments

As an addition to medication, psychosocial treatments—including certain forms of psychotherapy (or talk therapy)—are helpful in providing support, education, and guidance to people with bipolar disorder and their families. Studies have shown that psychosocial interventions can lead to increased mood stability, fewer hospitalizations, and improved functioning in several areas.[13] A licensed psychologist, social worker, or counselor typically provides these therapies and often works together with the psychiatrist to monitor a patient's progress. The number, frequency, and type of sessions should be based on the treatment needs of each person.

Psychosocial interventions commonly used for bipolar disorder are cognitive behavioral therapy, psychoeducation, family therapy, and a newer technique, interpersonal and social rhythm therapy. NIMH researchers are studying how these interventions compare to one another when added to medication treatment for bipolar disorder.

- Cognitive behavioral therapy helps people with bipolar disorder learn to change inappropriate or negative thought patterns and behaviors associated with the illness.

- Psychoeducation involves teaching people with bipolar disorder about the illness and its treatment, and how to recognize signs of relapse so that early intervention can be sought before a full-blown illness episode occurs. Psychoeducation also may be helpful for family members.

- Family therapy uses strategies to reduce the level of distress within the family that may either contribute to or result from the ill person's symptoms.

- Interpersonal and social rhythm therapy helps people with bipolar disorder both to improve interpersonal relationships and to regularize their daily routines. Regular daily routines and sleep schedules may help protect against manic episodes.

- As with medication, it is important to follow the treatment plan for any psychosocial intervention to achieve the greatest benefit.

Other Treatments

- In situations where medication, psychosocial treatment, and the combination of these interventions prove ineffective, or work too slowly to relieve severe symptoms such as psychosis or suicidal behaviors, electroconvulsive therapy (ECT) may be considered. ECT may also be considered to treat acute episodes when medical conditions, including pregnancy, make the use of medications too risky. ECT is a highly effective treatment for severe depressive, manic, and/or mixed episodes. The possibility of long-lasting memory problems, although a concern in the past, has been significantly reduced with modern ECT techniques. However, the potential benefits and risks of ECT, and of available alternative interventions, should be carefully reviewed and discussed with individuals considering this treatment and, where appropriate, with family or friends.[20]

- Herbal or natural supplements, such as St. John's wort (Hypericum perforatum), have not been well studied, and little is known about their effects on bipolar disorder. Because the FDA does not regulate their production, different brands of these supplements can contain different amounts of active ingredient. Before trying herbal or natural supplements, it is important to discuss them with your doctor. There is evidence that St. John's wort can reduce the effectiveness of certain medications.[21] In addition, like prescription antidepressants, St. John's wort may cause a switch into mania in some individuals with bipolar disorder, especially if no mood stabilizer is being taken.[22]

- Omega-3 fatty acids found in fish oil are being studied to determine their usefulness, alone and when added to conventional medications, for long-term treatment of bipolar disorder.[23]

Do Other Illnesses Co-Occur With Bipolar Disorder?

Alcohol and drug abuse are very common among people with bipolar disorder. Research findings suggest that many factors may contribute to these substance abuse problems, including self-medication of symptoms, mood symptoms either brought on or perpetuated by substance abuse, and risk factors that may influence the occurrence of both bipolar disorder and substance use disorders.[24] Treatment for co-occurring substance abuse, when present, is an important part of the overall treatment plan.

Anxiety disorders, such as post-traumatic stress disorder and obsessive-compulsive disorder, also may be common in people with bipolar disorder.[25, 26] Co-occurring anxiety disorders may respond to the treatments used for bipolar disorder, or they may require separate treatment.

How Can Individuals And Families Get Help For Bipolar Disorder?

Anyone with bipolar disorder should be under the care of a psychiatrist skilled in the diagnosis and treatment of this disease. Other mental health professionals, such as psychologists, psychiatric social workers, and psychiatric nurses, can assist in providing the person and family with additional approaches to treatment.

Help can be found at:

- University or medical school affiliated programs

- Hospital departments of psychiatry

- Private psychiatric offices and clinics

- Health maintenance organizations (HMOs)

- Offices of family physicians, internists, and pediatricians

- Public community mental health centers.

People with bipolar disorder may need assistance to get help.

> **♣ It's A Fact!!**
> **Bipolar Disorder Is A Long-Term Illness That Can Be Effectively Treated**
>
> Even though episodes of mania and depression naturally come and go, it is important to understand that bipolar disorder is a long-term illness that currently has no cure. Staying on treatment, even during well times, can help keep the disease under control and reduce the chance of having recurrent, worsening episodes.

- Often people with bipolar disorder do not realize how impaired they are, or they blame their problems on some cause other than mental illness.

- A person with bipolar disorder may need strong encouragement from family and friends to seek treatment. Family physicians can play an important role in providing referral to a mental health professional.

- Sometimes a family member or friend may need to take the person with bipolar disorder for proper mental health evaluation and treatment.

- A person who is in the midst of a severe episode may need to be hospitalized for his or her own protection and for much-needed treatment. There may be times when the person must be hospitalized against his or her wishes.

- Ongoing encouragement and support are needed after a person obtains treatment, because it may take a while to find the best treatment plan for each individual.

- In some cases, individuals with bipolar disorder may agree, when the disorder is under good control, to a preferred course of action in the event of a future manic or depressive relapse.

- Like other serious illnesses, bipolar disorder is also hard on spouses, family members, friends, and employers.

- Family members of someone with bipolar disorder often have to cope with the person's serious behavioral problems, such as wild spending sprees during mania or extreme withdrawal from others during depression, and the lasting consequences of these behaviors.

- Many people with bipolar disorder benefit from joining support groups such as those sponsored by the Depression and Bipolar Support Alliance (DBSA), the National Alliance for the Mentally Ill (NAMI), and the National Mental Health Association (NMHA). Families and friends can also benefit from support groups offered by these organizations.

References

1. Narrow WE. One-year prevalence of depressive disorders among adults 18 and over in the U.S.: NIMH ECA prospective data. Population estimates based on U.S. Census estimated residential population age 18 and over on July 1, 1998. Unpublished.

2. Regier DA, Narrow WE, Rae DS, et al. The de facto mental and addictive disorders service system. Epidemiologic Catchment Area prospective 1-year prevalence rates of disorders and services. *Archives of General Psychiatry*, 1993; 50(2): 85-94.

3. American Psychiatric Association. *Diagnostic and Statistical Manual for Mental Disorders, fourth edition (DSM-IV)*. Washington, DC: American Psychiatric Press, 1994.

4. Hyman SE, Rudorfer MV. Depressive and bipolar mood disorders. In: Dale DC, Federman DD, eds. *Scientific American®; Medicine. Vol. 3*. New York: Healtheon/WebMD Corp., 2000; Sect. 13, Subsect. II, p. 1.

5. Goodwin FK, Jamison KR. *Manic-depressive illness*. New York: Oxford University Press, 1990.

6. Geller B, Luby J. Child and adolescent bipolar disorder: a review of the past 10 years. *Journal of the American Academy of Child and Adolescent Psychiatry*, 1997; 36(9): 1168-76.

7. NIMH Genetics Workgroup. *Genetics and mental disorders*. NIH Publication No. 98-4268. Rockville, MD: National Institute of Mental Health, 1998.

8. Hyman SE. Introduction to the complex genetics of mental disorders. *Biological Psychiatry*, 1999; 45(5): 518-21.

9. Soares JC, Mann JJ. The anatomy of mood disorders—review of structural neuroimaging studies. *Biological Psychiatry*, 1997; 41(1): 86-106.

10. Soares JC, Mann JJ. The functional neuroanatomy of mood disorders. *Journal of Psychiatric Research*, 1997; 31(4): 393-432.

11. Sachs GS, Printz DJ, Kahn DA, Carpenter D, Docherty JP. The expert

☞ Remember!!

For More Information About Bipolar Disorder

Mental Health Information Center
Substance Abuse and Mental Health Services Administration
P.O. Box 42557
Washington, DC 20015
Toll-Free: 800-789-2647
Toll-Free TDD/TYY: 866-889-2647
Fax: 301-984-8796
Website: http://mentalhealth.samsha.gov

National Institute of Mental Health
Office of Communications
6001 Executive Blvd.
Room 8184, MSC 9663
Bethesda, MD 20892-9663
Toll-Free: 866-615-NIMH (6464)
Phone: 301-443-4513
Fax: 301-443-4279
TTY: 301-443-8431
Website: http://www.nimh.nih.gov
E-mail: nimhinfo@nih.gov

American Psychiatric Association (APA)
1000 Wilson Blvd., Suite 1825
Arlington, VA 22209-3901
Phone: 703-907-7300
Website: http://www.psych.org/index.cfm
E-mail: apa@psych.org

American Psychological Association
750 1st Street, N.E.
Washington, DC 20002-4242
Toll-Free: 800-374-2721
Phone: 202-336-5510
TDD/TYY: 202-336-6123
Website: http://www.apa.org

Child and Adolescent Bipolar Foundation
1187 Wilmette Ave., PMB 331
Wilmette, IL 60091
Phone: 847-256-8525
Fax: 847-920-9498
Website: http://www.bpkids.org

Depression and Bipolar Support Alliance
730 N. Franklin St., Suite 501
Chicago, IL 60610-7224
Toll-Free: 800-826-3632
Phone: 312-642-0049
Fax: 312-642-7243
Website: http://www.dbsalliance.org
E-mail: questions@dbsalliance.org

**Depression and Related Affective Disorders
Association (DRADA)**
2330 W. Joppa Rd., Suite 100
Lutherville, MD 21093
Phone: 410-583-2919
Website: http://www.drada.org
E-mail: drada@jhmi.edu

National Alliance for Research on Schizophrenia and Depression (NARSAD)
60 Cutter Mill Rd., Suite 404
Great Neck, NY 11021
Toll-Free: 800-829-8289
Fax: 516-487-6930
Website: http://www.narsad.org
E-mail: info@narsad.org

**National Foundation for Depressive Illness,
Inc. (NAFDI)**
P.O. Box 2257
New York, NY 10116
Toll-Free: 800-239-1265
Website: http://www.depression.org

consensus guideline series: medication treatment of bipolar disorder 2000. *Postgraduate Medicine*, 2000; Spec No:1-104.

12. Sachs GS, Thase ME. Bipolar disorder therapeutics: maintenance treatment. *Biological Psychiatry*, 2000; 48(6): 573-81.

13. Huxley NA, Parikh SV, Baldessarini RJ. Effectiveness of psychosocial treatments in bipolar disorder: state of the evidence. *Harvard Review of Psychiatry*, 2000; 8(3): 126-40.

14. Vainionpaa LK, Rattya J, Knip M, Tapanainen JS, Pakarinen AJ, Lanning P, Tekay A, Myllyla VV, Isojarvi JI. Valproate-induced hyperandrogenism during pubertal maturation in girls with epilepsy. *Annals of Neurology*, 1999; 45(4): 444-50.

15. Llewellyn A, Stowe ZN, Strader JR Jr. The use of lithium and management of women with bipolar disorder during pregnancy

and lactation. *Journal of Clinical Psychiatry*, 1998; 59(Suppl 6): 57-64; discussion 65.

16. Thase ME, Sachs GS. Bipolar depression: pharmacotherapy and related therapeutic strategies. *Biological Psychiatry*, 2000; 48(6): 558-72.

17. Suppes T, Webb A, Paul B, Carmody T, Kraemer H, Rush AJ. Clinical outcome in a randomized 1-year trial of clozapine versus treatment as usual for patients with treatment-resistant illness and a history of mania. *American Journal of Psychiatry*, 1999; 156(8): 1164-9.

18. Tohen M, Sanger TM, McElroy SL, Tollefson GD, Chengappa KN, Daniel DG, Petty F, Centorrino F, Wang R, Grundy SL, Greaney MG, Jacobs TG, David SR, Toma V. Olanzapine versus placebo in the treatment of acute mania. Olanzapine HGEH Study Group. *American Journal of Psychiatry*, 1999; 156(5): 702-9.

19. Rothschild AJ, Bates KS, Boehringer KL, Syed A. Olanzapine response in psychotic depression. *Journal of Clinical Psychiatry*, 1999; 60(2): 116-8.

20. U.S. Department of Health and Human Services. *Mental health: a report of the Surgeon General*. Rockville, MD: U.S. Department of Health and Human Services, Substance Abuse and Mental Health Services Administration, Center for Mental Health Services, National Institutes of Health, National Institute of Mental Health, 1999.

21. Henney JE. Risk of drug interactions with St. John's wort. From the Food and Drug Administration. *Journal of the American Medical Association*, 2000; 283(13): 1679.

22. Nierenberg AA, Burt T, Matthews J, Weiss AP. Mania associated with St. John's wort. *Biological Psychiatry*, 1999; 46(12): 1707-8.

23. Stoll AL, Severus WE, Freeman MP, Rueter S, Zboyan HA, Diamond E, Cress KK, Marangell LB. Omega 3 fatty acids in bipolar disorder: a preliminary double-blind, placebo-controlled trial. *Archives of General Psychiatry*, 1999; 56(5): 407-12.

24. Strakowski SM, DelBello MP. The co-occurrence of bipolar and substance use disorders. *Clinical Psychology Review*, 2000; 20(2): 191-206.

25. Mueser KT, Goodman LB, Trumbetta SL, Rosenberg SD, Osher FC, Vidaver R, Auciello P, Foy DW. Trauma and posttraumatic stress disorder in severe mental illness. *Journal of Consulting and Clinical Psychology*, 1998; 66(3): 493-9.

26. Strakowski SM, Sax KW, McElroy SL, Keck PE Jr, Hawkins JM, West SA. Course of psychiatric and substance abuse syndromes co-occurring with bipolar disorder after a first psychiatric hospitalization. *Journal of Clinical Psychiatry*, 1998; 59(9): 465-71.

Chapter 11

Suicide And Panic Disorder

Understanding Panic Disorder

Fear...heart palpitations...terror, a sense of impending doom... dizziness...fear of fear. The words used to describe panic disorder are often frightening. But there is great hope: Treatment can benefit virtually everyone who has this condition. It is extremely important for the person who has panic disorder to learn about the problem and the availability of effective treatments and to seek help.

What Is Panic Disorder?

In panic disorder, brief episodes of intense fear are accompanied by multiple physical symptoms (such as heart palpitations and dizziness) that occur repeatedly and unexpectedly in the absence of any external threat. These panic attacks, which are the hallmark of panic disorder, are believed to occur when the brain's normal mechanism for reacting to a threat—the so-called fight or flight response—becomes inappropriately aroused.

Most people with panic disorder also feel anxious about the possibility of having another panic attack and avoid situations in which they believe these

About This Book: Text in this chapter is excerpted from "Understanding Panic Disorder;" National Institute of Mental Health (NIMH), NIH Pub. No. 95-3509, updated June 21, 2001.

attacks are likely to occur. Anxiety about another attack, and the avoidance it causes, can lead to disability in panic disorder.

Who Has Panic Disorder?

In the United States, 1.6 percent of the adult population, or more than 3 million people, will have panic disorder at some time in their lives. The disorder typically begins in young adulthood, but older people and children can be affected. Women are affected twice as frequently as men. While people of all races and social classes can have panic disorder, there appear to be cultural differences in how individual symptoms are expressed.

Symptoms And Course Of Panic Disorder

Initial Panic Attack. Typically, a first panic attack seems to come "out of the blue," occurring while a person is engaged in some ordinary activity like driving a car or walking to work. Suddenly, the person is struck by a barrage of frightening and uncomfortable symptoms. These symptoms often include terror, a sense of unreality, or a fear of losing control.

✎ Weird Words

Agoraphobia: A fear of leaving home or familiar environments and avoidance of new situations often caused by the fear of experiencing a panic attack in the new situation.

Panic Attack: A brief time of intense fear that has multiple physical symptoms such as a racing heartbeat, chest pain, dizziness, breathing trouble, and flushing or chilling.

Panic Disorder: Panic attacks which happen repeatedly and unexpectedly.

Phobia: An unfounded but debilitating fear of a thing or an activity which leads to a panic attack.

Phrenophobia: The fear of losing one's mind.

This barrage of symptoms usually lasts several seconds, but may continue for several minutes. The symptoms gradually fade over the course of about an hour. People who have experienced a panic attack can attest to the extreme discomfort they felt and to their fear that they had been stricken with some terrible, life-threatening disease or were going crazy. Often people who are having a panic attack seek help at a hospital emergency room.

Initial panic attacks may occur when people are under considerable stress, from an overload of work, for example, or from the loss of a family member or close friend. The attacks may also follow surgery, a serious accident, illness, or childbirth. Excessive consumption of caffeine or use of cocaine or other stimulant drugs or medicines, such as the stimulants used in treating asthma, can also trigger panic attacks. Nevertheless panic attacks usually take a person completely by surprise. This unpredictability is one reason they are so devastating.

Sometimes people who have never had a panic attack assume that panic is just a matter of feeling nervous or anxious—the sort of feelings that everyone is familiar with. In fact, even though people who have panic attacks may not show any outward signs of discomfort, the feelings they experience are so overwhelming and terrifying that they really believe they are going to die, lose their minds, or be totally humiliated. These disastrous consequences don't occur, but they seem quite likely to the person who is suffering a panic attack.

Some people who have one panic attack, or an occasional attack, never develop a problem serious enough to affect their lives. For others, however, the attacks continue and cause much suffering.

Panic disorder. In panic disorder, panic attacks recur and the person develops an intense apprehension of having another attack. As noted earlier, this fear—called anticipatory anxiety or fear of fear—can be present most of the time and seriously interfere with the person's life even when a panic attack is not in progress. In addition, the person may develop irrational fears called phobias about situations where a panic attack has occurred. For example, someone who has had a panic attack while driving may be afraid to get behind the wheel again, even to drive to the grocery store.

♣ It's A Fact!!
Risk Factors Between Panic Disorder And Suicide

Research suggests that depression doesn't solely explain the relationship between panic disorder and suicide.

Several studies in recent years have suggested that people with panic disorder are more likely to attempt suicide than patients with other psychiatric conditions. One explanation was that panic disorder, when combined with clinical depression, made people more prone to suicide. The study appears in the June 2001 issue of the journal *Behaviour Research and Therapy*.

But the new study suggests that there are other anxiety-related factors that play an important role in whether patients with panic disorder consider suicide, said Brad Schmidt, an associate professor of psychology at Ohio State University.

"Depression is a very significant predictor of whether or not a patient with panic disorder will engage in some kind of suicide behavior," Schmidt said. "But depression alone doesn't account for it all."

The researchers found four mental health factors, aside from depression, that may predict suicidal behavior in a person with panic disorder. They include a patient's overall level of anxiety; fear of panic attacks; sensitivity to and avoidance of certain unpleasant physical sensations, such as heart palpitations; and phrenophobia—the fear of losing one's mind. In this study, suicidal behavior was defined as either thinking about or attempting suicide.

"There are specific components of anxiety that contribute to suicidal behavior, even though these factors are less substantial than depression," said Schmidt, a study co-author and also the director of the anxiety and stress disorders clinic at Ohio State.

Panic disorder is a psychiatric condition defined by sudden, unprovoked attacks of fear and panic.

The researchers asked 146 subjects with panic disorder to take a variety of tests in order to assess the extent of each patient's disorder. These tests included evaluations for depression, current thoughts of suicide, medical history, and panic-related symptoms, such as the frequency of panic attacks, phobias, and the intensity of anxiety symptoms.

Nineteen percent of the patients in the study were diagnosed with major depression. Of these, 43 percent reported current suicidal thoughts, compared to 10 percent of patients without a diagnosis of major depression.

Also, suicidal thoughts were more prevalent among patients diagnosed with agoraphobia—the fear of open areas and public places. More than half of the subjects (59 percent) were diagnosed with agoraphobia, and one in four of those reported thoughts of suicide, compared to 6 percent of the patients who were not agoraphobic.

The researchers found that suicidal ideation—thinking about committing suicide—was related to more than just depression alone. The perceived severity of an anxiety disorder may increase a patient's level of distress, in turn, increasing the chances that he or she will engage in suicidal behavior.

"Additional anxiety problems play an important role in the relationship between panic disorder and actual suicide attempts," Schmidt said. He and his colleagues found that a history of suicide attempts was associated with higher levels of anticipatory anxiety—or fear of panic attacks—and a tendency to be particularly sensitive to physical sensations that the patient deemed unpleasant.

They also found that the higher the overall level of anxiety, the more likely a person was to consider suicide.

Although additional anxiety factors may worsen a patient's state of mind, depression is still an important link between panic disorder and thoughts of suicide.

"While depression leaves patients at risk for the development of suicidal thoughts, the relationship between panic disorder and suicide is greatly reduced when depression is out of the picture," Schmidt said.

Schmidt co-authored the study with Kelly Woolaway-Bickel, a graduate student in psychology at Ohio State, and Mark Bates, of the Uniformed Services University of the Health Sciences in Bethesda, Md.

Source: This information is from "Risk Factors Beyond Depression May Be At Work In Panic Disorder," reprinted with permission from Ohio State University Research Communications, http://researchnews.osu.edu. © 2001 The Ohio State University.

People who develop these panic-induced phobias will tend to avoid situations that they fear will trigger a panic attack, and their lives may be increasingly limited as a result. Their work may suffer because they can't travel or get to work on time. Relationships may be strained or marred by conflict as panic attacks, or the fear of them, rule the affected person and those close to them.

Also, sleep may be disturbed because of panic attacks that occur at night, causing the person to awaken in a state of terror. The experience is so harrowing that some people who have nocturnal panic attacks become afraid to go to sleep and suffer from exhaustion. Also, even when a person does not experience nocturnal panic attacks, sleep may be disturbed because of chronic, panic-related anxiety.

Many people with panic disorder remain intensely concerned about their symptoms even after an initial visit to a physician yields no indication of a life-threatening condition. They may visit a succession of doctors seeking medical treatment for what they believe is heart disease or a respiratory problem. Or their symptoms may make them think they have a neurological disorder or some serious gastrointestinal condition. Some patients see as many as 10 doctors and undergo a succession of expensive and unnecessary tests in the effort to find out what is causing their symptoms.

This search for medical help may continue a long time, because physicians who see these patients frequently fail to diagnose panic disorder. When doctors do recognize the condition, they sometimes explain it in terms that suggest it is of no importance or not treatable. For example, the doctor may say, "There's nothing to worry about, you're just having a panic attack" or "It's just nerves." Although meant to be reassuring, such words can be dispiriting to the worried patient whose symptoms keep recurring. The patient needs to know that the doctor acknowledges the disabling nature of panic disorder and that it can be treated effectively.

Agoraphobia. Panic disorder may progress to a more advanced stage in which the person becomes afraid of being in any place or situation where escape might be difficult or help unavailable in the event of a panic attack. This condition is called agoraphobia. It affects about a third of all people with panic disorder.

Typically, people with agoraphobia fear being in crowds, standing in line, entering shopping malls, and riding in cars or public transportation. Often, these people restrict themselves to a zone of safety that may include only the home or the immediate neighborhood. Any movement beyond the edges of this zone creates mounting anxiety. Sometimes a person with agoraphobia is unable to leave home alone, but can travel if accompanied by a particular family member or friend. Even when they restrict themselves to safe situations, most people with agoraphobia continue to have panic attacks at least a few times a month.

People with agoraphobia can be seriously disabled by their condition. Some are unable to work, and they may need to rely heavily on other family members, who must do the shopping and run all the household errands, as well as accompany the affected person on rare excursions outside the safety zone. Thus the person with agoraphobia typically leads a life of extreme dependency as well as great discomfort.

♣ It's A Fact!!
Panic Attack Symptoms

- Terror—a sense that something unimaginably horrible is about to happen and one is powerless to prevent it

- Racing or pounding heartbeat

- Chest pains

- Dizziness, lightheadedness, nausea

- Difficulty breathing

- Tingling or numbness in the hands

- Flushes or chills

- Sense of unreality

- Fear of losing control, going crazy, or doing something embarrassing

- Fear of dying

Treatment For Panic Disorder

Treatment can bring significant relief to 70 to 90 percent of people with panic disorder, and early treatment can help keep the disease from progressing to the later stages where agoraphobia develops.

Before undergoing any treatment for panic disorder, a person should undergo a thorough medical examination to rule out other possible causes of the distressing symptoms. This is necessary because a number of other conditions, such as excessive levels of thyroid hormone, certain types of epilepsy, or cardiac arrhythmias, which are disturbances in the rhythm of the heartbeat, can cause symptoms resembling those of panic disorder.

Several effective treatments have been developed for panic disorder and agoraphobia. A form of psychotherapy called cognitive-behavioral therapy and medications are both effective for panic disorder. A treatment should be selected according to the individual needs and preferences of the patient. Any treatment that fails to produce an effect within 6 to 8 weeks should be reassessed.

When Panic Recurs

Panic disorder is often a chronic, relapsing illness. For many people, it gets better at some times and worse at others. If a person gets treatment, and appears to have largely overcome the problem, it can still worsen later for no apparent reason. These recurrences should not cause a person to despair or consider himself or herself a treatment failure. Recurrences can be treated effectively, just like an initial episode.

In fact, the skills that a person learns in dealing with the initial episode can be helpful in coping with any setbacks. Many people who have overcome panic disorder once or a few times find that, although they still have an occasional panic attack, they are now much better able to deal with the problem. Even though it is not fully cured, it no longer dominates their lives, or the lives of those around them.

Coexisting Conditions

Conditions that are frequently found to coexist with panic disorder include:

Simple Phobias. People with panic disorder often develop irrational fears of specific events or situations that they associate with the possibility of having a panic attack. Fear of heights and fear of crossing bridges are examples of simple phobias. Generally, these fears can be resolved through repeated exposure to the dreaded situations, while practicing specific cognitive-behavioral techniques to become less sensitive to them.

Social Phobia. This is a persistent dread of situations in which the person is exposed to possible scrutiny by others and fears acting in a way that will be embarrassing or humiliating. Social phobia can be treated effectively with cognitive-behavioral therapy or medications, or both.

Depression. About half of panic disorder patients will have an episode of clinical depression sometime during their lives. Major depression is marked by persistent sadness or feelings of emptiness, a sense of hopelessness, and other symptoms. When major depression occurs, it can be treated effectively with one of several antidepressant drugs, or, depending on its severity, by cognitive-behavioral therapies.

Obsessive-Compulsive Disorder (OCD). In OCD, a person becomes trapped in a pattern of repetitive thoughts and behaviors that are senseless and distressing but extremely difficult to overcome. Such rituals as counting, prolonged handwashing, and repeatedly checking for danger may occupy much of the person's time and interfere with other activities. Today, OCD can be treated effectively with medications or cognitive-behavioral therapies.

Alcohol Abuse. About 30 percent of people with panic disorder abuse alcohol. A person who has alcoholism in addition to panic disorder needs specialized care for the alcoholism along with treatment for the panic disorder. Often the alcoholism will be treated first.

Drug Abuse. As in the case of alcoholism, drug abuse is more common in people with panic disorder than in the population at large. In fact, about 17 percent of people with panic disorder abuse drugs. The drug problems often need to be addressed prior to treatment for panic disorder.

Suicidal Tendencies. Recent studies in the general population have suggested that suicide attempts are more common among people who have panic attacks than among those who do not have a mental disorder. Also, it appears that people who have both panic disorder and depression are at elevated risk for suicide. (However, anxiety disorder experts who have treated many patients emphasize that it is extremely unlikely that anyone would attempt to harm himself or herself during a panic attack.)

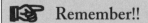 **Remember!!**

For More Information On Panic Disorder And Related Conditions

American Psychiatric Association
1000 Wilson Blvd., Suite 1825
Arlington, VA 22209-3901
Phone: 703-907-7300
Website: http://www.psych.org
E-mail: apa@psych.org

American Psychological Association
750 First Street, N.E.
Washington, DC 20002-4242
Toll-Free: 800-374-2721
Phone: 202-336-5500
TDD/TTY: 202-336-6123
Website: http://www.apa.org

Anxiety Disorders Association of America
8730 Georgia Ave., Suite 600
Silver Spring, MD 20910
Phone: 240-485-1001
Fax: 240-485-1035
Website: http://www.adaa.org

Association for the Advancement of Behavior Therapy
305 Seventh Avenue, 16th Floor
New York, NY 10001-6008
Phone: 212-647-1890
Fax: 212-647-1865
Website: http://www.aabt.org

National Alliance for the Mentally Ill
2107 Wilson Blvd., Suite 300
Colonial Place Three
Arlington, VA 22201-3042
Toll-Free: 800-950-NAMI (6264)
Phone: 703-524-7600
Fax: 703-524-9094
TDD: 703-516-7227
Website: http://www.nami.org

National Anxiety Foundation
3135 Custer Drive
Lexington, KY 40517-4001
Website: http://www.lexington-on-line.com/naf.html

Depression and Bipolar Support Alliance
730 North Franklin Street, Suite 501
Chicago, IL 60610-7224
Toll-Free: 800-826-3632
Phone: 312-642-0049
Fax: 312-642-7243
Website: http://www.dbsalliance.org

National Institute of Mental Health Publications List
5600 Fishers Lane, Room 7C-02
Rockville, MD 20857
Toll-Free: 866-615-6464
Phone: 301-443-4513
Fax: 301-443-4279
TTY: 301-443-8431
Website: http://infocenter.nimh.nih.gov
E-mail: nimhinfo@nih.gov

National Mental Health Association
2001 N. Beauregard St., 12th Floor
Alexandria, VA 22311
Toll-Free: 800-969-6642
Fax: 703-684-5968
TTY: 800-433-5959
Website: http://www.nmha.org

Anyone who is considering suicide needs immediate attention from a mental health professional or from a school counselor, physician, or member of the clergy. With appropriate help and treatment, it is possible to overcome suicidal tendencies.

There are also certain physical conditions that are often associated with panic disorder:

Irritable Bowel Syndrome. The person with this syndrome experiences intermittent bouts of gastrointestinal cramps and diarrhea or constipation, often occurring during a period of stress. Because the symptoms are so pronounced, panic disorder is often not diagnosed when it occurs in a person with irritable bowel syndrome.

Mitral Valve Prolapse. This condition involves a defect in the mitral valve, which separates the two chambers on the left side of the heart. Each time the heart muscle contracts in people with this condition, tissue in the mitral valve is pushed for an instant into the wrong chamber. The person with the disorder may experience chest pain, rapid heartbeat, breathing difficulties, and headache. People with mitral valve prolapse may be at higher than usual risk of having panic disorder, but many experts are not convinced this apparent association is real.

Finding Help For Panic Disorder

Often the person with panic disorder must undertake a strenuous search to find a therapist who is familiar with the most effective treatments for the condition. A list of places to start follows. The Anxiety Disorders Association of America can provide a list of professionals in your area who specialize in the treatment of panic disorder and other anxiety disorders.

Self-help and support groups are the least expensive approach to managing panic disorder, and are helpful for some people. A group of about 5 to 10 people meet weekly and share their experiences, encouraging each other to venture into feared situations and cope effectively with panic attacks. Group members are in charge of the sessions. Often family members are invited to attend these groups, and at times a therapist or other panic disorder expert may be brought in to share insights with group members. Information on

self-help groups in specific areas of the country can be obtained from the
Anxiety Disorders Association of America.

References

Barlow, D.H., and Craske, M.G. *Mastery of Your Anxiety and Panic*. Albany,
NY: Graywind Publications, 1988.

Beck, A.T., and Emery, G., with Greenberg, R. *Anxiety Disorders and Phobias: A Cognitive Perspective*. New York: Basic Books, 1985.

Gold, M.S. *The Good News About Panic, Anxiety, and Phobias*. New York:
Bantam, 1989.

Greist, J.H., and Jefferson, J.W. *Panic Disorder and Agoraphobia: A Guide*.
Madison, WI: Anxiety Disorders Center and Information Centers, University of Wisconsin, 1992.

Hecker, J.E., and Thorpe, G.L. *Agoraphobia and Panic: A Guide to Psychological Treatment*. Needham Heights, MA: Allyn and Bacon, 1992.

Katon, W. *Panic Disorder in the Medical Setting*. NIH Pub. No. 93-3482.
Washington, DC: Supt. of Docs., U.S. Govt. Print. Off., 1993.

Kernodle, W.D. *Panic Disorder*. Richmond, VA: William Byrd Press, 1991.

Klerman, G.L., et al., eds. *Panic Anxiety and Its Treatments*. Washington,
DC: American Psychiatric Press, 1993.

Mathews, A.M.; Gelder, M.G.; and Johnston, D.W. *Agoraphobia: Nature
and Treatment*. New York and London: Guilford Press, 1981.

National Institutes of Health. *NIH Consensus Development Conference Statement, Vol. 9, No. 2. Treatment of Panic Disorder*. Bethesda, MD: NIH, September 1991.

Rachman, S., and Maser, J.D. *Panic: Psychological Perspectives*. Hillsdale, NJ:
Erlbaum Associates, 1988.

Sheehan, D.V. *The Anxiety Disease*. New York: Bantam, 1986.

Wilson, R.R. Don't Panic: *Taking Control of Anxiety Attacks*. New York: Harper
and Row, 1986.

Chapter 12

Post-Traumatic Stress Disorder In People At Risk For Suicide

What Is Post-Traumatic Stress Disorder?

Post-traumatic Stress Disorder, or PTSD, is a psychiatric disorder that can occur following the experience or witnessing of life-threatening events such as military combat, natural disasters, terrorist incidents, serious accidents, suicide, or violent personal assaults like rape. People who suffer from PTSD often relive the experience through nightmares and flashbacks, have difficulty sleeping, and feel detached or estranged, and these symptoms can be severe enough and last long enough to significantly impair the person's daily life.

PTSD is marked by clear biological changes as well as psychological symptoms. PTSD is complicated by the fact that it frequently occurs in conjunction with related disorders such as depression, substance abuse, problems of memory and cognition, and other problems of physical and mental health. The disorder is also associated with impairment of the person's ability to function in social or family life, including problems at school or work, family discord, marital problems and divorces, and difficulties in parenting.

About This Chapter: This chapter includes excerpts from "What is Post-Traumatic Stress Disorder" updated May 2003, "How is PTSD Measured?" updated September 2003, and "Treatment of PTSD" updated February 2004, from the National Center for Post-Traumatic Stress Disorder (PTSD).

Understanding PTSD

PTSD is not a new disorder. There are written accounts of similar symptoms that go back to ancient times, and there is clear documentation in the historical medical literature starting with the Civil War, when a PTSD-like disorder was known as Da Costa's Syndrome. There are particularly good descriptions of post-traumatic stress symptoms in the medical literature on combat veterans of World War II and on Holocaust survivors.

Careful research and documentation of PTSD began in earnest after the Vietnam War. The National Vietnam Veterans Readjustment Study estimated in 1988 that the prevalence of PTSD in that group was 15.2% at that time and that 30% had experienced the disorder at some point since returning from Vietnam. PTSD has subsequently been observed in all veteran populations that have been studied, including World War II, Korean conflict, and Persian Gulf populations, and in United Nations peacekeeping forces deployed to other war zones around the world.

PTSD is not only a problem for veterans, however. Although there are unique cultural- and gender-based aspects of the disorder, it occurs in men

---

♣ It's A Fact!!
Post-Traumatic Stress Disorder With
Major Depression Increases Suicide Risk

The March 2003 *American Journal of Psychiatry* reported a study led by Maria A. Oquendo, M.D. which evaluated the connection between post-traumatic stress disorder, depression, and suicide risk. Hospital patients who were diagnosed with major depression were evaluated to see if they had post-traumatic stress disorder, suicidal behavior, or other clinical risk factors for suicidal acts.

The results of this study indicate that patients experiencing both a major depressive episode and post-traumatic stress disorder are more likely to have attempted suicide. Women with both disorders are more likely to have attempted suicide than men with both disorders.

—JBS

♣ It's A Fact!!

Traumatic Events Increase Suicide Risk In Partial PTSD

Many more people have been affected by traumatic events than have been counted in statistical reports of people with PTSD. These people have not been included in the counts of people with PTSD because they have some, but not all of the symptoms of PTSD. Dr. Randall Marshall of New York State Psychiatric Institute and Columbia University led the study which was reported in the September 2001 *American Journal of Psychiatry*. Dr. Marshall found that even partial PTSD raised the risk of suicidal thoughts in people who had experienced traumatic events.

—JBS

and women, adults and children, Western and non-Western cultural groups, and all socioeconomic levels. A national study of American civilians conducted in 1995 estimated that the lifetime prevalence of PTSD was 5% in men and 10% in women.

How Does PTSD Develop?

Most people who are exposed to a traumatic, stressful event experience some of the symptoms of PTSD in the days and weeks following exposure. Available data suggest that about 8% of men and 20% of women go on to develop PTSD, and roughly 30% of these individuals develop a chronic form that persists throughout their lifetimes.

The course of chronic PTSD usually involves periods of symptom increase followed by remission or decrease, although some individuals may experience symptoms that are unremitting and severe.

How Is PTSD Assessed?

In recent years, a great deal of research has been aimed at developing and testing reliable assessment tools. It is generally thought that the best way to diagnose PTSD—or any psychiatric disorder, for that matter—is to combine findings from structured interviews and questionnaires with physiological assessments. A multi-method approach especially helps address concerns that some patients might be either denying or exaggerating their symptoms.

How Common Is PTSD?

An estimated 7.8 percent of Americans will experience PTSD at some point in their lives, with women (10.4%) twice as likely as men (5%) to develop PTSD. About 3.6 percent of U.S. adults aged 18 to 54 (5.2 million people) have PTSD during the course of a given year. This represents a small portion of those who have experienced at least one traumatic event; 60.7% of men and 51.2% of women reported at least one traumatic event. The traumatic events most often associated with PTSD for men are rape, combat exposure, childhood neglect, and childhood physical abuse. The most traumatic events for women are rape, sexual molestation, physical attack, being threatened with a weapon, and childhood physical abuse.

> ✤ **It's A Fact!!**
> The National Center for PTSD reports that rates of PTSD in children and adolescents who have witnessed a traumatic event vary from 3% to 100%. For example, studies have shown that as many as 100% of children who witness a parental homicide, suicide, or sexual assault develop PTSD.
>
> —JBS

Who Is Most Likely To Develop PTSD?

1. Those who experience intense stress; find life to be unpredictable; feel they cannot control the events, people, or responsibilities in their life; who have experienced sexual abuse or violence; or who feel betrayed.

2. Those with prior factors such as genetics (inherited mental disorders), early age of onset and longer-lasting childhood trauma, lack of a working social support system, and stressful life events that happen at the same time which make them more susceptible to PTSD.

3. Those who report greater perceived threat or danger, suffering, upset, terror, and horror or fear.

4. Those with a social environment that produces shame, guilt, stigmatization, or self-hatred.

Common Parts Of PTSD Treatment

Treatment for PTSD typically begins with a detailed evaluation and the development of a treatment plan that meets the unique needs of the survivor. Generally, PTSD-specific treatment is begun only after the survivor has been safely removed from a crisis situation. If a survivor is still being exposed to trauma (such as ongoing domestic or community violence, abuse, or homelessness), is severely depressed or suicidal, is experiencing extreme panic or disorganized thinking, or is in need of drug or alcohol detoxification, it is important to address these crisis problems as a part of the first phase of treatment.

- It is important that the first phase of treatment include educating trauma survivors and their families about how persons get PTSD, how PTSD affects survivors and their loved ones, and other problems that commonly come along with PTSD symptoms.

- Exposure to the event via imagery allows the survivor to re-experience the event in a safe, controlled environment, while also carefully examining his or her reactions and beliefs in relation to that event.

- One aspect of the first treatment phase is to have the survivor examine and resolve strong feelings such as anger, shame, or guilt, which are common among survivors of trauma.

✎ Weird Words

Cognitions: Mental processes used to acquire knowledge such as thinking, learning, and memory.

Cohesion: A uniting with a group created by a common experience.

Empathy: Understanding someone's emotions and feelings.

Stigmatization: Disrespecting a person through negative talk or gossip about physical or mental characteristics which they may or may not have.

Trauma Narrative: The explanation or telling of a person's traumatic experience.

- Another step in the first phase is to teach the survivor to cope with post-traumatic memories, reminders, reactions, and feelings without becoming overwhelmed or emotionally numb. Trauma memories usually do not go away entirely as a result of therapy, but become manageable with the mastery of new coping skills.

Therapeutic Approaches Commonly Used To Treat PTSD

Cognitive-behavioral therapy (CBT) involves working with cognitions to change emotions, thoughts, and behaviors. Exposure therapy is one form of CBT that is unique to trauma treatment. It uses careful, repeated, detailed imagining of the trauma (exposure) in a safe, controlled context to help the survivor face and gain control of the fear and distress that was overwhelming during the trauma. Along with exposure, CBT for trauma includes:

- learning skills for coping with anxiety (such as breathing retraining or biofeedback) and negative thoughts (cognitive restructuring),

- managing anger,

- preparing for stress reactions (stress inoculation),

- handling future trauma symptoms,

- addressing urges to use alcohol or drugs when trauma symptoms occur (relapse prevention), and

> **✔ Quick Tip**
> Understanding that PTSD is a medically recognized anxiety disorder that occurs in normal individuals under extremely stressful conditions is essential for effective treatment.

- communicating and relating effectively with people (social skills or marital therapy).

Pharmacotherapy (medication) can reduce the anxiety, depression, and insomnia often experienced with PTSD, and in some cases, it may help relieve the distress and emotional numbness caused by trauma memories. Several kinds of antidepressant drugs have contributed to patient improvement in most (but not all) clinical trials, and some other classes of drugs have shown promise. At this time, no particular drug has emerged as a definitive treatment for PTSD. However, medication is clearly useful for symptom relief, which makes it possible for survivors to participate in psychotherapy.

Eye Movement Desensitization and Reprocessing (EMDR) is a relatively new treatment for traumatic memories that involves elements of exposure therapy and cognitive-behavioral therapy combined with techniques (eye movements, hand taps, sounds) that create an alternation of attention back and forth across the person's midline. While the theory and research are still evolving for this form of treatment, there is some evidence that the therapeutic element unique to EMDR, attentional alternation, may facilitate the accessing and processing of traumatic material.

Group treatment is often an ideal therapeutic setting because trauma survivors are able to share traumatic material within the safety, cohesion, and empathy provided by other survivors. As group members achieve greater understanding and resolution of their trauma, they often feel more confident and able to trust. As they discuss and share how they cope with trauma-related shame, guilt, rage, fear, doubt, and self-condemnation, they prepare themselves to focus on the present rather than the past. Telling one's story (the trauma narrative) and directly facing the grief, anxiety, and guilt related to trauma enables many survivors to cope with their symptoms, memories, and other aspects of their lives.

Brief psychodynamic psychotherapy focuses on the emotional conflicts caused by the traumatic event, particularly as they relate to early life experiences. Through the retelling of the traumatic event to a calm, empathic, compassionate, and nonjudgmental therapist, the survivor achieves a greater sense of self-esteem, develops effective ways of thinking and coping, and learns to deal more successfully with intense emotions. The therapist helps the survivor identify current life situations that set off traumatic memories and worsen PTSD symptoms.

Psychiatric Disorders That Commonly Co-Occur With PTSD

Psychiatric disorders that commonly co-occur with PTSD include depression, alcohol/substance abuse, panic disorder, and other anxiety disorders. Although crises that threaten the safety of the survivor or others must be addressed first, the best treatment results are achieved when both PTSD and the other disorder(s) are treated together rather than one after the other. This is especially true for PTSD and alcohol/substance abuse.

Complex PTSD

Complex PTSD (sometimes called Disorder of Extreme Stress) is found among individuals who have been exposed to prolonged traumatic circumstances, especially during childhood, such as childhood sexual abuse. Developmental research is revealing that many brain and hormonal changes may occur as a result of early, prolonged trauma, and these changes contribute to difficulties with memory, learning, and regulating impulses and emotions. Combined with a disruptive, abusive home environment that does not foster healthy interaction, these brain and hormonal changes may contribute to severe behavioral difficulties (such as impulsivity, aggression, sexual acting out, eating disorders, alcohol/drug abuse, and self-destructive actions), emotional regulation difficulties (such as intense rage, depression, or panic), and mental difficulties (such as extremely scattered thoughts, dissociation, and amnesia). As adults, these individuals often are diagnosed with depressive disorders, personality disorders, or dissociative disorders. Treatment often takes much longer than with regular PTSD, may progress at a much slower rate, and requires a sensitive and structured treatment program delivered by a trauma specialist.

☞ Remember!!

PTSD and depression are often unrecognized and untreated. Depression is a suicide risk factor. When depression is combined with PTSD, a person's suicide risk is further increased. If you are suffering from even some of the symptoms of PTSD, talk with someone about getting help. Treatment will help you cope with PTSD and depression.

Chapter 13

Schizophrenia And Suicide

Depression And Suicide In Schizophrenia

Patients with schizophrenia frequently suffer from more than one psychiatric disorder. More than half will experience some form of depression during their lifetime. This combination is often associated with impaired social adjustment, treatment non-compliance, multiple hospitalizations, and relapse for psychosis. The rate of suicide among individuals with schizophrenia is about 10 percent, highlighting the importance of recognizing and treating depression associated with schizophrenia.

Is It Depression?

The incidence of depression during or immediately following an acute psychotic episode is very high, occurring in about 25% of patients with schizophrenia. Depressive symptoms may also appear just before a psychotic relapse. Negative symptoms of schizophrenia (inability to experience pleasure, lack of energy and motivation, social withdrawal, and impaired abstract thinking) can have a significant overlap with symptoms of depression making it difficult to recognize. Also, some depressive symptoms may be confused with side effects of antipsychotic medications such as akinesia, (apathy and

About This Chapter: This information is reprinted with permission from the Mental Illness Research, Education, and Clinical Center of the VA Desert Pacific Healthcare Network, http://www.mirecc.org. © 2001-2004.

diminished spontaneous movement and speech) or akathisia, (motor restlessness) which can produce dysphoria (negative moods). Additionally, a depressed mood is often seen in persons who are abusing or withdrawing from drugs or alcohol as well as in medical conditions, such as thyroid disorders. Deficits in perception, cognition, and communication skills in patients with schizophrenia often interfere with the detection of depression and risk for suicide.

Paul, a 33 year old male veteran with schizophrenia was able to function in social relationships but unable to work. Divorced with a young daughter, Paul was doing quite well on antipsychotic medication until his ex-wife moved to another state, taking his daughter, who he saw on weekends. At first, Paul spent his weekends with his mother, helping her with yard work. Gradually, he began to spend less and less time with his mother and more and more time at his own home watching television. Whenever his mother suggested that he telephone or write to his daughter, Paul would reply, "What's the use?" Paul began to neglect his grooming and began to hear voices again. At his mother's urging, Paul sought professional help and was diagnosed

✎ Weird Words

Schizophrenia: A common type of psychosis, characterized by abnormalities in perception, content of thought, and thought processes (hallucinations and delusions) and by extensive withdrawal of interest from other people and the outside world, with excessive focusing on one's own mental life; now considered a group or spectrum of disorders rather than a single entity.*

Non-Compliance: When a patient does not follow the course of treatment recommended by the doctor or other health care professional.

Psychosis: A mental and behavioral disorder causing gross distortion or disorganization of a person's mental capacity, affective response, and capacity to recognize reality, communicate, and relate to others to the degree of interfering with the person's capacity to cope with the ordinary demands of everyday life. Also called psychotic disorder.*

Psychotic Relapse: Return of the symptoms of a psychotic disorder after a period of improvement.

Source: Definitions noted with an asterisk (*) are from *Stedman's Medical Dictionary, 27ᵗʰ Edition*, Copyright © 2000 Lippincott Williams & Wilkins. All rights reserved.

with depression. He was placed on an older, often called typical antipsychotic medication. Although the medication controlled the voices he heard it left Paul feeling tired and lethargic most of the time. Paul was sleeping or watching television large amounts of the day. Paul's mother noticed the changes in his activities and wondered if Paul was depressed. Paul's psychiatrist determined that Paul's behavior was a result of the side effects from the anti-psychotic medication, not depression because Paul did not feel particularly sad or hopeless. He prescribed one of the newer, atypical antipsychotic medications and Paul began to feel more like himself again.

One symptom that can differentiate a depressive episode from negative symptoms of schizophrenia is sadness. People with clinical depression frequently experience sadness, whereas people with negative symptoms of schizophrenia do not. Those who develop persistent depressive symptoms not related to psychotic episodes are more likely to have clinical depression. Clinical depression is a psychiatric disorder in which a person has a persistent (greater than 2 weeks) sad mood and/or an inability to derive pleasure from previously enjoyable activities. Changes in appetite, energy levels, and sleeping patterns are common, as are feelings of guilt, worthlessness, and hopelessness. People with clinical depression may have thoughts about death and suicide. Whether it is depression as part of a psychotic episode or a more persistent clinical depression, it is important to obtain a thorough evaluation by a mental health professional to determine the causative factors of these symptoms and how best to treat them.

Suicide

Untreated depression is a major risk factor for suicide, the eighth leading cause of death in the U.S. Suicide claims the lives of 30,000 Americans per year, outnumbering the murder rate by 3:2. Suicide impacts more than 180,000 persons in the U.S. each year taking into account the effect a suicide has on the surviving family members.

Paul's ex-wife returned with their daughter, they were getting along well and discussing reconciliation. Suddenly, Paul's ex-wife changed her mind and decided to move out of state once again. This second loss sent Paul spiraling into depression. He lost 10 pounds in one month, spent most of his days sleeping, and most of his nights crying or pacing. Paul felt hopeless, worthless, and began to wonder if life was worth living. He quit taking his antipsychotic medication and began to hear voices again. One morning, after drinking a few beers in front of the television, Paul ingested a lethal dose of medication. Fortunately, his mother found him, unconscious but still alive, and he was successfully treated for the overdose of medication. During his hospital stay Paul was stabilized on antipsychotic and antidepressant medication and began participating in a psychotherapy group where he learned how to cope with feelings of sadness, worthlessness, and hopelessness. The group helped him to change his thinking patterns. Paul has not heard voices or felt depressed for several months now, and is currently also participating in a vocational rehabilitation program where he is learning how to cope with feelings of sadness, worthlessness, and hopelessness. The group helped him to change his thinking patterns.

The highest risk of suicide occurs in the presence of multiple co-existing conditions, particularly combinations of mood or psychotic disorders with alcohol or drugs. Substance and alcohol abuse alone or in combination with psychiatric disorders are found in 25% of suicides. Major depressive disorder and bipolar disorder are associated with about half of all suicides. Patients with depression and schizophrenia are nearly three times more likely to attempt suicide than people with clinical depression alone and may be less likely to communicate suicidal intent to health care professionals. They are also more likely to use highly lethal methods in their suicide attempts. To date, there are no definitive measures to predict suicide. Researchers have identified factors that place individuals

> ♣ **It's A Fact!!**
>
> According to Lewis Judd, M.D., psychiatry department chair at the University of California, San Diego, studies show schizophrenia has the highest suicide rate of any mental disorder. At least 37% of people with schizophrenic disorder make at least one suicide attempt. Schizophrenia combined with bipolar disorder has a lifetime suicide attempt rate of 70.6%.
>
> —JBS

at higher risk for suicide, but as with suicide in general, the progression to suicide among people with schizophrenia is complex.

In general, the risk of suicide rises with advanced age, especially after the age of 60. By the age of 75, the risk for suicide doubles. This increase may be related to factors such as retirement, widowhood, social isolation, declining vigor and health, and other losses.

Suicide Prevention

Researchers believe that both depression and suicidal behavior can be linked to decreases in the neurotransmitter serotonin in the brain. Low levels of this brain chemical have been found in patients with depression, impulsive disorders, a history of violent suicide attempts, and also in postmortem brains of suicide victims. This has led to the use of a group of antidepressants called SSRIs (selective serotonin reuptake inhibitors) to treat depression in people with and without schizophrenia. The newer antipsychotic medications may also relieve some depressive symptoms in people with depression and schizophrenia. Psychotherapy, such as cognitive-behavioral therapy, in conjunction with medication, has also been found to be an effective treatment for depression. Mental Illness Research, Education, and Clinical Care (MIRECC) researchers are currently conducting studies to test the effectiveness of medications and psychotherapies for depression in people with schizophrenia.

Risk And Protective Factors For Suicide

Protective Factors From Suicide

- Intact social supports, marriage
- Active religious affiliation or faith
- Presence of dependent young children
- Ongoing supportive relationship with a caregiver
- Absence of depression or substance abuse
- Living close to medical and mental health resources
- Awareness that suicide is a product of illness
- Proven problem-solving and coping skills

♣ It's A Fact!!
Schizophrenia: The Myths, The Signs, The Statistics

Schizophrenia: The Signs

- Disordered or jumbled thinking which makes it hard to concentrate and to remember things.

- Hearing voices. One or several voices are heard definitely and regularly. The voices are so real that the person may often talk back to them.

- False beliefs that can't be shaken.

- Some people are convinced that they are living a completely different life from the life they are actually living—they may think they are very rich, very powerful, very intelligent, or that they are somebody else. Some people believe that others are trying to harm them.

- A person's emotions may change. They may show inappropriate emotions—laughing at something sad, or appear not to have any emotions at all.

- The loss of a sense of bodily boundaries.

- Inability to experience pleasure.

- Lack of motivation.

- High anxiety.

Schizophrenia: Let's Dispel The Myths

- Schizophrenia is not split personality or multiple personality disorder.

- Treatments now available for schizophrenia only control some of the symptoms.

- Schizophrenia is a persistent, long-term brain disorder.

- People have the impression that those with schizophrenia are looked after by government as a matter of course. This is a mistaken impression. Many people with schizophrenia find it difficult to get treatment, and those who refuse treatment because of the confusion in their minds more often never get treatment at all.

- People with schizophrenia are not necessarily violent, but left untreated a minority may become so. People with schizophrenia are more likely to be reclusive and retiring.

- People with schizophrenia are more likely to do harm to themselves than to others.

- Any anti-social behavior shown by a person with schizophrenia is usually not willful, but rather a result of this brain disorder.

Schizophrenia: The Statistics

- In a city of 3 million, 30,000 people will have experienced schizophrenia.

- One in 4,000 new cases of schizophrenia occur each year anywhere in the world.

- The incidence of schizophrenia is the same throughout the world: 1 in 100.

- Your likelihood of getting schizophrenia is one in a hundred.

- It appears to strike men and women equally.

- The usual onset is between the ages of 15 and 30.

- In most developed countries, people with schizophrenia occupy eight percent of hospital beds.

- One in ten people with schizophrenia commits suicide.

- One in four people with schizophrenia attempts suicide

The main enemy of the untreated schizophrenic is time. The person deteriorates. He/She must use up an inordinate amount of energy dealing with paranoid delusions and with the chaotic lifestyle that results from being only marginally able to take care of oneself. It is the art of schizophrenia to sabotage any positive gestures of help. (Source: The story of a street person, "Remembering My Brother," by Elizabeth Swados. New York Times Magazine, August 18, 1991.)

General Risk Factors For Suicide

- Young and elderly men

- Native American or Caucasian

- Self-reported hopelessness

- Deteriorating health

- Significant loss (emotional, social, physical, or financial security)

- Current or past substance abuse

- Family history of suicide

- Easy access to a firearm

Schizophrenia-Related Suicide Risk Factors

- Long-term illness with many relapses

- Symptoms and poor functioning upon discharge

- Awareness of illness, fear of deterioration

- Excessive dependence or loss of faith in treatment

- Depressed mood, hopelessness, hostility

- Prominent positive symptoms

☞ **Remember!!**
Schizophrenia with mood disorders greatly
increases a person's suicide risk. It is important to
seek treatment, continue medications, and follow
doctor or health care provider instructions
when seeking help for schizophrenia.

Chapter 14

Use Of Alcohol And Other Drugs Increases Teen Suicide Risk

Teens And Alcohol

Drinking among teenagers is a serious problem in the United States.

- Alcohol is the most commonly used drug among teens. A recent survey of students found that:

  - 52% of eighth graders (and 80% of high-school seniors) have used alcohol at some time; and

  - 25% of eighth graders (and 62% of high-school seniors) have been drunk.[1]

- Even though it is illegal for teens to drink, most say that it is easy to get alcohol. 71% of eighth graders and 95% of high-school seniors say that it would be easy to get alcohol if they wanted some.[2]

- Although many teenagers try alcohol, most teens do not get drunk on a regular basis. Only 8% of eighth graders (and 32% of high-school seniors) say they have been drunk in the past month.[3]

About This Chapter: Text in this chapter includes excerpts from "Teens and Alcohol," National Youth Violence Prevention Resource Center, 2002; and "Substance Use and the Risk of Suicide Among Youths," Substance Abuse and Mental Health Services Administration (SAMHSA), July 12, 2002.

- Most teens disapprove of frequent heavy drinking. 81% of eighth graders and 65% of high-school seniors say they disapprove of drinking heavily once or twice each weekend.[4]

- Teens often underestimate the risk that drinking can pose. In a recent survey, only 56% of eighth graders and 43% of high-school seniors said that they thought drinking heavily once or twice a weekend was a great risk.[5]

What Are Some Of The Real Risks?

- Drinking alcohol increases the risk that a teen will commit or be a victim of a serious crime, such as assault, rape, or murder.[6]

- Drinking alcohol increases teens' risk of death from car crashes and drowning.[7, 8]

- Drinking alcohol increases the likelihood that a teen will engage in risky unprotected sex.[9, 10]

- Teens who drink are more likely than other teens to attempt suicide.[11]

- If a teen drinks a large amount of alcohol in a short period of time, alcohol poisoning can occur, leading to coma or even death.

> **✤ It's A Fact!!**
> The National Strategy for Suicide Prevention reports that between 40 and 60% of those who die by suicide are intoxicated at the time of death. An estimated 18–66% of those who die by suicide have some alcohol in their blood at the time of death.

The younger teens are when they begin to drink, the greater the risk for addiction. People who begin drinking before the age of 15 are four times more likely to be dependent on alcohol as adults than those who wait until age 21. More than 40% of those who start drinking at age 14 or younger become dependent on alcohol as adults.[12]

Teens That Drink Are Also More Likely To Attempt Suicide

Alcohol use among teenagers has been associated with considering, planning, attempting, and completing suicide. In one study of teen suicide, drug and alcohol abuse was the most common characteristic of those who attempted suicide; 70 percent of these teenagers frequently used alcohol and/or other drugs.[13] However, research has not proven that drinking actually causes suicidal behavior, only that the two behaviors are associated.[14]

What You Can Do

Get the facts about alcohol and drinking. Many teens are not aware of basic facts about alcohol. For example, did you know that:

- one drink can make you fail a breath test;

- one 12-ounce beer has about as much alcohol as a 1.5-ounce shot of liquor, a 5-ounce glass of wine, or a wine cooler; and

- mixing alcohol with medications or illegal drugs is extremely dangerous and can lead to accidental death.

Learn about different ways to turn down a drink. Sometimes, watching TV, or listening to people talk, it's easy to believe that everyone is drinking. In fact, most teens don't drink on a regular basis, and drinking doesn't make you cool. If someone offers you a drink just say, "No thanks," "I don't drink," or "I'm not into that." You may want to try suggesting another activity instead.

Learn to recognize the signs of a drinking problem in a friend (or yourself). If a friend has one or more of the following warning signs, he or she may have a problem with alcohol:

- getting drunk on a regular basis

- lying about how much alcohol he or she is using or hiding alcohol

- believing that alcohol is necessary to have fun

- having frequent hangovers

- feeling run-down, depressed, or even suicidal

- having blackouts—forgetting what he or she did while drinking

- having problems at school or getting in trouble with the law

- giving up activities he or she used to do, such as playing sports or doing homework, and shunning friends who don't drink

♣ It's A Fact!!
Firearms, Alcohol, And Suicide: A Deadly Connection

The statistics speak for themselves. According to the Minnesota Department of Health, in Minnesota, suicide ranks as the second leading cause of death of young people between the ages of 10–34—only unintentional injuries occur more frequently. Research shows that firearms remain the most commonly used suicide method among youth, regardless of race or gender, accounting for almost two of every three completed suicides.

Although poison and cutting/piercing instruments were used most frequently to attempt suicide, a firearm is the tool most frequently used in completed suicide by both men and women of all ages, and for boys and girls ages 10–14.[1] In 1997, twenty 15–19 year old Minnesotans (18 males and 2 females) committed suicide with a firearm; in 1998 there were 19 (17 males and 2 females).[2]

Firearms Need To Be Removed From The Homes Of At-Risk Youth

Research concludes that the availability of guns in the home, regardless of firearm type or method of safe storage, appears to increase the risk of suicide among adolescents.[3] Research maintains that youth would be less likely to substitute an alternative suicide method if guns were not easily accessible. Method substitution may be less likely to occur in adolescents and young adults, possibly because of the prominent role that impulsivity and substance abuse play in youthful suicide. The vast majority (92%) of firearm suicide attempts result in immediate fatality.[4] Suicide attempts by other means, such as ingestion of poison or exposure to high quantities of carbon monoxide, allow time for a change of heart and/or medical intervention.

There Is A Connection Between Alcohol And Suicide And Firearms

The literature strongly suggests that alcohol is a contributing factor in a large number of suicides for both men and women.[5] However, alcohol's role in suicides remains unclear. Between 18 percent and 66 percent of suicide victims have alcohol in their blood at the time of death.[6] Suicide victims who had been drinking, but not necessarily intoxicated, were 4.9 times more likely to have used firearms than those who had not been drinking.[7]

Why Don't We Know More About Suicide And Alcohol?

There are two main reasons why little is known about the connection between alcohol and suicide.

1. Blood alcohol concentration (BAC) screening is not routine in medical treatment settings, unless the presence of alcohol would alter the course of treatment; and

2. Researchers must go back to the autopsy report in suicides to determine if alcohol was in the bloodstream. Currently, this information is not documented on a death certificate.

References

1. Hoyert, et. Al. Deaths: Final data for 1997. Centers for Disease Control and Prevention. *National Vital Statistics Report*. June 30, 1999. 47: 19. 71.

2. Minnesota Department of Health, Division of Health Statistics.

3. Brent, D.A., et. Al. The Presence and Accessibility of Firearms in the Homes of Adolescent Suicides. *Journal of the American Medical Association*. 1991. 266: 21. 2989 - 2995.

4. Wintemute et. al. The Choice of Weapons in Firearms Suicide. *American Journal of Public Health*. July, 1977. 78: 7. 284.

5. Caces, F. and Harford, T. Time Series Analysis of Alcohol Consumption and Suicide Mortality in the United States, 1934-1987. *Journal of Studies on Alcohol*. July, 1998. 59. 455-461.

6. Roizen, 1998.

7. Brent, et. Al. Alcohol, Firearms, and Suicide Among Youth: Temporal trends.

✤ It's A Fact!!

Alcoholism And Suicide

- Alcoholics have a much higher rate of death by suicide than do members of the general population.

- Those alcoholics with a history of suicide attempts appear to have a significantly more severe course of alcohol dependence than other alcoholics.

- The fathers, mothers, and siblings of alcoholics who had attempted suicide also showed a significantly higher prevalence of suicide attempts.

Source: "Suicidal Behavior Among Alcoholics," Addiction Technology Transfer Center National Office, 2002.

References

1. Institute for Social Research, University of Michigan, *Monitoring the Future Study*, 2000 Data From In-School Surveys of 8th, 10th, and 12th Grade Students, Table 1.

2. Institute for Social Research, University of Michigan, *Monitoring the Future Study*, 2000 Data From In-School Surveys of 8th, 10th, and 12th Grade Students, Tables 12 and 13.

3. Institute for Social Research, University of Michigan, *Monitoring the Future Study*, 2000 Data From In-School Surveys of 8th, 10th, and 12th Grade Students, Table 2.

4. Institute for Social Research, University of Michigan, *Monitoring the Future Study*, 2000 Data From In-School Surveys of 8th, 10th, and 12th Grade Students, Tables 10 and 11.

5. Institute for Social Research, University of Michigan, *Monitoring the Future Study*, 2000 Data From In-School Surveys of 8th, 10th, and 12th Grade Students, Tables 8 and 9.

6. National Institute on Alcohol Abuse and Alcoholism, *Ninth Special Report to the U.S. Congress on Alcohol and Health*, Bethesda, MD: U.S. Department of Health and Human Services, 1997.

7. National Institute on Alcohol Abuse and Alcoholism. (1996). *Alcohol Alert* No. 31: Drinking and Driving. Bethesda, MD: NIAAA.

8. Office of the Inspector General. (1992). *Report to the Surgeon General, Youth and Alcohol: Dangerous and Deadly Consequences*, Washington, D.C.: U.S. Department of Education.

9. Fergusson, D.M., & Lynskey, M.T. (1996). Alcohol misuse and adolescent sexual behaviors and risk taking. Pediatrics 98(1): 91-96.

10. Strunin, L., & Hingson, R. (1992). Alcohol, drugs, and adolescent sexual behavior. *International Journal of the Addictions* 27(2): 129-146.

11. White, H.R. (1997). Longitudinal perspective on alcohol use and aggression during adolescence. In: Galanter, M., ed. *Recent Developments in Alcoholism*. Vol. 13. New York: Plenum Press, pp. 81-103.

12. Grant, B.F. (1998). The impact of a family history of alcoholism on the relationship between age of onset of alcohol use and DSM-IV alcohol dependence: Results from the National Longitudinal Alcohol Epidemiologic Survey, *Alcohol Health and Research World*, 22.

13. Office of the Inspector General. (1992). *Report to the Surgeon General, Youth and Alcohol: Dangerous and Deadly Consequences*, Washington, D.C.: U.S. Department of Education.

14. National Institute on Alcohol Abuse and Alcoholism. (1997). Youth Drinking: Risk Factors and Consequences, *Alcohol Alert* No. 37.

Substance Use And The Risk Of Suicide Among Youths

The National Household Survey on Drug Abuse (NHSDA) asks youths aged 12 to 17 whether they had thought seriously about killing themselves or tried to kill themselves during the 12 months before the survey interview.[1] For the purpose of this report, youths who thought about or tried to

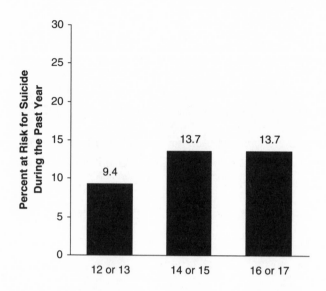

Figure 14.1. *Percentages Of Youths Aged 12–17 At Risk For Suicide During The Past Year, By Age: 2000.*

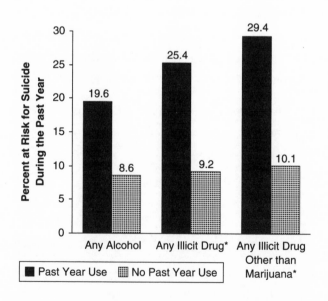

Figure 14.2. *Percentages Of Youths Aged 12–17 At Risk For Suicide During The Past Year, By Past Year Alcohol Or Illicit Drug Use: 2000.*

♣ It's A Fact!!

Alcohol use interacts with conditions such as depression and stress to contribute to suicide, the third leading cause of death among people between the ages of 14 and 25. In one study, 37 percent of eighth grade females who drank heavily reported attempting suicide, compared with 11 percent who did not drink.

Source: "Underage Drinking: A Major Public Health Challenge," *Alcohol Alert*, No. 59, April 2003, National Institute on Alcohol Abuse and Alcoholism (NIAAA).

kill themselves during the past year were considered to be at-risk for suicide. Responses were analyzed by geographic regions for comparative purposes.[2]

Respondents were also queried about their use of alcohol and illicit drugs during the 12 months before the survey interview. "Any illicit drug" refers to marijuana/hashish, cocaine (including crack), inhalants, hallucinogens, heroin, or prescription-type drugs used nonmedically. Youths were also asked whether they had received treatment or counseling services during the past year for emotional or behavioral problems that were not caused by alcohol or drugs.[3] Respondents who received treatment or counseling were asked to identify reasons for the last time they received these services.[4]

Suicide Risk Among Youths

Suicide is an important cause of mortality among youths in the United States.[5] The 2000 NHSDA estimated that almost 3 million youths were at risk for suicide during the past year. Of youths at risk for suicide, 37 percent actually tried to kill themselves during the past year. Females (16 percent) were almost twice as likely as males (8 percent) to be at risk for suicide during the past year. The likelihood of suicide risk was also greater among youths aged 14 to 17 than it was among those aged 12 or 13 (Figure 14.1). The likelihood of suicide risk was similar among white, black, Hispanic, and Asian youths.

Substance Use And Suicide Risk

Prior research has associated substance use with an increased risk of suicide among youths.[6] The 2000 NHSDA found that youths who reported alcohol or illicit drug use during the past year were more likely than those who did not use these substances to be at risk for suicide during this same time period. For instance, youths who reported past year use of any illicit drug other than marijuana (29 percent) were almost three times more likely than youths who did not (10 percent) to be at risk for suicide during this time period (Figure 14.2).

Regional Differences Of Suicide Risk

Regionally, youths from the West (14 percent) were more likely to be at risk for suicide during the past year than those who lived in the Midwest (12 percent) or Northeast (11 percent) (Figure 14.3). The risk of suicide was similar among youths from large metropolitan, small metropolitan, and non-metropolitan counties.

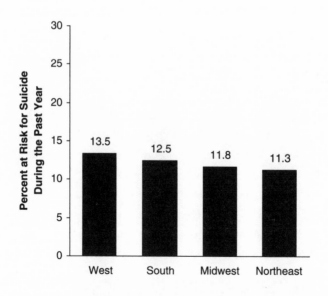

Figure 14.3. Percentages Of Youths Aged 12–17 At Risk For Suicide During The Past Year, By Geographic Region: 2000.

Mental Health Treatment Utilization Among Suicidal Youths

Research has demonstrated that the most effective way to prevent suicide is through the early identification and treatment of those at risk.[6] Yet, according to the 2000 NHSDA, only 36 percent of youths at risk for suicide during the past year received mental health treatment during this same time period. Fewer than one-fifth of youths at risk for suicide received help from a private therapist, psychologist, psychiatrist, social worker, or counselor (Table 14.1). More than 15 percent received treatment from school counselors, school psychologists, or having regular meetings with teachers. Among youths at risk for suicide who received mental health treatment, 38 percent reported suicidal thoughts or attempts as the reason for the last time they received these services.[7]

Table 14.1. Percentages Of Youths Aged 12–17 At Risk For Suicide During The Past Year Reporting That They Received Mental Health Services During This Same Time Period, By Location Of Treatment: 2000.

Location of Treatment	Percent Reporting That They Received Mental Health Services During the Past Year
Any treatment	35.5
Private therapist, psychologist, psychiatrist, social worker, or counselor	19.4
School counselors, school psychologists, or having regular meetings with teachers	15.1
Mental health clinic or center	6.5
In-home therapist, counselor, or family preservation worker	6.3
Pediatrician or other family doctor	5.3
Overnight or longer stay in any type of hospital	5.2
Special education classes while in a regular classroom or in a special classroom, a special program, or in a special school	4.6
Partial day hospital or day treatment program	3.8
Overnight or longer stay in a residential treatment center	3.5
Overnight or longer stay in foster care or in a therapeutic foster care home	2.0

End Notes

1. Respondents were asked whether they tried to kill themselves during the past year if they reported thinking seriously about killing themselves during the same time period and/or they answered affirmatively to at least one of the following questions: (a) "During the past 12 months, has there been a time when nothing was fun for you and you just weren't interested in anything?" (b) "During the past 12 months, has there been a time when you had less energy than you usually do?" or (c) "During the past 12 months, has there been a time when you felt you couldn't do anything well or that you weren't as good-looking or as smart as other people?"

2. Regions include the following groups of States:

   • **Northeast Region:** Maine, New Hampshire, Vermont, Massachusetts, Rhode Island, Connecticut, New York, New Jersey, Pennsylvania.

   • **Midwest Region:** Wisconsin, Illinois, Michigan, Indiana, Ohio, North Dakota, South Dakota, Nebraska, Kansas, Minnesota, Iowa, Missouri.

   • **South Region:** Alabama, Kentucky, Mississippi, Tennessee, West Virginia, Virginia, Maryland, Delaware, District of Columbia, North Carolina, South Carolina, Georgia, Florida, Texas, Oklahoma, Arkansas, Louisiana.

   • **West Region:** Idaho, Nevada, Arizona, New Mexico, Utah, Colorado, Wyoming, Montana, California, Oregon, Washington, Hawaii, Alaska.

3. Respondents were asked about treatment or counseling services provided by any of the following: Overnight or longer stay in any type of hospital; overnight or longer stay in a residential treatment center; overnight or longer stay in foster care or in a therapeutic foster care home; treatment or counseling at a partial day hospital or day treatment program; visiting a mental health clinic or center; visiting a private therapist, psychologist, psychiatrist, social worker, or counselor; treatment or counseling from

an in-home therapist, counselor, or family preservation worker; visiting a pediatrician or other family doctor; receiving special education services while in a regular classroom or in a special classroom, a special program, or in a special school; or talking to school counselors, school psychologists, or having regular meetings with teachers.

4. Respondents were asked to select reasons from a list of options, which included: 1) Thought about killing self or tried to kill self, 2) felt depressed, 3) felt very afraid or anxious, 4) were breaking rules or "acting out," 5) had eating problems, and 6) some other reason.

5. Catallozzi, M., Pletcher, J.R., & Schwarz, D.F. (2001). Prevention of suicide in adolescents. *Current Opinions in Pediatrics*, 13, 417-422.

6. National Institute of Mental Health. (1999, November 26). "Suicide Facts." Retrieved April 2, 2002 from http://www.nimh.nih.gov/publicat/suicidefacts.cfm.

7. Youths who reported they received mental health services through special education services while in a regular classroom or in a special classroom, a special program, or in a special school were not asked the reason for the last time they received these services and were totally excluded from this analysis.

Figure And Table Notes

*Any illicit drug refers to marijuana/hashish, cocaine (including crack), heroin, hallucinogens, inhalants, or prescription-type drugs used non-medically. Any illicit drug other than marijuana refers to any of these listed drugs, regardless of marijuana/hashish use; marijuana/hashish users who also have used any of the other drugs listed are included.

Source (table and all figures): Substance Abuse and Mental Health Services Administration (SAMHSA) 2000 NHSDA.

The National Household Survey on Drug Abuse (NHSDA) is an annual survey sponsored by the Substance Abuse and Mental Health Services Administration (SAMHSA). The 2000 data are based on information obtained from nearly 72,000 persons aged 12 or older, including more than 25,000

youths aged 12 to 17. The survey collects data by administering questionnaires to a representative sample of the population through face-to-face interviews at their place of residence.

☞ **Remember!!**

If you recognize signs of drug
or alcohol abuse in a friend or
yourself, professional help may be
necessary. Call the National Clearing-
house for Alcohol and Drug Information at 800-729-6686 for information
and referrals. Don't try to handle this
on your own. Talk with an adult you
can trust, such as your parents or a
trusted family member, a teacher,
a school counselor, your clergy,
or a professional at a mental health center.

Chapter 15

Body Image Problems And Eating Disorders

Body Image Problems

It's Monday morning and the ritual has started already. You're taking a shower, but something has caught your eye in the mirror. Did your nose grow overnight? It's always been a honker. But today, it's all over your face. Makeup, you decide, is the solution, so you spend another 45 minutes after your shower experimenting with nose-slimming techniques and blush. Perhaps there's something you can do with your hair to camouflage your nose, you think. On second thought, maybe going to school today isn't such a great idea after all. You're already running late, and people will just stare at your nose all day anyway. If only you could get your parents to spring for plastic surgery . . .

Does that—or something like that—sound familiar? Almost everyone wishes that something about their body was a bit different. This is particularly

About This Chapter: This chapter includes "Body Image Problems," reviewed by Katharine Phillips, M.D., and Paul Robins, Ph.D. This information was provided by TeensHealth, one of the largest resources online for medically reviewed health information written for parents, kids, and teens. For more articles like this one, visit www.TeensHealth.org, or www.KidsHealth.org. © 2000 The Nemours Center for Children's Health Media, a division of The Nemours Foundation. Additional text under the heading "Eating Disorders" is excerpted from "Eating Disorders: Facts About Eating Disorders and the Search for Solutions," National Institute of Mental Health (NIMH), NIH Publication No. 01-4901, updated August 2002.

true for teens whose bodies are going through all sorts of changes caused by puberty. But imagine being totally obsessed with something you felt you had to change. And imagine that the thing you wanted to change wasn't even a big thing, but you couldn't stop thinking about it.

This kind of obsession with a particular body part is called body dysmorphic disorder (BDD). Described by Brown University's Katharine Phillips, M.D., as the disease of imagined ugliness, BDD can cause teens to drop out of school, quit their jobs, neglect their social lives, and in the most severe cases, attempt suicide.

Defining Body Dysmorphic Disorder

"Thirty to 40% of the population has some kind of dissatisfaction with their bodies," says Carol Watkins, MD, of the Northern County Psychiatric Associates in Baltimore, Maryland. This is especially true for teens whose bodies are changing rapidly. "But BDD occurs when a person gets really preoccupied that there's something wrong with a particular part of the body." BDD occurs in only a small percentage of those teens who experience "normal" dissatisfaction.

✎ Weird Words

Anorexia: Diminished appetite; aversion to food.

Bulimia: A chronic abnormal disorder involving repeated and secretive episodic bouts of eating characterized by uncontrolled rapid ingestion of large quantities of food over a short period of time (binge eating), followed by self-induced vomiting, use of laxatives or diuretics, fasting, or vigorous exercise in order to prevent weight gain; often accompanied by feelings of guilt, depression, or self-disgust.

Body Dysmorphic Disorder (BDD): Psychosomatic (somatoform) disorder characterized by preoccupation with some imagined defect in appearance in a normal-appearing person.

Eating Disorder: Group of mental disorders including anorexia nervosa, bulimia nervosa, pica, and rumination disorder of infancy.

Obsessive: A recurrent and persistent idea, thought, or impulse to carry out an act that is ego-dystonic, that is experienced as senseless or repugnant, and that the individual cannot voluntarily suppress.

Source: From *Stedman's Medical Dictionary, 27th Edition*, Copyright © 2000 Lippincott Williams & Wilkins. All rights reserved.

Teens with BDD obsess about an imagined or slight defect in appearance. Most often, they focus on what they perceive as a facial flaw, but they can also worry about other body parts, such as short legs or breast size or body shape. Just as teens with eating disorders obsess about their weight, teens with BDD worry about an aspect of their appearance. "[Teens with BDD worry] their hair is thinning, their face is terribly scarred—when in fact they look perfectly fine. And they worry they will be considered superficial or vain if they tell people about their concerns," Dr. Phillips says.

Because few people with BDD are willing to talk about their concerns or seek help, it's hard to know exactly how common BDD is. Dr. Phillips believes that as many as one in 50 people, mainly women in their 30s, may have the disorder. Other researchers believe the number of people with BDD is even less. And BDD also affects teens—about 70% of cases begin before age 18.

What Causes BDD?

The causes of BDD are unclear, but there are several theories. One theory is that the disorder is caused by a chemical imbalance in the brain, perhaps involving serotonin, that leads to the obsession with perceived body flaws. The causes of that imbalance are unknown. Other theories focus on psychological, behavioral, or cultural factors as the cause of BDD. For example, our culture puts a lot of emphasis on body image and that may play a role.

What is known is that BDD sufferers have tendencies toward being obsessive (so preoccupied with a certain thought or thoughts that the person can't just shake the thought and move on). There is also evidence that people with BDD suffer from depression. So a combination of factors may contribute to a person having BDD.

Signs And Symptoms Of BDD

People with mild to moderate symptoms of BDD usually spend a great deal of time grooming themselves in the morning. Throughout the day, they may frequently check their appearance in mirrors or windows. In addition, they may repeatedly seek reassurance from people around them that they look okay.

"It's normal for adolescents to worry about pimples and look in the mirror," Dr. Watkins says. "It's not normal, however, to hide in a room because of it. Or to seek plastic surgery." It's also not normal to measure the "flawed" body part repeatedly or to spend large sums of money on makeup to cover the problem. And those teens with BDD who find plastic surgeons willing to perform surgery are often not satisfied with the results.

Although teens with mild BDD usually continue to go to school, the obsessions can interfere with their daily lives. "I spoke with one adult who told me that for an entire school year she kept her hand over her nose while at school. This act prevented her from volunteering any responses in class," says Terri Fernandez-Tyson, a researcher who studies BDD at Arizona State University.

Teens with severe symptoms may drop out of school, quit their jobs, or refuse to leave their homes. In the most severe cases, teens with severe BDD may consider or attempt suicide.

✔ Quick Tip
Getting Help For BDD

Body dysmorphic disorder, like other obsessions, can interfere with your life—robbing it of pleasure and draining your energy. An experienced psychologist or psychiatrist who is knowledgeable about BDD can help you break the grip of the disorder so that you can fully enjoy your life.

Diagnosing And Treating BDD

BDD is diagnosed through an interview with a psychiatrist or psychologist, and a questionnaire may be used to help the doctor determine if a teen has BDD. The Body Dysmorphic Disorder Questionnaire, a nine-item quiz, focuses on a person's concerns about his or her physical appearance. Another questionnaire used to diagnose BDD, the Body Dysmorphic Disorder Examination (BDDE), contains 34 questions that evaluate six tendencies in a teen:

1. The preoccupation with and evaluation of appearance.

2. The degree of self-consciousness and feelings of discomfort in public.

3. The tendency to overvalue appearance in determining overall self-worth.

4. The avoidance of social situations and physical contact with others.

5. The altering of one's appearance through grooming, dress, or cosmetics.

6. The tendency to frequently check one's appearance, perform repetitive grooming, and seek reassurance from others.

But all the assessment tools in the world don't make it easy to diagnose BDD. "People with BDD tend to be ashamed and secretive and will seek a dermatologist's or a plastic surgeon's help before going to a psychiatrist," Dr. Watkins says. Teens who do seek treatment from mental health professionals are likely to report feelings of depression and anxiety and may not talk to the health professional about their feelings about their bodies. As a result, the condition may actually go undiagnosed.

Once BDD has been diagnosed, however, there are effective treatments, including medication and cognitive behavior therapy. The medications sometimes used to treat BDD are also sometimes used to treat depression and anxiety. These medications are usually not habit-forming and can significantly relieve BDD symptoms.

Cognitive behavior therapy—when a therapist helps a teen examine and change faulty beliefs, resist compulsive behaviors, and face stressful situations—has also been found to be an effective treatment for BDD. "If they think their hair is thinning and everyone is looking at them, you send them into a social situation where they think people are looking at their hair and coach them on how they should respond," Dr. Watkins says. "You start with baby steps—first you cover up mirrors, then you teach them not to look in mirrors."

Eating Disorders

Eating is controlled by many factors, including appetite, food availability, family, peer, and cultural practices, and attempts at voluntary control. Dieting to a body weight leaner than needed for health is highly promoted by current fashion trends, sales campaigns for special foods, and in some activities and professions. Eating disorders involve serious disturbances in eating behavior, such as extreme and unhealthy reduction of food intake or severe overeating, as well as feelings of distress or extreme concern about body shape or weight. Researchers are investigating how and why initially voluntary behaviors, such as eating smaller or larger amounts of food than usual, at some point move beyond control in some people and develop into an eating disorder.

✤ It's A Fact!!

Eating disorders frequently co-occur with other psychiatric disorders such as depression, substance abuse, and anxiety disorders.[1] People who suffer from eating disorders can experience a wide range of physical health complications, including serious heart conditions and kidney failure which may lead to death. Therefore, it is critically important to recognize eating disorders as real and treatable diseases.

Eating disorders are not due to a failure of will or behavior; rather, they are real, treatable medical illnesses in which certain maladaptive patterns of eating take on a life of their own. The main types of eating disorders are anorexia nervosa and bulimia nervosa.[1] A third type, binge-eating disorder, has been suggested but has not yet been approved as a formal psychiatric diagnosis.[2] Eating disorders frequently develop during adolescence or early adulthood, but some reports indicate their onset can occur during childhood or later in adulthood.[3]

Females are much more likely than males to develop an eating disorder. Only an estimated 5 to 15 percent of people with anorexia or bulimia[4] and an estimated 35 percent of those with binge-eating disorder[5] are male.

Anorexia Nervosa

An estimated 0.5 to 3.7 percent of females suffer from anorexia nervosa in their lifetime.[1] Symptoms of anorexia nervosa include:

- Resistance to maintaining body weight at or above a minimally normal weight for age and height.

- Intense fear of gaining weight or becoming fat, even though underweight.

- Disturbance in the way in which one's body weight or shape is experienced, undue influence of body weight or shape on self-evaluation, or denial of the seriousness of the current low body weight.

- Infrequent or absent menstrual periods (in females who have reached puberty).

People with anorexia see themselves as overweight even though they are dangerously thin. The process of eating becomes an obsession. Unusual eating habits develop, such as avoiding food and meals, picking out a few foods and eating these in small quantities, or carefully weighing and portioning food. People with anorexia may repeatedly check their body weight, and many engage in other techniques to control their weight, such as intense and compulsive exercise, or purging by means of vomiting and abuse of laxatives, enemas, and diuretics. Girls with anorexia often experience a delayed onset of their first menstrual period.

> ✤ **It's A Fact!!**
>
> The most common causes of death in people with anorexia are complications of the disorder, such as cardiac arrest or electrolyte imbalance, and suicide.

The course and outcome of anorexia nervosa vary across individuals: some fully recover after a single episode; some have a fluctuating pattern of weight gain and relapse; and others experience a chronically deteriorating course of illness over many years. The mortality rate among people with anorexia has been estimated at 0.56 percent per year, or approximately 5.6 percent per decade, which is about 12 times higher than the annual death rate due to all causes of death among females ages 15–24 in the general population.[6]

Bulimia Nervosa

An estimated 1.1 percent to 4.2 percent of females have bulimia nervosa in their lifetime.[1] Symptoms of bulimia nervosa include:

- Recurrent episodes of binge eating, characterized by eating an excessive amount of food within a discrete period of time and by a sense of lack of control over eating during the episode.

- Recurrent inappropriate compensatory behavior in order to prevent weight gain, such as self-induced vomiting or misuse of laxatives, diuretics, enemas, or other medications (purging); fasting; or excessive exercise.

- The binge eating and inappropriate compensatory behaviors both occur, on average, at least twice a week for 3 months.

- Self-evaluation is unduly influenced by body shape and weight.

♣ **It's A Fact!!**
Eating Disorders Linked To Suicide Risk

One third of anorexic women and 30% of bulimic women have attempted suicide according to a study reported in the May 2004 journal *General Hospital Psychiatry*. Dr. Gabriella Milos led the researchers at the University Hospital Zurich who found that women who had an eating disorder who also had attempted suicide usually had at least one other psychiatric condition. The group also concluded that these findings show that impulse control problems (including binging and purging) are an important risk factor for suicide attempts. The results showed that women with anorexia who had suicidal thoughts were young when the eating disorder began and were more concerned with their appearance and fearful of weight gain than those without suicidal thoughts.

—JBS

Because purging or other compensatory behavior follows the binge-eating episodes, people with bulimia usually weigh within the normal range for their age and height. However, like individuals with anorexia, they may fear gaining weight, desire to lose weight, and feel intensely dissatisfied with their bodies. People with bulimia often perform the behaviors in secrecy, feeling disgusted and ashamed when they binge, yet relieved once they purge.

Treatment Strategies[1]

Eating disorders can be treated and a healthy weight restored. The sooner these disorders are diagnosed and treated, the better the outcomes are likely to be. Because of their complexity, eating disorders require a comprehensive treatment plan involving medical care and monitoring, psychosocial interventions, nutritional counseling, and when appropriate, medication management. At the time of diagnosis, the clinician must determine whether the person is in immediate danger and requires hospitalization.

Treatment of anorexia calls for a specific program that involves three main phases:

1. Restoring weight lost to severe dieting and purging.

2. Treating psychological disturbances such as distortion of body image, low self-esteem, and interpersonal conflicts.

3. Achieving long-term remission and rehabilitation, or full recovery.

Early diagnosis and treatment increases the treatment success rate. Use of psychotropic medication in people with anorexia should be considered only after weight gain has been established. Certain selective serotonin reuptake inhibitors (SSRIs) have been shown to be helpful for weight maintenance and for resolving mood and anxiety symptoms associated with anorexia.

The acute management of severe weight loss is usually provided in an inpatient hospital setting, where feeding plans address the person's medical and nutritional needs. In some cases, intravenous feeding is recommended. Once malnutrition has been corrected and weight gain has begun, psychotherapy (often cognitive-behavioral or interpersonal psychotherapy) can help people with anorexia overcome low self-esteem and address distorted thought and behavior patterns. Families are sometimes included in the therapeutic process.

The primary goal of treatment for bulimia is to reduce or eliminate binge eating and purging behavior. To this end, nutritional rehabilitation, psychosocial intervention, and medication management strategies are often employed. Establishment of a pattern of regular, non-binge meals, improvement of attitudes related to the eating disorder, encouragement of healthy but not excessive exercise, and resolution of co-occurring conditions such as mood or anxiety disorders are among the specific aims of these strategies. Individual psychotherapy (especially cognitive-behavioral or interpersonal psychotherapy), group psychotherapy that uses a cognitive-behavioral approach, and family or marital therapy have been reported to be effective. Psychotropic medications, primarily antidepressants such as the selective serotonin reuptake inhibitors (SSRIs), have been found helpful for people with bulimia, particularly those with significant symptoms of depression or anxiety, or those who have not responded adequately to psychosocial treatment alone. These medications also may help prevent relapse. The treatment goals and strategies for binge-eating disorder are similar to those for bulimia, and studies are currently evaluating the effectiveness of various interventions.

☞ **Remember!!**
People with body image or eating disorders often do not recognize or admit that they are ill. As a result, they may strongly resist getting and staying in treatment. Family members or other trusted individuals can be helpful in ensuring that the person with a body image or eating disorder receives needed care and rehabilitation. For some people, treatment may be long term.

References

1. American Psychiatric Association Work Group on Eating Disorders. Practice guideline for the treatment of patients with eating disorders (revision). *American Journal of Psychiatry*, 2000; 157(1 Suppl): 1-39.

2. American Psychiatric Association. *Diagnostic and Statistical Manual for Mental Disorders, fourth edition (DSM-IV)*. Washington, DC: American Psychiatric Press, 1994.

3. Becker AE, Grinspoon SK, Klibanski A, Herzog DB. Eating disorders. *New England Journal of Medicine*, 1999; 340(14): 1092-8.

4. Andersen AE. Eating disorders in males. In: Brownell KD, Fairburn CG, eds. *Eating disorders and obesity: a comprehensive handbook*. New York: Guilford Press, 1995; 177-87.

5. Spitzer RL, Yanovski S, Wadden T, Wing R, Marcus MD, Stunkard A, Devlin M, Mitchell J, Hasin D, Horne RL. Binge eating disorder: its further validation in a multisite study. *International Journal of Eating Disorders*, 1993; 13(2): 137-53.

6. Sullivan PF. Mortality in anorexia nervosa. *American Journal of Psychiatry*, 1995; 152(7): 1073-4.

Chapter 16

Self-Injury In Teens

Worried About Self-Injury?

What Is Self-Injury?

Self-injury is a way of dealing with very difficult feelings that build up inside. People deal with these feelings in various ways. Here are some examples:

- cutting or burning themselves,
- bruising themselves,
- taking an overdose of tablets,
- pulling hair, or
- picking skin.

Some people think that the seriousness of the problem can be measured by how bad the injury is. This is not the case—a person who hurts themselves a bit can be feeling just as bad as someone who hurts themselves a lot.

Self-injury can affect anyone. It is a lot more common than people think. Many people hurt themselves secretly for a long time before finding the courage to tell someone.

Why Do People Do It?

Everyone has problems in their lives and often people look for help. But sometimes it's hard to cope or even to put feelings into words. If they get bottled up inside, the pressure goes up and up until they feel like they might explode. This is the point where some people injure themselves.

What Makes People So Stressed?

There are lots of things:

- problems to do with race, culture, or religion
- money
- bullying
- growing up
- sexuality
- problems with friends
- bereavement
- housing problems
- pressures at school or work
- abuse
- pressure to fit in

♣ It's A Fact!!

A recent study of college under-graduates (Gratz, Conrad, and Roemer, 2002) asked study partici-pants about specific self-harm be-haviors and found alarmingly high rates. Although the high rates may have been due in part to the broad spectrum of self-harm behaviors that were assessed (e.g., severe scratching and interfering with the healing of wounds were included), the numbers are certainly cause for concern.

- 18% reported having harmed themselves more than 10 times in the past,
- 10% reported having harmed themselves more than 100 times in the past, and
- 38% endorsed a history of deliberate self-harm.

Source: "Self-Harm," National Center for Post-Traumatic Stress Disorder (PTSD), December 2003.

When a lot of problems come together, they can feel too much. If you're also feeling vulnerable, it's hard to cope as well as you normally do.

Thinking About Stopping

There are lots of reasons why you might want to stop injuring yourself, although you might not know what else to do to help you cope. Here are some feelings that you might recognize.

- **Embarrassed** in case people think you're weird.

- **Depressed** about anything ever getting better.

- **Guilty** because you can't stop harming yourself, even if you want to.

- **Afraid** that you might end up dead.

- **Isolated**. You don't know who to talk to.

- **Helpless**. You don't know what to do for the best.

- **Hating yourself** for not being what people want.

- **Upset**. You can't keep your feelings in, or may be you can't let them out.

- **Worried** in case people think you're just attention-seeking.

- **Out of control**. You might not know why you hurt yourself and wonder if you're going mad.

- **Scared** because you don't know why you do it and/or it's getting worse.

✎ Weird Words

Non-Lethal: Not causing death.

Self-Harm: Deliberate physical injury to oneself. Also called self-injury, self-abuse, or self-mutilation.

Suicide Attempt: A life-threatening action which is stopped when help arrives or the attempter is found and given treatment before he or she dies.

Helping Yourself

If you have worries that make you want to injure yourself, you might want help to change. This section is about what you can do to help yourself.

Thinking About Why You Do It

Lots of people don't know why they harm themselves and it can be scary to become aware of how you feel and why. Stopping self-injury is easier if you can find other ways of coping. To do this, you'll first need to have a clear idea of why you do it. Many people find it useful to talk to someone who is trained to help.

Here are some questions that may be helpful for you to think about:

- What was happening when you first began to feel like injuring yourself?

- What seems to trigger the feeling now?

- Are you always at a certain place or with a particular person?

- Do you have frightening memories or thoughts and feel you can't tell anyone?

- Is there anything else that makes you want to hurt yourself?

What Helps You Not Hurt Yourself?

What helps you to cope when you feel upset? Some people find it helpful to be with a friend, talk to someone they trust, or make a phone call. Others find it helps to

♣ It's A Fact!!
Suicide Attempts By Self-Mutilators

Self-mutilators perceived their suicide attempts as less lethal, with a greater likelihood of rescue and with less certainty of death. In addition, suicide attempters with a history of self-mutilation had significantly higher levels of depression, hopelessness, aggression, anxiety, impulsivity, and suicide ideation. They exhibited more behaviors consistent with borderline personality disorder and were more likely to have a history of childhood abuse. Self-mutilators had more persistent suicide ideation, and their pattern for suicide was similar to their pattern for self-mutilation, which was characterized by chronic urges to injure themselves.

Source: Reprinted with permission from Abstract: p. 427, *American Journal of Psychiatry*, March 2001. Copyright 2001 American Psychiatric Association.

do something they enjoy, listen to music or write feelings down in a diary. What helps you?

Deciding To Get Help

Sometimes, however hard you try to stop injuring yourself on your own, you can't. If you feel like this, it probably means that you need to talk to someone you can trust. This needs to be someone who will listen to you, talk about how you feel, and give practical help. There could be a real risk that you could harm yourself permanently or perhaps even die.

Who Can You Trust To Listen?

- Brother
- Aunt
- Parent or caregiver
- Sister
- Social worker
- Friend's parent or caregiver
- Uncle
- Youth Worker
- Doctor
- School Nurse
- Grandparent
- Friend
- Teacher

✔ Quick Tip

When self-injury becomes a way of coping with stress it is a sign that there are problems that need sorting out. Help or support may be needed from family, friends, or others. People who harm themselves are more likely to commit suicide in the future if they do not get help for the underlying problems.

When you have thought of someone to talk to, it helps to be prepared:

1. Where and when would you tell them?

2. Would you tell them face to face, by phone, or letter?

3. What would you say?

4. You could practice by saying it out loud, somewhere you feel safe.

5. Picture how the person might respond if you told them.

Table 16.1. Nonfatal Self-Inflicted Injuries Treated In Hospital Emergency Departments—United States, 2000. Estimated number*, percentage[t], and rate per 100,000 population of nonfatal self-inflicted injuries treated in hospital emergency departments, by selected characteristics—United States 2000.

Characteristic	Male No.	Male %	Male Rate^	Female No.	Female %	Female Rate^	Total No.	Total %	Total Rate^
Age group (years)									
0–9	262**	0.2**	—.**	196**	0.1**	—.**	458**	0.2**	—.**
10–14	3,860	3.4	37.9	10,066	6.6	103.6	13,926	5.3	70.0
15–19	20,326	18.1	198.7	31,200	20.6	322.7	51,526	19.5	259.0
20–24	20,044	17.8	212.5	23,761	15.7	261.5	43,805	16.6	236.6
25–34	26,967	24.0	145.4	33,654	22.2	178.2	60,630	23.0	161.9
35–44	25,215	22.4	113.1	33,276	21.9	147.2	58,492	22.1	130.3
45–54	11,939	10.6	65.7	12,887	8.5	67.7	24,806	9.4	66.7
55 and up	3,828	3.4	14.8	6,637	4.4	20.2	10,465	4.0	17.8
Race/Ethnicity[tt]									
White, non-Hispanic	69,156	61.5	71.8	94,259	62.2	93.9	163,414	61.9	83.1
Black	10,128	9.0	60.4	12,575	8.3	67.8	22,703	8.6	64.3
Hispanic	8,339**	7.4**	—.**	9,483**	6.3**	—.**	17,822**	6.7**	—.**
Other, non-Hispanic	2,802**	2.5**	—.**	3,409**	2.2**	—.**	6,211**	2.4**	—.**
Unknown	22,025**	19.6**	—.**	31,932**	21.1**	—.**	53,957**	20.4**	—.**
Cause									
Cut/pierce	32,670	29.1	24.3	32,586	21.5	23.2	65,256	24.7	23.7
Poisoning	61,503	54.7	45.7	108,739	71.7	77.3	170,222	64.5	61.8
Firearm	2,658**	2.4**	—.**	358**	0.2**	—.**	3,016**	1.1**	—.**
Other	14,905	13.3	11.1	8,991	5.9	6.4	23,896	9.0	8.7
Unknown	714**	0.6**	—.**	984**	0.6**	—.**	1,698**	0.6**	—.**
Injury category									
Probable suicide	65,395	58.2	48.6	93,061	61.4	66.1	158,466	60.0	57.6
Possible suicide	12,873	11.4	9.6	14,422	9.5	10.2	27,294	10.3	9.9
Unclear/unknown	34,182	30.4	25.4	44,176	29.1	31.4	78,358	29.7	28.5
Total	112,450	100.0	83.6	151,658	100.0	107.7	264,108	100.0	95.9

* Includes weighted data for persons of unknown sex.
[t] Some percentages do not total 100% because of rounding.
^ per 100,000 population
** National estimate might be unstable because it is based on fewer than 20 cases or the coefficient of variation is less that 30%.
[tt] Black includes Hispanic and non-Hispanic; Hispanic excludes black Hispanic. Rates should be interpreted with caution because of high percentage of unknowns.

Source: Table 1 "Nonfatal Self-Inflicted Injuries Treated In Hospital Emergency Departments—United States, 2000," *MMWR Weekly* May 24, 2002/ 51(20); 436-8.

Think of a way to look after yourself if they respond in a way which isn't what you'd hoped. Remember, the first person you speak to might not be able to help. This may not be their fault—or yours. Don't give up—it is important that you try again.

What If You Can't Talk To Someone You Know?

If there is no-one you feel you can trust at the moment, you could try a telephone help line. They can make you feel more relaxed and able to speak than you might think—and it's up to you when you finish the conversation.

It's sometimes easier to talk to someone trained to help, who doesn't know you. There are a lot of places that offer advice and help. You could contact a youth counseling service.

Your doctor or school nurse should be able to advise you about what support is available locally. They could refer you to someone who has experience in helping people who self-injure.

> **✔ Quick Tip**
> If you feel your life is in danger it is very important to get help. You can make an emergency appointment to see your doctor, or call 1-800-DON'T-CUT.

The person you see will want to help—and won't think you are stupid, mad, or wasting their time. The service is confidential (they should explain what this means and also the rare times when they will have to tell someone else)—no one else will know what you've talked about. They are used to talking to people who have all sorts of worries, even if you're not sure what to say.

Although it can take a lot of courage and determination, it's important to keep trying. You will find the right person to help you in the end.

Friends And Family—How You Can Help

If you are worried about someone who is self-injuring and want to help, this section tells you some things you can do. Friends and family have a really important part to play. You can help by:

- Noticing that someone is self-injuring

- Offering to listen and support

- Getting help when it's needed

It may be difficult to understand why someone injures themselves. You may feel shocked, angry, or even guilty. It can also be hard to know how to help. Here are some suggestions:

- Keep an open mind—don't judge or jump to conclusions

- Make time to listen and take them seriously

- Help them to find their own way of managing their problems

- Help them work out who else can help

- Offer to go with them to tell someone, or offer to tell someone for them

- Carry on with the ordinary activities you do together

- Don't be offended if they don't want to handle things your way

- Don't tease them—respect their feelings

- Support any positive steps they take

What To Do If The Situation Looks Dangerous

> ✔ **Quick Tip**
> If a person is involved in any life-threatening behavior, do not leave them alone. Call 911 for help.

Someone may tell you that they are hurting themselves and ask you to keep it a secret. This can put you in a very difficult situation. Of course, it's important to respect their wish for privacy. But if you think their life is in danger it is important to get help as soon as you can.

You may be able to work out together who would be the best person to tell. If not, try and let them know that you had to tell someone, and why.

Remember that your feelings matter too.

- Look after yourself—make sure you get the support you need.

- Remember—even those trained to work with people who self-injure need support, so it's okay if you do too.

- Try to carry on with your other activities and relationships.

- You don't have to be available for them all the time.

- If they hurt themselves it is their responsibility, not yours, even if they say it is.

☞ Remember!!

Don't let self-abuse get worse. Help is available. To get started contact:

SAFE (Self-Abuse Finally Ends)
Toll-Free: 800-DON'T-CUT
(800-366-8288)
Website: http://
www.selfinjury.com

Part Three

Treatment Options For A Person Thinking Of Suicide

Chapter 17

You've Just Been Diagnosed With A Mood Disorder...What Now?

Just Diagnosed? You're Not Alone.

If you've just been diagnosed with depression, bipolar disorder, or another mood disorder such as dysthymia or cyclothymia, you are not alone. Mood disorders affect more than 22 million Americans. They are treatable, and they don't have to prevent you from living the life you want. Having a mood disorder does not mean you're weak, flawed, or crazy.

Some people have said they felt relieved to know what was wrong when they were first diagnosed with a mood disorder, and glad to know it could be treated. Others said they felt afraid, embarrassed, or angry. Whatever you are feeling, one of the best things you can do to help yourself in your recovery is to learn all you can about your illness. This chapter will tell you some basic facts about mood disorders and help you work toward living with your diagnosis. If you are seeking help for your child, friend, or other family member, this chapter can help you understand mood disorders and communicate more easily with his or her health care providers.

About This Chapter: Reprinted with permission from the Depression and Bipolar Support Alliance (DBSA), © 2004. All rights reserved. For additional information, including assistance in finding a support group or mental health professional, contact the Depression and Bipolar Support Alliance at 800-826-3632, or visit their website at http://www.dbsalliance.org.

Questions For Your Doctor

♣ It's A Fact!!

A skilled and interested doctor will address most of your concerns, but you may want to ask additional questions. Don't leave the doctor's office until all of your questions are answered. Take notes if things seem complicated. If necessary, bring a list of questions with you to your doctor. Here is a list to start with:

- What's the name of my medication and how will it help me?

- What dosage(s) of medication do I need to take?

- At what time(s) of day should I take them? Do I need to take them with food?

- Do I need to avoid any specific foods, medications supplements (vitamins, herbals), or activities while I am taking this medication?

- What should I do if I forget to take my medication?

- Is there a generic form of my medication available? Would it be right for me?

- What side effects might I have? What can I do about them?

- How can I reach you in an emergency?

- How long will it take for me to feel better? What type of improvement should I expect?

- Are there any specific risks I should worry about? How can I prevent them? How can I recognize them?

- If my medication needs to be stopped for any reason, how should I do it? (Never stop taking your medication without first talking to your doctor.)

- How often will I need to come in for medication management? How long will my appointments take?

- Should I also have talk therapy? What type do you recommend? Is it possible that I could be treated with talk therapy and no medication?

- Is there anything I can do to help my treatment work better, such as changing my diet, physical activity, sleep patterns, or lifestyle?

- If my current treatment isn't helpful, what are my alternatives? What is my next step?

- What risks do I need to consider if I want to become pregnant?

- Add questions of your own.

What's Happening To Me?

Mood disorders are physical illnesses that affect the brain. Their exact cause is not known, but it is known that an imbalance in brain chemicals plays a role. These illnesses also have a genetic component, meaning they can run in families. However, they are not caused by having a bad childhood or anything you may have done—they are not your fault, and they are nothing to be ashamed of.

Many people have trouble understanding mood disorders and other illnesses that affect the brain. You may have heard, or even thought, that people with mental illnesses were dangerous or unable to lead normal lives. These beliefs are not true.

You have been diagnosed with an illness. But you are still you—now you can explain and change some of your feelings, thoughts, and actions. The hopelessness, anxiety, anger, sleeplessness, racing thoughts, or other symptoms that have been causing problems now have an explanation and a treatment—you don't have to put up with them any more. Getting treatment does not mean you have failed in any way, it means that you have the strength, courage, and sense to look for a way to feel better and cope better with life.

Though there is not yet a cure for mood disorders, your symptoms can be managed with the right treatment. Think of your mood disorder the same way you think of illnesses such as asthma or diabetes. No one would ever ask someone else to think positive in response to the low blood sugar of diabetes or breathing trouble of asthma, and no one would think twice about getting the necessary treatment for these illnesses. When treated, a mood disorder does not have to prevent you from living a healthy, productive life.

Do I Need To See More Than One Health Care Provider?

Sometimes you will need to see one health care provider for psychotherapy or talk therapy (this may be a psychiatrist, psychologist, therapist, social worker, or other professional) and a medical doctor to prescribe medication (this may be your primary care doctor or a psychiatrist). If you have more than one person treating you, let them know how they can reach one another. It is best for all of you to work together to find the right treatment plan for you.

Facts About Mood Disorders   ♣ It's A Fact!!

What Are Mood Disorders?

Mood disorders are treatable medical conditions involving extreme changes in mood, thought, energy, and behavior. A person with bipolar disorder, also known as manic depression, has moods that usually alternate between mania, or an extremely up mood, and depression, or an extremely down mood. These changes or mood swings can last for hours, days, weeks, or even months. A person with major (unipolar) depression has periods of down mood, and may have crying spells, significant changes in appetite and sleep, loss of energy, and other symptoms.

Mood disorders are not character flaws or signs of personal weakness. A person cannot snap out of or control the mood changes caused by mood disorders. Mood disorders have many symptoms, including:

Manic episode: A distinct period of elevated, enthusiastic, or irritable mood which includes at least three of the following symptoms:

- Increased physical and mental activity and energy
- Exaggerated optimism and self-confidence
- Grandiose thoughts, inflated sense of self-importance
- Excessive irritability
- Aggressive behavior
- Decreased need for sleep without feeling tired
- Racing speech, racing thoughts
- Impulsiveness, poor judgment
- Reckless behavior such as spending sprees, impulsive business decisions, erratic driving, and sexual indiscretions
- In severe cases, delusions and hallucinations

Hypomanic episode: Similar to manic episode, but less severe and without delusions or hallucinations. It is clearly different from a non-depressed mood with an obvious change in behavior that is unusual or out-or-character.

Major depressive episode: A period of two weeks or more during which at least five of the following symptoms are present.

- Prolonged sadness or unexplained crying spells
- Significant changes in appetite and sleep patterns
- Irritability, anger, agitation

continued

- Worry, anxiety

- Pessimism, indifference

- Loss of energy, persistent exhaustion

- Unexplained aches and pains

- Feelings of guilt, worthlessness, and/or hopelessness

- Inability to concentrate, indecisiveness

- Inability to take pleasure in former interests, social withdrawal

- Excessive consumption of alcohol or use of chemical substances

- Recurring thoughts of death or suicide

Mixed state (also called mixed mania): A period during which symptoms of manic and a depressive episode are present at the same time.

Dysthymia, another mood disorder, is a milder form of depression characterized by changes in eating or sleeping patterns, and a down, irritable, or self-critical mood that is present more of the time than not. People with dysthymia may say they are "just that way" or "have always been that way."

Cyclothymia, another mood disorder, is a milder form of bipolar disorder characterized by alternating hypomanic episodes and less severe episodes of depression. The severity of this illness may change over time.

Rapid cycling occurs when a person has four or more manic hypomanic, mixed, or depressive episodes within a 12-month period. For many people, rapid cycling is temporary.

What Is The Difference Between A Mood Disorder And Ordinary Mood Swings?

The three main things that make a mood disorder different from ordinary mood swings are:

Intensity: Mood swings that come with a mood disorder are usually more severe than ordinary mood swings.

Length: A bad mood is usually gone in a few days, but mania or depression can last weeks or months. When a person suffers from rapid cycling, high and low moods can come and go quickly, but the person does not usually return to a stable mood for a long period of time.

Interference with life: The extremes in mood that come with mood disorders can cause serious problems. For example, depression can make a person unable to get out of bed or go to work, or mania can cause a person to go for days without sleep or spend money he or she does not have.

What Are The Benefits Of Psychotherapy?

You may need extra help coping with unhealthy relationships or harmful lifestyle choices that contribute to your illness. Psychotherapy (talk therapy) can be very helpful for this. Choose a therapist with whom you feel comfortable, and whose judgment you trust. Therapy may not always be easy, since you will be talking about parts of your life that may be emotionally painful. However, the goal of therapy is for you to develop skills and behaviors that will help you cope with difficult situations and help you to become aware of, and possibly prevent, episodes of depression or mania.

When looking for a therapist, be sure to find one who has experience treating someone with your mood disorder. There are many types of therapy to choose from—most therapists use a combination of types. Behavioral therapy concentrates on current behaviors, cognitive therapy focuses on your thoughts, and inter-personal therapy looks at your relationships with others. Group therapy involves several, usually unrelated, people working with the same therapist and each other. In family or couples therapy, your loved ones may join you. One approach is not necessarily better than another—the best choice is the one that works for you.

Do I Need To Take Medication?

The decision to take medication is entirely up to you and your doctor. Many people are unwilling to take medication at first—some worry that it will change their personality or be addictive—neither of these beliefs is true. Medications for mood disorders are prescribed to keep your moods stable and keep you from having episodes of depression or mania that would interfere with your life. You don't need to tell anyone you are taking medication if you don't want to, unless your medication makes you unable to do your job or fulfill other important obligations. It might surprise you, however, to find out how many people you know are taking or have taken medication for a mood disorder.

What If My Medication Doesn't Work?

No two people will respond the same way to the same medication. Sometimes you and you doctor will need to try several different medications or a combination of medications in order to provide the improvement you need. Finding the right medication plan can take time. Don't lose hope!

Keep your own records of treatment, including the name of the medication, the dosages used, the length of time you took them, and your positive or negative experiences. Many options are available today, and more effective medications with fewer side effects are being researched.

✔ Quick Tip

Never stop taking your medication or change your dosage without first talking to your doctor.

It may also take some time for you to adjust to your medication. Most medications take two to six weeks before a person feels their full effect. So, though it may be difficult, it's important to be patient and wait for a medication to take effect.

Many of the medications that affect the brain may also affect other systems of the body, and cause side effects such as dry mouth, constipation, sleepiness, blurred vision, weight gain, weight loss, dizziness, or sexual dysfunction. Some side effects go away within days or weeks, while others can be long-term. Don't be discouraged by side effects; there are ways to reduce or eliminate them. Sometimes there are things you can do, such as changing the time you take your medication to help with sleepiness or sleeplessness, or taking it with food to help with nausea. Sometimes another medication can be prescribed to block an unwanted side effect, or your dosage can be adjusted to reduce the side effect to a tolerable level. Other times your medication must be changed.

Tell your doctor about any side effects you are having. The decision to change or add medication must be made by you and your doctor together. Tell your doctor before you begin taking any additional medication, including over-the-counter medications or natural/herbal supplements.

If side effects from medicine cause you to become very ill (with symptoms such as fever, sore throat, rash, yellowing of your skin, pain in your abdomen or any other area, breathing or heart problems, or other severe changes that concern you), contact your doctor or a hospital emergency room right away.

What Can I Do To Improve Communication With My Health Care Provider(s)?

It is important that you have an open, trusting relationship with your health care provider and feel confident in his or her knowledge, skill, and interest in helping you. You should never feel intimidated by your doctor or feel as if you're wasting his or her time. It's also important that you share all the information your doctor needs to help you. A complete medical history including your medication allergies, prior experiences with medication, and any alcohol or drug use, is important to guiding your treatment. Sometimes your doctor will also ask for your family history.

No matter who you are or what illness you have, you deserve to have the best treatment possible. If, after some time has passed, you feel the same way you did before treatment or worse, you have the right to ask for a second opinion. You have no obligation to stay with your current health care professional.

How Can I Spot My Warning Signs?

Each person is different, and each person has different triggers or stressors that may cause their symptoms of depression or mania to get worse. For some people, a trigger can be an argument with a friend or family member; for others, it can be visiting a particular place, having too much to do, or major life events such as moving or changing jobs. As you learn more about your illness, your triggers, and your mind and body chemistry, you may be able to spot new episodes and get help before they get out of control Ask your family and friends to tell you if they notice any signs that you might be having an episode. Use a journal, personal calendar, and/or the following tools to track your moods.

My Symptoms Of Depression/Dysthymia

- Pessimistic outlook—feeling like everything is going wrong and always will

- Less interest in things I usually care about; less ability to laugh or feel joy

- Crying more often, sometimes for no apparent reason

- Anxiety, worry, mental paralysis

- Exhaustion, need for more sleep, or inability to get up in the morning

- Excessive guilt—feeling like everything is my fault or like I am a bad person

- Feelings of emptiness, worthlessness, or hopelessness

- Unexplained aches and pains

Symptoms are different for everyone. Some people feel like sleeping all the time when they become depressed; others have trouble sleeping and stay up late feeling worried. What are your warning symptoms?

My Symptoms Of Mania/Hypomania

- Thoughts speeding up, obsessions, unable to stop the flood of thoughts coming into my mind

- Being hyper, extra-talkative, extra-active

- Feeling extremely confident

- Paranoia, worry, anxiety

- Irritability, temper outbursts

- Big plans or ideas (while such ideas can lead to good things, it's important to be aware of sudden grandiose ideas or overconfidence that seems to come out of nowhere)

- Less need for sleep, much more energy than usual

My Stressors

Record the stressful event, your reaction to it, and possible ways to cope when you are stressed.

When you're feeling manic or hypomanic, ask someone else to hold onto your car keys, credit cards, and checkbook until your mood is more stable. If one of your symptoms is spending too much money, ask someone to go to the store with you and help you to stay within your budget.

When you've figured out what your warning symptoms are, take action as soon as you spot them. Don't wait for an episode to become full-blown and cause a crisis. Call your doctor or therapist and let him or her know the symptoms you're having. Ask a close friend or family member to stay with you until you are feeling more stable.

What If I Start To Feel Suicidal?

It's especially important to have a plan in place to help yourself if you start to feel suicidal—and to make a promise to yourself that you'll use it. Make a list of the phone numbers of trusted friends, health care providers, and crisis hot lines you can call if or when you are having trouble. Your life is important, and as strong as suicidal thoughts may seem, they are a temporary and treatable symptom of your illness. The best thing you can do for yourself is get help as soon as you start having these thoughts—don't wait for them to become unbearable. One national crisis hot line you can use is 800-442-4673. You can also check your local phone directory or ask your health care providers for a local crisis line number.

In addition to telling someone right away when you feel suicidal, make sure you can't get hold of any weapons, old medications, or any thing else you could use to hurt yourself. Get a friend to help you throw away all medications you are no longer taking. Have someone else hold onto your car keys when you are feeling suicidal. Don't use alcohol or illegal drugs, because they can make you more likely to act on impulse.

How Can I Manage The Cost Of Treatment?

There is no easy answer to this question. Sadly, illnesses such as mood disorders are sometimes not insured at the same level as other illnesses. Sometimes coverage for mental health conditions is not offered at all. Legislation is pending in Congress to give people with group insurance equal coverage for mental and physical health issues. Of course, this does not help people who don't have insurance. Here are some things you can do to try to reduce the cost of your treatment.

- Talk to your health care provider(s) and try to work out lower fees or a payment plan.

✔ Quick Tip
My Plan For Life

I Promise Myself

If I start to think about suicide, or am in any other type of crisis, I will contact these family members or friends—make a list of at least three people with their phone numbers.

I Will Also

- Call my doctor or a suicide hot line, or go to a hospital if necessary.

- Remember that when I feel suicidal, my brain is lying to me and making things seem worse than they are. Suicidal thoughts are not based on reality; they are a symptom of my illness.

- Remember that my life is valuable and worthwhile, even if it doesn't feel that way right now.

- Stick with my prescribed treatment plan.

- Remember to take my medications.

- Remember to see my counselor, therapists, or psychiatrist.

- Remember to call my doctor if I don't feel safe or if I'm having problems.

- Get in contact with other people who have a mood disorder.

- Stay away from alcohol and illegal drugs.

- Have someone take away my car keys and anything I could use to hurt myself.

- Stay aware of my moods, know my warning signs and get help early.

- Be kind to myself.

- Use community or state-provided services, many of which offer a sliding payment scale.

- Space out your allowable psychotherapy visits over time and work on developing skills you can use between visits.

- Ask your doctor to contact the pharmaceutical company that makes your medication and see if you are eligible to receive free medication. Ask if your doctor has any samples of your medication to give you.

- Ask your doctor to contact your insurance company to ask if they will allow more treatment for you.

- If you are having a hard time getting insurance because you've had treatment for mental illness, your state may have a risk pool, which offers insurance for hard-to-insure individuals. You may find additional information at www.healthinsurance.org/riskpoolinfo.html.

- Get help before there is a crisis. A brief appointment to talk about how you're feeling or adjust your medication costs less than a hospital stay. Attend a Depression and Bipolar Support Alliance (DBSA) support group, which is free of charge. There you'll meet understanding people who can share coping skills to help you through difficult times.

☞ Remember!!
There Is Help, There Is Hope

Patience is a great help in recovery. It's needed when adjusting to the effects of a new treatment, when getting to know a new group of people, when waiting for your mind and body to feel better after having an episode. If you've lived with symptoms of a mood disorder for years, you may have already developed patience—from hanging on and waiting for depression or mania to pass. Sometimes you may be asked to have patience and not give up during the most difficult times in your life. This can be very difficult, but it is also the most important. Always remember, you are not alone, there is help, and there is hope. With treatment and support, you can feel better.

How Do DBSA Support Groups Help?

When you are newly diagnosed, it's helpful to have reliable, knowledge-able people around you who know what you are going through and can help answer the question, "What next?" and other questions you have. DBSA group participants are people with mood disorders and their families who share experience, discuss coping skills, and offer hope to one another in a safe and confidential environment. DBSA support groups provide the caring and assistance that is important to lasting recovery. People who go to DBSA groups say that the groups:

- Provide a safe and welcoming place for mutual acceptance, understanding, and self-discovery.

- Give them the opportunity to reach out to others and benefit from the experience of those who have been there.

- Motivate them to follow their treatment plans.

- Help them to understand that mood disorders do not define who they are.

- Help them rediscover their strengths and humor.

People who had been attending DBSA groups for more than a year were also less likely to have been hospitalized for their mood disorder during that year, according to a DBSA survey.

How Do I Talk To Others About My Illness?

Many people are afraid to discuss their illness with others. Some people worry that their friends may not accept them, their family might become distant, or their employer might fire them. Telling others about your mood disorder is completely your choice. Some of your close friends and family members may have already become concerned about mood swings you've had, so they might be glad to hear you're getting help. Other people in your life might have wrong or hurtful beliefs about mental illness and you may choose not to tell them.

When you do tell others, do so with an attitude that is calm and optimistic, and show them that you are determined to work on managing your symptoms and getting well. If you need to, reassure them that you are not dangerous—to yourself or to them. Often, people will reflect a good attitude back to you. Regardless of others' reactions, keep in mind that you are not damaged—you are the same person you have always been.

You may have done things while in a manic or depressed state that you need to apologize for. While you can offer your illness as an explanation, be sure to let people know that you are working to keep those kinds of things from happening again.

Sharing your illness with employers or co-workers can also be difficult. Unfortunately, stigma still exists, and if you believe this stigma would threaten your job, it may be best to say nothing about your illness, unless you need special accommodations such as reduced hours or extended time off.

Sometimes families have a hard time accepting a mood disorder diagnosis. Some parents believe that having a son or daughter with a mood disorder means they are bad parents. Others will have the belief that a person should be able to control mood swings, or just snap out of it. Do your best to educate your family and friends by giving them brochures, books, or video tapes about mood disorders. Even if they still do not change their beliefs, keep reminding yourself that you are not flawed and you are not wrong for seeking treatment.

Your family may need support, too. Encourage them to seek counseling, therapy, or support groups for themselves, or consider having some family sessions with a therapist, so that each member of the family can share reactions, feelings, and worries in a safe environment.

Chapter 18

Going To A Therapist

At first glance, Ben, Andy, Rachel, and Emily don't seem to have much in common. Ben is totally into basketball and playing guitar, whereas Andy is a quiet guy who passes his time in front of his computer. Rachel is a straight-A student and student council rep, and Emily is an average student who loves drama and painting. They dress differently and hang with different friends, they live in different neighborhoods, and they aren't even in the same year in high school.

But these teens do share an important similarity—they've all gone to therapy for help with dealing with their problems. Although their reasons for going to therapy are very different, all of them are relieved that they've found someone who can help them sort things out.

About This Chapter: This information was provided by TeensHealth, one of the largest resources online for medically reviewed health information written for parents, kids, and teens. For more articles like this one, visit www.TeensHealth.org, or www.KidsHealth.org. © 2001 The Nemours Center for Children's Health Media, a division of The Nemours Foundation. Additional text under its own heading is from "How to Find Help Through Psychotherapy," available at http://helping.apa.org/therapy/psychotherapy.html. © 1998 American Psychological Association. Reprinted with permission. Reviewed in June 2004 by Dr. David A. Cooke, M.D., Diplomate, American Board of Internal Medicine.

What Is Therapy—And What Do Therapists Do?

The dictionary defines therapy as the treatment of a disorder or illness. There are many different kinds of therapy; you've probably heard people discussing physical therapy, art therapy, or even gene therapy. In this chapter, however, therapy refers to psychotherapy—the treatment of behavioral and emotional concerns (these concerns are sometimes called mental or emotional disorders).

A psychotherapist (therapist for short) is a person who has been professionally trained to help people with emotional and behavioral problems and disorders. These problems can include things like significant problems with friends and family or problems with depression, anxiety, obsessive-compulsive disorder, or attention deficit hyperactivity disorder. There are several different types of therapists. The letters following a therapist's name sometimes tell you the kind of training he or she has received:

- **Psychiatrists** (MD or DO) are licensed medical doctors who have advanced training in psychotherapy and pharmacology (the science of using drugs as medicine). They are the only mental health care providers who can prescribe medications.

- **Clinical psychologists** (PhD, PsyD, or EdD) are therapists who have received doctorate degrees. They have advanced training in the practice of psychology, and many specialize in treating teens and their families.

- **Clinical social workers** (LCSW, ACSW, LICSW, or CSW) have master's degrees and training in counseling individuals and groups.

What are some reasons that people go to therapists?

There are times when life can get very difficult or complicated. Sometimes when people are trying as hard as they can to get through a rough time, they find that they just can't cope by themselves. They need help to sort out their feelings and find solutions to their problems. That's an example of a time when therapy can help.

The teen years can be particularly tough. Some teens have to deal with family problems, like divorce or the death or illness of a family member. Some may not get along with a parent, stepparent, or sibling. Some face a lot of pressure to get good grades at school; others have problems with their self-esteem. Some teens have to deal with a chronic illness like diabetes or mental health problems such as depression or bipolar disorder; others may be trying to overcome abusive situations or eating disorders. These are some of the many reasons that a teen might go to therapy. There's nothing wrong with getting help when you're faced with problems you can't solve alone. In fact, it's just the opposite. The right move is to ask an adult you trust—like a parent, school counselor, or doctor—to assist you in finding a therapist who can help you.

What happens during therapy?

During your first visit to a therapist, he or she will probably ask you to talk in general terms about what's going on with you. The therapist will probably explain a little bit about what you'll cover in your sessions and suggest how frequently you should meet. This may be once a week, every other week, or once a month. It's important that you stick to whatever schedule you agree on and go to your appointments, so that you have enough time with your therapist to work out your concerns.

Some teens worry that a therapist will tell their parents about what they discuss during therapy. That makes it hard for them to talk openly about their situations. Therapists respect the privacy of their patients, and keep everything that they're told confidential. They won't talk about what you've told them with anyone else unless you give your permission. The only exception would be if the therapist felt that you might harm yourself or someone else. If the issue of privacy and confidentiality worries you, be sure to ask your therapist about it during your first meeting. It's difficult for therapy to be effective if you don't feel that you can trust your therapist.

Because every person is different, therapists use various ways to treat people. They may use just one kind of therapy, or they may combine different types (using medication and "talk" therapy together, for example). Therapeutic strategies can include:

- **Relaxation training**: In this approach, the therapist helps people learn to relax their minds and their bodies so that they can cope with stress and maintain daily activities. This strategy helps people take control of their own situations.

- **Stress management**: In this type of therapy, people learn to recognize the signs of stress and to find ways of dealing with stress.

- **Cognitive-behavioral therapy**: This kind of therapy helps people identify negative ways of thinking and change them to more positive approaches. For example, a teen who is convinced that he will always fail when taking a test could identify his self-defeating thought patterns and learn a more positive, effective way of thinking.

- **Individual therapy**: In individual therapy, the therapist meets one-on-one with the teen to work on a problem such as depression.

- **Family therapy**: In this type of therapy, a teen goes to therapy with some or all of his family members, which helps to improve communication among them. The treatment focuses on problem-solving techniques.

No matter what approach your therapist takes, he or she will monitor your progress to determine if the strategy is working. If you're uncomfortable with the therapy—or, as sometimes happens, with the particular therapist you're going to—be sure to tell your parents. If you feel that therapy isn't helping, it may be better to try a different therapist or a different kind of therapy.

✔ **Quick Tip**

Therapy can be a positive experience with many benefits. You'll probably find that you learn a lot about yourself, and that therapy can help you grow as a person. You'll also discover ways of coping with difficult situations—not only those that you're facing today, but also those that you may face in the future.

Does this mean I'm crazy (or a freak)?

If you're considering therapy or going to a therapist now, you may wonder if there's something wrong with you. But there's nothing wrong with asking for help when you need it. It takes a lot of courage—and maturity—to look for solutions to your problems instead of allowing them to become worse.

You don't have to hide the fact that you're going to a therapist—but you don't have to tell anyone, either, if you'd prefer not to. Getting help with an emotional problem is the same as getting help with a medical problem like diabetes. You might want to tell a few friends about it, but you may not want to tell anyone, especially if you feel that they won't understand. Either way, it's your decision, and you should do whatever you're most comfortable with.

How To Find Help Through Psychotherapy

Millions of Americans have found relief from depression and other emotional difficulties through psychotherapy. Even so, some people find it hard to get started or stay in psychotherapy. This brief question-and-answer guide provides some basic information to help individuals take advantage of outpatient (non-hospital) psychotherapy.

Why do people consider using psychotherapy?

Psychotherapy is a partnership between an individual and a professional such as a psychologist who is licensed and trained to help people understand their feelings and assist them with changing their behavior. According to the National Institute of Mental Health, one-third of adults in the United States experience an emotional or substance abuse problem. Nearly 25 percent of the adult population suffers at some point from depression or anxiety.

People often consider psychotherapy, also known as therapy, under the following circumstances:

- They feel an overwhelming and prolonged sense of sadness and help-lessness, and they lack hope in their lives.

- Their emotional difficulties make it hard for them to function from day to day. For example, they are unable to concentrate on assignments and their job performance suffers as a result.

• Their actions are harmful to themselves or to others. For instance, they drink too much alcohol and become overly aggressive.

• They are troubled by emotional difficulties facing family members or close friends.

What does research show about the effectiveness of psychotherapy?

Research suggests that therapy effectively decreases patients' depression and anxiety and related symptoms—such as pain, fatigue, and nausea. Psychotherapy has also been found to increase survival time for heart surgery and cancer patients, and it can have a positive effect on the body's immune system. Research increasingly supports the idea that emotional and physical health are very closely linked and that therapy can improve a person's overall health status.

There is convincing evidence that most people who have at least several sessions of psychotherapy are far better off than untreated individuals with emotional difficulties. One major study showed that 50 percent of patients noticeably improved after eight sessions while 75 percent of individuals in psychotherapy improved by the end of six months. Psychotherapy with children is similar in effectiveness to psychotherapy with adults.

If I begin psychotherapy, how should I try to gain the most from it?

There are many approaches to outpatient psychotherapy and various formats in which it may occur—including individual, group, and family psychotherapy. Despite the variations, all psychotherapy is a two-way process that works especially well when patients and their therapists communicate openly. Research has shown that the outcome of psychotherapy is improved when the therapist and patient agree early about what the major problems are and how psychotherapy can help.

You and your therapist both have responsibilities in establishing and maintaining a good working relationship. Be clear with your therapist about your expectations and share any concerns that may arise. Psychotherapy works best when you attend all scheduled sessions and give some forethought to what you want to discuss during each one.

✔ Quick Tip

How do I find a qualified therapist?

Selecting a therapist is a highly personal matter.

A professional who works very well with one individual may not be a good choice for another person. There are several ways to get referrals to qualified therapists such as licensed psychologists, including the following:

- Talk to close family members and friends for their recommendations, especially if they have had a good experience with psychotherapy.

- Many state psychological associations operate referral services which put individuals in touch with licensed and competent mental health providers. (Call the American Psychological Association's Practice Directorate at 202-336-5800 for the name and phone number of the appropriate state organization.)

- Ask your primary care physician (or other health professional) for a referral. Tell the doctor what's important to you in choosing a therapist so he or she can make appropriate suggestions.

- Inquire at your church or synagogue.

- Look in the phone book for the listing of a local mental health association or community mental health center and check these sources for possible referrals.

Ideally, you will end up with more than one lead. Call and request the opportunity, either by phone or in person, to ask the therapist some questions. You might want to inquire about his or her licensure and level of training, approach to psychotherapy, participation in insurance plans, and fees. Such a discussion should help you sort through your options and choose someone with whom you believe you might interact well.

How can I evaluate whether therapy is working well?

As you begin psychotherapy, you should establish clear goals with your therapist. Perhaps you want to overcome feelings of hopelessness associated with depression. Or maybe you would like to control a fear that disrupts your daily life. Keep in mind that certain tasks require more time to accomplish than others. You may need to adjust your goals depending on how long you plan to be in psychotherapy.

After a few sessions, it's a good sign if you feel the experience truly is a joint effort and that you and the therapist enjoy a good rapport. On the other hand, you should be open with your therapist if you find yourself feeling 'stuck' or lacking direction once you've been in psychotherapy awhile.

There may be times when a therapist appears cold and disinterested or doesn't seem to regard you positively. Tell your therapist if this is the situation, or if you question other aspects of his or her approach. If you find yourself thinking about discontinuing psychotherapy, talk with your therapist. It might be helpful to consult another professional, provided you let your therapist know you are seeking a second opinion.

☞ **Remember!!**

Psychotherapy isn't easy. But patients who are willing to work in close partnership with their therapist often find relief from their emotional distress and begin to lead more productive and fulfilling lives.

Patients often feel a wide range of emotions during psychotherapy. Some qualms about psychotherapy that people may have result from the difficulty of discussing painful and troubling experiences. When this happens, it can actually be a positive sign indicating that you are starting to explore your thoughts and behaviors.

You should spend time with your therapist periodically reviewing your progress (or your concern that you are not making sufficient headway). Although there are other considerations affecting the duration of psychotherapy, success in reaching your primary goals should be a major factor in deciding when your psychotherapy should end.

Chapter 19

Psychotherapy For Teens

Psychotherapy is a form of treatment that can help teens and families understand and resolve problems, modify behavior, and make positive changes in their lives. There are several types of psychotherapy that involve different approaches, techniques, and interventions. At times, a combination of different psychotherapy approaches may be helpful. In some cases a combination of medication with psychotherapy may be more effective.

Psychotherapy is not a quick fix or an easy answer. It is a complex and rich process that can reduce symptoms, provide insight, and improve a child or adolescent's functioning and quality of life. Child and adolescent psychiatrists are trained in different forms of psychotherapy, and if indicated, are able to combine these forms of treatment with medications to alleviate the child or adolescent's emotional and/or behavioral problems.

Questions And Answers About Child And Adolescent Psychiatry

Not all people grow from infancy through their adolescent years without experiencing some bumps along the way. While every person is unique and special, sometimes they encounter problems with feelings or behaviors that cause disruption in their lives and the lives of those around them. Child and Adolescent Psychiatrists are physicians specifically trained to treat children and adolescents with these problems.

Why do parents and families bring their child or teenager to a child and adolescent psychiatrist?

Parents and families often worry when their child or teenager seems to have a problem which causes them to be sad, disruptive, rebellious, inattentive, unable to cope with things, or to get involved with drugs and alcohol. They may be concerned about their child or adolescent's development, eating and /or sleeping patterns, and how they are getting along with family, friends, and at school. Many families first discuss their concerns with a family physician, school counselor, or clergy. Following this, the family may be referred to or seek out a Child and Adolescent Psychiatrist. The Child and Adolescent Psychiatrist is uniquely qualified to understand the full range of factors associated with emotional difficulties and mental disorders that can affect children and adolescents.

Are parents and families responsible for their child's problem?

Parents and families often have this worry. Some families even delay seeking help for their child for fear that they will be blamed. Feeling responsible for the child's problems or distress is a normal sign of caring and attachment. There can be multiple causes for many of the problems that children and adolescents experience. Sometimes the cause of a problem is not known, but all disorders are treatable. A Child and Adolescent Psychiatrist will help parents and families understand that they should not blame themselves for their child or adolescent's problem and resolve the feelings of "Why me? Why my child?"

What about stigma?

Parents and families are sometimes concerned about their child being labeled with a psychiatric disorder. Just as children and adolescents may become physically ill, they may experience emotional and behavioral problems. Many problems can be completely overcome and symptoms can almost always be improved with treatment. Once a child starts to improve, many parents feel good telling their friends and relatives: "Yes, my child did have a significant problem, but we got the help we needed."

What kind of evaluation is offered?

As a physician, the Child and Adolescent Psychiatrist begins by carefully listening to your concerns about your teen and the family. The Child and Adolescent Psychiatrist also reviews the full medical history with parents, and frequently will ask to obtain additional information from other members of the family, the school, the child or adolescent's personal physician, and other significant adults in the life of the child or adolescent. The Child and Adolescent Psychiatrist talks with parents and families about how to anticipate and answer their child or adolescent's questions about the psychiatric examination. The meeting with the child or adolescent may involve talking, drawing, or playing with toys to help your child or adolescent's doctor better understand what is going on. Questions may be asked about the child or adolescent's view of the problem, as well as how the child is getting along with family, friends, teachers, and students in school. An assessment is made of the child or adolescent's strengths as well as their problems.

What if a physical problem is causing the symptoms?

As a physician, the Child and Adolescent Psychiatrist is trained to recognize physical disorders that may be affecting how people think, feel, and behave. In addition, the Child and Adolescent Psychiatrist considers how emotions, feeling, thinking, and behaving may influence your child or adolescent's physical health. As a physician, the Child and Adolescent Psychiatrist is qualified to take medical responsibility for the plan of psychiatric treatment and will consult with your child or adolescent's family physician to develop a comprehensive treatment plan.

What kind of treatment is offered?

The individual plan of psychiatric treatment will take into account your child or adolescent's problems as well as the strengths that are identified in your child's personality, your family, the school, and other community resources. Child and Adolescent Psychiatrists use a variety of treatment techniques; e.g., psychotherapies, behavior therapies, medications, interventions with the school and family, etc. The Child and Adolescent Psychiatrist will discuss your child or adolescent's treatment plan with you and your teen. This discussion includes the advantages and disadvantages of various treatment approaches as well as availability of programs and services in your community.

How long does psychiatric treatment usually take?

Some children and adolescents will respond to short-term treatment (for example, up to 12 sessions). When the disorder(s) has persisted for a long time or is complicated, a longer term of treatment may be needed. A few disorders which are chronic may require continuing care. You should discuss

---

♣ It's A Fact!!
Different Types Of Psychotherapy In Alphabetical Order

- **Cognitive Behavior Therapy (CBT)** helps improve a teen's moods and behavior by examining confused or distorted patterns of thinking. During CBT the teen learns that thoughts cause feelings and moods which can influence behavior. For example, if a teen is experiencing unwanted feelings or has problematic behaviors, the therapist works to identify the underlying thinking that is causing them. The therapist then helps the teen replace this thinking with thoughts that result in more appropriate feelings and behaviors. Research shows that CBT can be effective in treating depression and anxiety.

- **Dialectical Behavior Therapy (DBT)** can be used to treat older adolescents who have chronic suicidal feelings/thoughts, engage in intentional self-harm, or have Borderline Personality Disorder. DBT emphasizes taking responsibility for one's problems and helps the person examine how they deal with conflict and negative feelings. This often involves a combination of group and individual sessions.

- **Family Therapy** focuses on helping the family function in more positive and constructive ways by exploring patterns of communication and providing support and education. Family therapy sessions can include the child or adolescent along with parents, siblings, and grandparents. Couples therapy is a specific type of family therapy that focuses on a couple's communication and interactions (e.g., parents having marital problems).

continued

the duration and goals of treatment with your Child and Adolescent Psychiatrist after the initial diagnostic evaluation.

How much does psychiatric treatment cost?

The fees of the Child and Adolescent Psychiatrist are based on both the complexity of the treatment and the amount of time involved. Fees vary in different parts of the country. Psychiatric treatment sessions may be scheduled on a regular basis and length of sessions can vary depending on the treatment plan. Issues regarding finances and payment plans should be discussed openly and frankly with the Child and Adolescent Psychiatrist from the beginning of treatment.

continued from previous page

- **Group Therapy** uses the power of group dynamics and peer interactions to increase understanding and improve social skills. There are many different types of group therapy (e.g. psychodynamic, social skills, substance abuse, multi-family, parent support, etc.)

- **Interpersonal Therapy (IPT)** is a brief treatment specifically developed and tested for depression. The goals of IPT are to improve interpersonal functioning by decreasing the symptoms of depression. IPT has been shown to be effective in adolescents with depression.

- **Play Therapy** involves the use of toys, blocks, dolls, puppets, drawings, and games to help the child recognize, identify, and verbalize feelings. The psychotherapist observes how the child uses play materials and identifies themes or patterns to understand the child's problems. Through a combination of talk and play the child has an opportunity to better understand and manage their conflicts, feelings, and behavior.

- **Psychodynamic Psychotherapy** emphasizes understanding the issues that motivate and influence a teen's behavior, thoughts, and feelings. It can help identify a teen's typical behavior patterns, defenses, and responses to inner conflicts and struggles. Psychoanalysis is a specialized, more intensive form of psychodynamic psychotherapy which usually involves several sessions per week. Psychodynamic psychotherapies are based on the assumption that a teen's behavior and feelings will improve once the inner struggles are brought to light.

Will my health insurance plan cover the cost?

You must read your contract or call your insurance plan office to find out the details about health insurance benefits and the extent of psychiatric services covered by your plan. Most health plans cover some portion of evaluations, consultation, and treatment services provided by a Child and Adolescent Psychiatrist. However, benefits and coverage for mental health treatments are frequently limited or restricted by insurance plans. If your health insurance plan does not cover these services and if finances appear to be a barrier in seeking necessary psychiatric services, you should discuss this matter frankly with the Child and Adolescent Psychiatrist.

Will information and treatment be confidential?

Most state laws protect the confidentiality of communication between patients and physicians. Child and Adolescent Psychiatrists will not discuss information about you and your child or adolescent with others without your consent except as required by law.

Who is a Child and Adolescent Psychiatrist?

Child and Adolescent Psychiatrists are physicians who specialize in evaluating, diagnosing, and treating children and adolescents with psychiatric disorders which cause problems with feeling, thinking, and behavior. They are specially trained and qualified to treat infants, children, adolescents, and adults as individuals, couples, families, and groups. They practice in a variety of settings, including independently in offices, on the staffs of hospitals, clinics, HMOs, etc.

What training does a Child and Adolescent Psychiatrist have?

A Child and Adolescent Psychiatrist has 9 to 10 years of special training. Child psychiatric training includes: 4 years of medical school after which the Doctor of Medicine (M.D.) degree is awarded; 1 year of supervised general medical practice in an approved residency program in a hospital, 2 or 3 years of supervised training in general psychiatry in an approved residency, and then 2 additional years of supervised training working with children, adolescents, and their families in an approved Child and Adolescent Psychiatry residency.

The Child and Adolescent Psychiatrist is a physician licensed to practice medicine. After completing their training, the Child and Adolescent Psychiatrist is eligible to take an examination to become Board certified in General Psychiatry by the American Board of Psychiatry and Neurology. After successfully completing this examination, the Child and Adolescent Psychiatrist becomes eligible for an additional examination to become Board certified in Child and Adolescent Psychiatry.

How can I find a Child and Adolescent Psychiatrist?

Ask your pediatrician, family physician, school counselor, or clergy for a referral to a child and adolescent psychiatrist; Or look in the Yellow Pages listing of Physicians and Surgeons under Psychiatry (Child). You may also contact a community hospital, state or county medical society, or the Division of Child and Adolescent Psychiatry in any medical school or university.

☞ **Remember!!**

Psychotherapy may be a long, hard process, but it offers a hopeful treatment for anyone experiencing emotional or behavioral problems.

Chapter 20

Treatment Strategies For Depression And Bipolar Disorder

How are mood disorders treated?

A good treatment plan often includes medication to stabilize mood, talk therapy to help with coping skills, and support from a peer-run group like Depression and Bipolar Support Alliance (DBSA) to help you manage your illness. Seeking treatment does not mean you are weak or a failure, it means you have the strength and courage to look for a way to feel better. Getting treatment for depression or bipolar disorder is no different than getting treatment for diabetes, asthma, high blood pressure, or arthritis. Don't let feelings of shame or embarrassment keep you from getting help.

What is psychotherapy (talk therapy)?

Psychotherapy can be an important part of treatment. A good therapist can help you cope with the feelings you are having and change the patterns that contribute to your illness. Behavioral therapy concentrates on your actions; cognitive therapy focuses on your thoughts; and interpersonal therapy looks at your relationships with others. Your loved ones may join you in sessions of family or couples therapy. Group therapy involves several, usually unrelated people working with the same therapist and each other. Many therapists use a combination of approaches. One approach is not necessarily better than another—the best choice is the one that works best for you.

How is medication used to treat depression and bipolar disorder?

There are many safe, effective medications that may be prescribed to relieve symptoms of depression or bipolar disorder. You and your doctor will work together to find the right medication or combination of medications for you. This process may take some time, so don't lose hope. No two people will respond the same way to a medication, and many people need to try several before they find the best one(s). Different treatments may be needed at different times in a person's life. Keep your own records of treatment—how you feel each day, what medications (and dosages) you take and how they affect you—to help your doctor develop a treatment plan for you. DBSA's Personal Calendar available at www.DBSAlliance.org or by calling DBSA can be very helpful with this.

Your doctor may start your treatment with a medication approved to treat mood disorders. He or she might also add other medications which have been approved by the FDA as safe and effective treatments for other illnesses of the brain, but have not yet been specifically approved to treat depression or bipolar disorder. This is called off-label use, and can be helpful for people whose symptoms don't respond to traditional treatments.

What should I do if I experience side effects?

Many of the medications that affect the brain may also affect other systems of the body, and cause side effects such as dry mouth, constipation, sleepiness, blurred vision, weight gain, weight loss, dizziness, or sexual problems. Some side effects become less or go away within days or weeks, while others can be long-term.

Multisystemic Therapy

♣ **It's A Fact!!**

Multisystemic Therapy (MST) is a mental health service that focuses on changing how youth suffering from mental illness function in their natural settings—that is, at home, in school, and in their neighborhoods.[1, 2, 3] It is designed to promote positive social behavior while decreasing problematic behavior, including delinquency, depression, or substance abuse. Therapy is approached as a combined effort between youth, the family, and the MST therapist. The family and teen set treatment goals and the therapist suggests strategies to accomplish them.

Specific treatments are used within MST. The interventions are individualized to the family's strengths and weaknesses and address the needs of the young person, family, school, peers, and neighborhood. Therapists working in the home have small caseloads and are available 24 hours a day, 7 days a week. Treatment teams usually consist of professional counselors, crisis caseworkers, and psychiatrists or psychologists who provide clinical supervision.

MST has helped youth with reduced symptoms of internalizing distress and depression. Importantly, families who received MST were significantly more satisfied with their treatment than were families whose children were hospitalized.

In addition, MST was successful in preventing a significant proportion of adolescents from being hospitalized. Further, the use of hospitalization was not offset by increases in the use of other restrictive placement options.

References

1. Henggeler SW, Schoenwald SK, Borduin CM, et al. *Multisystemic treatment of antisocial behavior in children and adolescents.* New York: Guilford Press, 1998.

2. Borduin CM, Mann BJ, Cone LT, et al. Multisystemic treatment of serious juvenile offenders: long-term prevention of criminality and violence. *Journal of Consulting and Clinical Psychology*, 1995; 63(4): 569-78.

3. Henggeler SW, Melton GB, Smith LA. Family preservation using multisystemic therapy: an effective alternative to incarcerating serious juvenile offenders. *Journal of Consulting and Clinical Psychology*, 1992; 60(6): 953-61.

Additional Information

Multisystemic Therapy Services
Website: http://www.mstservices.com

Source: "Youth In A Difficult World," National Institute of Mental Health (NIMH), updated: January 1, 2001.

✔ Quick Tip

Contact your doctor or a hospital emergency room right away
if side effects cause you to become very ill with symptoms such as fever,
rash, jaundice (yellow skin or eyes), breathing problems, heart problems (skipped
beats, racing), or other severe changes that concern you. This includes any
changes in your thoughts, such as hearing voices, seeing things,
or having thoughts of death or suicide.

Don't be discouraged by side effects; there are ways to reduce or get rid of them. It may help to change the time you take your medication to help with sleepiness or sleeplessness, or take it with food to help with nausea. Sometimes another medication can be prescribed to block an unwanted side effect, or your dosage can be adjusted to reduce the side effect to a tolerable level. Other times your medication must be changed. Tell your doctor about any side effects you are having. The decision to change or add medication must be made together by you and your doctor; you should never stop taking your medication or change your dosage without talking to your doctor first.

Be sure your doctor knows about all the medications you are taking for your mood disorder and any other physical illnesses you have. This includes over-the-counter or natural/herbal treatments. Even natural treatments may interact with your medications and change the way they work.

What if I don't feel better?

If you don't feel better right away, remember that it isn't your fault, and you haven't failed. Never be afraid to get a second opinion if you don't feel your treatment is working as well as it should. Here are some reasons your treatment may not be giving you the results you need.

Not enough time: Often a medication may not appear to work, when the reality is that it may not have had enough time to take effect. Most medications for mood disorders must be taken for two to four weeks before you begin to see results. Some can take as long as six to eight weeks before you feel their full effect. So, though it may not be easy, give your medication time to start working.

Dosage too low: With most medications used to treat mood disorders, the actual amount reaching the brain can be very different from one person to the next. A medication must reach the brain to be effective, so if your dose is too low and not enough reaches your brain, you might incorrectly assume the medication doesn't work, when you actually just need your doctor to adjust your dosage.

Different type (class) of medication needed: Your doctor may need to prescribe a different type of medication, or add one or more different types of medication to what you are currently taking.

Not taking medications as prescribed: A medication can have poor results if it is not taken as prescribed. Even if you start to feel better, keep taking your medication so you can keep feeling better. If you often forget to take your medications, consider using an alarm or pager to remind you, or keeping track of what you have taken using a pillbox with one or more compartments for each day. It may also be helpful for you to keep a written checklist of medications and times taken, or to take your medication at the same time as a specific event: a meal, a television show, bedtime, or the start or end of a work day.

Side effects: Some people stop taking their medication or skip doses because the side effects bother them. Even if your medication is working, side effects may keep you from feeling better. In some case, side effects can be similar to symptoms of depression or mania, making it difficult to tell the difference between the illness and the effects of the medication. If you have trouble with side effects, they don't go away within a few weeks, and the suggestions mentioned earlier don't help, talk to your doctor about changing the medication, but don't stop taking it on your own.

Medication interactions: Medications used to treat other illnesses may interfere with the medication you are taking for your depression or bipolar disorder. For example, some medications may keep others from reaching high enough levels in the blood, or cause your body to get rid of them before they have a chance to work. Ask your doctor or pharmacist about the possible interactions of each newly-prescribed medication with other medications you are taking.

Other medical conditions: Sometimes a medication may not work for reasons not related to your mood disorder. Medical conditions such as hypothyroidism, chronic fatigue syndrome, and brain injury can limit the effectiveness of your medication. Sometimes normal aging or menopause can change your brain chemistry and make it necessary to change your dosage or your medication. It's a good idea to have a complete physical examination and discuss your complete medical history with your doctor.

Substance abuse: Alcohol or illegal drug abuse may interfere with the treatment of depression or bipolar disorder. For example, alcohol reduces the effectiveness of some antidepressants. The combination of alcohol or drugs with your medication(s) may lead to serious or dangerous side effects. It can also be difficult to benefit from talk therapy if you are under the influence of alcohol or other drugs. If you are having trouble stopping drinking or using drugs, you may want to consider seeking help from a 12-step recovery program or a treatment center.

Non-response: Response to any medication, especially those for depression and bipolar disorder, can be very different for each individual. A certain percentage of people won't respond to a particular medication at all. If you are one of these people, don't give up hope. There are many treatment strategies available for you and your doctor to try.

☞ Remember!!

Treating a mood disorder can take several weeks or months of therapy and/or medication. Do not give up. Treatment allows most people to live a normal life. Continue to work with your doctor to find the best treatment plan for you.

Chapter 21

Medications For Treatment Of Mental Health Disorders

This chapter is intended to inform you, but it is not a "do-it-yourself" manual. Leave it to the doctor, working closely with you, to diagnose mental illness, interpret signs and symptoms of the illness, prescribe and manage medication, and explain any side effects. This will help you ensure that you use medication most effectively and with minimum risk of side effects or complications.

Introduction

Anyone can develop a mental illness—you, a family member, a friend, or a neighbor. Some disorders are mild; others are serious and long-lasting. These conditions can be diagnosed and treated. Most people can live better lives after treatment. And psychotherapeutic medications are an increasingly important element in the successful treatment of mental illness.

Medications for mental illnesses were first introduced in the early 1950s with the antipsychotic chlorpromazine. Other medications have followed. These medications have changed the lives of people with these disorders for the better.

About This Book: This chapter includes text from "Medications," National Institute of Mental Health (NIMH), NIH Publication No. 02-3929, 2002.

✎ **Weird Words**

Neurotransmitters: A chemical released by a cell which helps the brain cells communicate.

Off-Label: Use medicine for a purpose other than the approved use.

Potency: Strength of a specific amount of a medicine.

Psychotherapeutic Medications: Medicine used to relieve the symptoms of mental health disorders.

Side Effect: An unexpected, often undesired effect from taking medicine.

Psychotherapeutic medications also may make other kinds of treatment more effective. Someone who is too depressed to talk, for instance, may have difficulty communicating during psychotherapy or counseling, but the right medication may improve symptoms so the person can respond. For many patients, a combination of psychotherapy and medication can be an effective method of treatment.

Another benefit of these medications is an increased understanding of the causes of mental illness. Scientists have learned much more about the workings of the brain as a result of their investigations into how psychotherapeutic medications relieve the symptoms of disorders such as psychosis, depression, anxiety, obsessive-compulsive disorder, and panic disorder.

Relief From Symptoms

Just as aspirin can reduce a fever without curing the infection that causes it, psychotherapeutic medications act by controlling symptoms. Psychotherapeutic medications do not cure mental illness, but in many cases, they can help a person function despite some continuing mental pain and difficulty coping with problems. For example, drugs like chlorpromazine can turn off the voices heard by some people with psychosis and help them to see reality more clearly. And antidepressants can lift the dark, heavy moods of depression. The degree of response—ranging from a little relief of symptoms to complete relief—depends on a variety of factors related to the individual and the disorder being treated.

How long someone must take a psychotherapeutic medication depends on the individual and the disorder. Many depressed and anxious people may need medication for a single period—perhaps for several months—and then never need it again. People with conditions such as schizophrenia or bipolar disorder (also known as manic-depressive illness), or those whose depression or anxiety is chronic or recurrent, may have to take medication indefinitely.

Like any medication, psychotherapeutic medications do not produce the same effect in everyone. Some people may respond better to one medication than another. Some may need larger dosages than others do. Some have side effects, and others do not. Age, sex, body size, body chemistry, physical illnesses and their treatments, diet, and habits such as smoking are some of the factors that can influence a medication's effect.

Medications For Mental Illness

This chapter describes medications by their generic (chemical) names and in parentheses by their trade names (brand names used by pharmaceutical companies). They are divided into four large categories—antipsychotic, antimanic, antidepressant, and antianxiety medications. Medications that specifically affect children and teens are discussed, and a chart at the end of the chapter shows the trade and generic names of medications commonly prescribed for children and adolescents.

Antipsychotic Medications

A person who is psychotic is out of touch with reality. People with psychosis may hear voices or have strange and illogical ideas (for example, thinking that others can hear their thoughts, or are trying to harm them, or that they are the President of the United States or some other famous person). They may get excited or angry for no apparent reason, or spend a lot of time by themselves, or in bed, sleeping during the day and staying awake at night. The person may neglect appearance, not bathing or changing clothes, and may be hard to talk to—barely talking or saying things that make no sense. They often are initially unaware that their condition is an illness.

These kinds of behaviors are symptoms of a psychotic illness such as schizophrenia. Antipsychotic medications act against these symptoms. These medications cannot cure the illness, but they can take away many of the symptoms or make them milder. In some cases, they can shorten the course of an episode of the illness as well.

There are a number of antipsychotic (neuroleptic) medications available. These medications affect neurotransmitters that allow communication between nerve cells. One such neurotransmitter, dopamine, is thought to be relevant to schizophrenia symptoms. All these medications have been shown to be effective for schizophrenia. The main differences are in the potency—that is, the dosage (amount) prescribed to produce therapeutic effects—and the side effects. Some people might think that the higher the dose of medication prescribed, the more serious the illness; but this is not always true.

The 1990s saw the development of several new drugs for schizophrenia, called atypical antipsychotics. Because they have fewer side effects than the older drugs, today they are often used as a first-line treatment. The first atypical antipsychotic, clozapine (Clozaril), was introduced in the United States in 1990. In clinical trials, this medication was found to be more effective than conventional or typical antipsychotic medications in individuals with treatment-resistant schizophrenia (schizophrenia that has not responded to other drugs), and the risk of tardive dyskinesia (a movement disorder) was lower. However, because of the potential side effect of a serious blood disorder—agranulocytosis (loss of the white blood cells that fight infection)—

✔ Quick Tip

If you are taking more than one medication, and at different times of the day, it is essential that you take the correct dosage of each medication. An easy way to make sure you do this is to use a 7-day pillbox, available in any pharmacy, and to fill the box with the proper medication at the beginning of each week. Many pharmacies also have pillboxes with sections for medications that must be taken more than once a day.

patients who are on clozapine must have a blood test every 1 or 2 weeks. The inconvenience and cost of blood tests and the medication itself have made maintenance on clozapine difficult for many people. Clozapine, however, continues to be the drug of choice for treatment-resistant schizophrenia patients.

Several other atypical antipsychotics have been developed since clozapine was introduced. The first was risperidone (Risperdal), followed by olanzapine (Zyprexa), quetiapine (Seroquel), and ziprasidone (Geodon). Each has a unique side effect profile, but in general, these medications are better tolerated than the earlier drugs.

All these medications have their place in the treatment of schizophrenia, and doctors will choose among them. They will consider the person's symptoms, age, weight, and personal and family medication history.

Dosages And Side Effects

Some drugs are very potent and the doctor may prescribe a low dose. Other drugs are not as potent and a higher dose may be prescribed.

Unlike some prescription drugs, which must be taken several times during the day, some antipsychotic medications can be taken just once a day. In order to reduce daytime side effects such as sleepiness, some medications can be taken at bedtime. Some antipsychotic medications are available in "depot" forms that can be injected once or twice a month.

Most side effects of antipsychotic medications are mild. Many common ones lessen or disappear after the first few weeks of treatment. These include drowsiness, rapid heartbeat, and dizziness when changing position.

Just as people vary in their responses to antipsychotic medications, they also vary in how quickly they improve. Some symptoms may diminish in days; others take weeks or months. Many people see substantial improvement by the sixth week of treatment. If there is no improvement, the doctor may try a different type of medication. The doctor cannot tell beforehand which medication will work for a person. Sometimes a person must try several medications before finding one that works.

✔ **Quick Tip**

Questions For Your Doctor

You and your family can help your doctor find the right medications for you. The doctor needs to know your medical history, other medications being taken, and life plans such as hoping to have a baby. After taking the medication for a short time, you should tell the doctor about favorable results as well as side effects. The Food and Drug Administration (FDA) and professional organizations recommend that the patient or a family member ask the following questions when a medication is prescribed:

- What is the name of the medication, and what is it supposed to do?

- How and when do I take it, and when do I stop taking it?

- What foods, drinks, or other medications should I avoid while taking the prescribed medication?

- Should it be taken with food or on an empty stomach?

- Is it safe to drink alcohol while on this medication?

- What are the side effects, and what should I do if they occur?

- Is a Patient Package Insert for the medication available?

Multiple Medications

Antipsychotic medications can produce unwanted effects when taken with other medications. Therefore, the doctor should be told about all medicines being taken, including over-the-counter medications and vitamin, mineral, and herbal supplements, and the extent of alcohol use. Some antipsychotic medications interfere with antihypertensive medications (taken for high blood pressure), anticonvulsants (taken for epilepsy), and medications used for Parkinson's disease. Other antipsychotics add to the effect of alcohol and other central nervous system depressants such as antihistamines, antidepressants, barbiturates, some sleeping and pain medications, and narcotics.

Antimanic Medications

Bipolar disorder is characterized by cycling mood changes: severe highs (mania) and lows (depression). Episodes may be predominantly manic or depressive, with normal mood between episodes. Mood swings may follow each other very closely, within days (rapid cycling), or may be separated by months to years. The highs and lows may vary in intensity and severity and can co-exist in mixed episodes.

When people are in a manic high, they may be overactive, overly talkative, have a great deal of energy, and have much less need for sleep than normal. They may switch quickly from one topic to another, as if they cannot get their thoughts out fast enough. Their attention span is often short, and they can be easily distracted. Sometimes people who are high are irritable or angry and have false or inflated ideas about their position or importance in the world. They may be very elated, and full of grand schemes that might range from business deals to romantic sprees. Often, they show poor judgment in these ventures. Mania, untreated, may worsen to a psychotic state.

In a depressive cycle the person may have a low mood with difficulty concentrating; lack of energy, with slowed thinking and movements; changes in eating and sleeping patterns (usually increases of both in bipolar depression); feelings of hopelessness, helplessness, sadness, worthlessness, guilt; and sometimes, thoughts of suicide.

Lithium

The medication used most often to treat bipolar disorder is lithium. Lithium evens out mood swings in both directions—from mania to depression, and depression to mania—so it is used not just for manic attacks or flare-ups of the illness, but also as an ongoing maintenance treatment for bipolar disorder.

Although lithium will reduce severe manic symptoms in about 5 to 14 days, it may be weeks to several months before the condition is fully controlled. Antipsychotic medications are sometimes used in the first several days of treatment to control manic symptoms until the lithium begins to take effect. Antidepressants may also be added to lithium during the depressive phase of bipolar disorder. If given in the absence of lithium or another mood stabilizer, antidepressants may provoke a switch into mania in people with bipolar disorder.

A person may have one episode of bipolar disorder and never have another, or be free of illness for several years. But for those who have more than one manic episode, doctors usually give serious consideration to maintenance (continuing) treatment with lithium.

Regular blood tests are an important part of treatment with lithium. If too little is taken, lithium will not be effective. If too much is taken, a variety of side effects may occur. The range between an effective dose and a toxic one is small. Blood lithium levels are checked at the beginning of treatment to determine the best lithium dosage. Once a person is stable and on a maintenance dosage, the lithium level should be checked every few months. How much lithium people need to take may vary over time, depending on how ill they are, their body chemistry, and their physical condition.

Side Effects Of Lithium

When people first take lithium, they may experience side effects such as drowsiness, weakness, nausea, fatigue, hand tremor, or increased thirst and urination. Some may disappear or decrease quickly, although hand tremor may persist. Weight gain may also occur. Dieting will help, but crash diets should be avoided because they may raise or lower the lithium level. Drinking low-calorie or no-calorie beverages, especially water, will help keep weight down. Kidney changes—increased urination and, in children, enuresis (bed wetting)—may develop during treatment. These changes are generally manageable and are reduced by lowering the dosage. Because lithium may cause the thyroid gland to become underactive (hypothyroidism) or sometimes enlarged (goiter), thyroid function monitoring is a part of the therapy. To restore normal thyroid function, thyroid hormone may be given along with lithium.

Anything that lowers the level of sodium in the body—reduced intake of table salt, a switch to a low-salt diet, heavy sweating from an unusual amount of exercise or a very hot climate, fever, vomiting, or diarrhea—may cause a lithium buildup and lead to toxicity. It is important to be aware of conditions that lower sodium or cause dehydration and to tell the doctor if any of these conditions are present so the dose can be changed.

Lithium, when combined with certain other medications, can have unwanted effects. Some diuretics—substances that remove water from the body—increase the level of lithium and can cause toxicity. Other diuretics, like coffee and tea, can lower the level of lithium. Signs of lithium toxicity may include nausea, vomiting, drowsiness, mental dullness, slurred speech, blurred vision, confusion, dizziness, muscle twitching, irregular heartbeat, and, ultimately, seizures. A lithium overdose can be life-threatening. People who are taking lithium should tell every doctor who is treating them, including dentists, about all medications they are taking.

With regular monitoring, lithium is a safe and effective drug that enables many people, who otherwise would suffer from incapacitating mood swings, to lead normal lives.

♣ **It's A Fact!!**
If a person is feeling better or even completely well, their medication should not be stopped without talking to the doctor. It may be necessary to stay on the medication to continue feeling well. If, after consultation with the doctor, the decision is made to discontinue the medication, it is important to continue to see the doctor while tapering off medication.

Anticonvulsants

Some people with symptoms of mania who do not benefit from or would prefer to avoid lithium have been found to respond to anticonvulsant medications commonly prescribed to treat seizures. The anticonvulsant valproic acid (Depakote, divalproex sodium) is the main alternative therapy for bipolar disorder. It is as effective in non-rapid-cycling bipolar disorder as lithium and appears to be superior to lithium in rapid-cycling bipolar disorder.[2] Although valproic acid can cause gastrointestinal side effects, the incidence is low. Other adverse effects occasionally reported are headache, double vision, dizziness, anxiety, or confusion. Because in some cases valproic acid has caused liver dysfunction, liver function tests should be performed before therapy and at frequent intervals thereafter, particularly during the first 6 months of therapy.

Other anticonvulsants used for bipolar disorder include carbamazepine (Tegretol), lamotrigine (Lamictal), gabapentin (Neurontin), and topiramate (Topamax). The evidence for anticonvulsant effectiveness is stronger for acute mania than for long-term maintenance of bipolar disorder. Some studies suggest particular efficacy of lamotrigine in bipolar depression. At present, the lack of formal FDA approval of anticonvulsants other than valproic acid for bipolar disorder may limit insurance coverage for these medications.

Most people who have bipolar disorder take more than one medication. Along with the mood stabilizer—lithium and/or an anticonvulsant—they may take a medication for accompanying agitation, anxiety, insomnia, or depression. It is important to continue taking the mood stabilizer when taking an antidepressant because research has shown that treatment with an antidepressant alone increases the risk that the patient will switch to mania or hypomania, or develop rapid cycling.[5] Sometimes, when a bipolar patient is not responsive to other medications, an atypical antipsychotic medication is prescribed. Finding the best possible medication, or combination of medications, is of utmost importance to the patient and requires close monitoring by a doctor and strict adherence to the recommended treatment regimen.

Antidepressant Medications

Major depression, the kind of depression that will most likely benefit from treatment with medication, is more than just the blues. It is a condition that lasts 2 weeks or more, and interferes with a person's ability to carry on daily tasks and enjoy activities that previously brought pleasure. Depression is associated with abnormal functioning of the brain. An interaction between genetic tendency and life history appears to determine a person's chance of becoming depressed. Episodes of depression may be triggered by stress, difficult life events, side effects of medications, or medication/substance withdrawal, or even viral infections that can affect the brain.

✔ Quick Tip

Watch For Worsening Depression And Suicidality During Treatment With Antidepressant Medications

In March 2004 the Food and Drug Administration (FDA) requested stronger warning statements for drugs used in the treatment of depression warning that patients need to watch for worsening of depression or suicidality, especially at the beginning of therapy or when the dose either increases or decreases. The drugs that are the focus of this warning are: fluoxetine (Prozac); sertraline (Zoloft); paroxetine (Paxil); fluvoxamine (Luvox); citalopram (Celexa); escitalopram (Lexapro); bupropion (Wellbutrin); venlafaxine (Effexor); nefazodone (Serzone); and mirtazapine (Remeron).

Anxiety, agitation, panic attacks, insomnia, irritability, hostility, impulsivity, severe restlessness, hypomania, mania, or suicidal thoughts have been reported in patients being treated with antidepressants. If you or someone you know is taking antidepressants and experiences these symptoms, contact your health care provider immediately.

Among antidepressants, only fluoxetine (Prozac) is approved for the treatment of pediatric major depressive disorder. Fluoxetine (Prozac), sertraline (Zoloft), and fluvoxamine (Luvox) are approved for pediatric obsessive compulsive disorder. None of these drugs is approved as the only therapy for use in treating bipolar depression, either in adults or children.

Source: "FDA Public Health Advisory," March 22, 2004, U.S. Food and Drug Administration.

Depressed people will seem sad, or down, or may be unable to enjoy their normal activities. They may have no appetite and lose weight (although some people eat more and gain weight when depressed). They may sleep too much or too little, have difficulty going to sleep, sleep restlessly, or awaken very early in the morning. They may speak of feeling guilty, worthless, or hopeless; they may lack energy or be jumpy and agitated. They may think about killing themselves and may even make a suicide attempt. Some depressed people have delusions (false, fixed ideas) about poverty, sickness, or sinfulness that are related to their depression. Often feelings of depression are worse at a particular time of day, for instance, every morning or every evening.

Not everyone who is depressed has all these symptoms, but everyone who is depressed has at least some of them, co-existing, on most days. Depression can range in intensity from mild to severe. Depression can co-occur with other medical disorders such as cancer, heart disease, stroke, Parkinson's disease, Alzheimer's disease, and diabetes. In such cases, the depression is often overlooked and is not treated. If the depression is recognized and treated, a person's quality of life can be greatly improved.

Antidepressants are used most often for serious depressions, but they can also be helpful for some milder depressions. Antidepressants are not uppers or stimulants, but rather take away or reduce the symptoms of depression and help depressed people feel the way they did before they became depressed.

The past decade has seen the introduction of many new antidepressants that work as well as the older ones but have fewer side effects. Some of these medications primarily affect one neurotransmitter, serotonin, and are called selective serotonin reuptake inhibitors (SSRIs). These include fluoxetine (Prozac), sertraline (Zoloft), fluvoxamine (Luvox), paroxetine (Paxil), and citalopram (Celexa).

The late 1990s ushered in new medications that, like the tricyclics, affect both norepinephrine and serotonin but have fewer side effects. These new medications include venlafaxine (Effexor) and nefazodone (Serzone).

Other newer medications chemically unrelated to the other antidepressants are the sedating mirtazapine (Remeron) and the more activating bupropion (Wellbutrin). Wellbutrin has not

> **✔ Quick Tip**
>
> **Check With Your Doctor Before You Stop Antidepressant Medication**
>
> You should consult your doctor to discuss the best course of action if you observe worsening depression, the emergence of suicidal thinking, or if you are experiencing other symptoms that you are concerned might be related to taking your medication. If your doctor advises that your medication should be stopped, be sure to follow your doctor's advice about how to accomplish this.
>
> Source: "Questions and Answers on Antidepressant Use in Children, Adolescents, and Adults," U.S. Food and Drug Administration, March 22, 2004.

been associated with weight gain or sexual dysfunction, but is not used for people with, or at risk for, a seizure disorder.

Each antidepressant differs in its side effects and in its effectiveness in treating an individual person, but the majority of people with depression can be treated effectively by one of these antidepressants.

Side Effects Of Antidepressant Medications

Antidepressants may cause mild, and often temporary, side effects (sometimes referred to as adverse effects) in some people. Typically, these are not serious. However, any reactions or side effects that are unusual, annoying, or that interfere with functioning should be reported to the doctor immediately. The most common side effects of tricyclic antidepressants, and ways to deal with them, are as follows:

✔ Quick Tip

Some people gain weight while taking medications and need to pay extra attention to diet and exercise to control their weight. Other side effects may include a decrease in sexual ability or interest, problems with menstrual periods, sunburn, or skin rashes. If a side effect occurs, the doctor should be told. He or she may prescribe a different medication, change the dosage or schedule, or prescribe an additional medication to control the side effects.

- Dry mouth—it is helpful to drink sips of water; chew sugarless gum; brush teeth daily.

- Constipation—bran cereals, prunes, fruit, and vegetables should be in the diet.

- Bladder problems—emptying the bladder completely may be difficult, and the urine stream may not be as strong as usual. Older men with enlarged prostate conditions may be at particular risk for this problem. The doctor should be notified if there is any pain.

- Sexual problems—sexual functioning may be impaired; if this is worrisome, it should be discussed with the doctor.

- Blurred vision—this is usually temporary and will not necessitate new glasses. Glaucoma patients should report any change in vision to the doctor.

♣ It's A Fact!!

What We Know About Antidepressant Medication For Teens

- SSRIs (serotonin reuptake inhibitors) are considered an improvement over older antidepressants because they are better tolerated and are safer if taken in an overdose (which is an issue for patients at risk for suicide). They have been extensively tested in adult populations and have been proven to be safe and effective for adults. Fluoxetine, sertraline, and fluvoxamine are approved by the FDA for the treatment of Obsessive-Compulsive Disorder because studies have shown they are safe and effective for adolescents with this disorder.

- Use of SSRIs has risen dramatically in the past several years in children and adolescents age 10–19. Some research points out that this increase has coincided with a significant decrease in suicide rates in this age group, but it is not known if SSRIs are directly responsible for this improvement.

- Fluoxetine has also been shown to be safe and helpful in treating depression in children 8 years and older in two different studies—one supported by NIMH and the other supported by Eli Lilly, the manufacturer of the drug. The studies found that it reduced depression for many children better than a placebo (a fake pill) and it did not increase suicide or suicidal thinking. However, fluoxetine failed to improve depression in at least one-third of patients. Also, about one in 10 children experienced adverse side effects such as agitation and mania.

- The other SSRIs, such as sertraline, citalopram, and paroxetine, have not been approved for treatment of depression in children or adolescents, though they have often been prescribed to children by physicians in "off-label use"—a use other than the approved use.

Source: "Antidepressant Medications for Children: Information for Parents and Caregivers," National Institute of Mental Health (NIMH), April 23, 2004.

- Dizziness—rising from the bed or chair slowly is helpful.

- Drowsiness as a daytime problem—this usually passes soon. A person who feels drowsy or sedated should not drive or operate heavy equipment. The more sedating antidepressants are generally taken at bedtime to help sleep and to minimize daytime drowsiness.

- Increased heart rate—pulse rate is often elevated. Older patients should have an electrocardiogram (EKG) before beginning tricyclic treatment.

The newer antidepressants, including SSRIs, have different types of side effects, as follows:

- Sexual problems—fairly common, but reversible, in both men and women. The doctor should be consulted if the problem is persistent or worrisome.

- Headache—this will usually go away after a short time.

- Nausea—may occur after a dose, but it will disappear quickly.

- Nervousness and insomnia (trouble falling asleep or waking often during the night)—these may occur during the first few weeks; dosage reductions or time will usually resolve them.

- Agitation (feeling jittery)—if this happens for the first time after the drug is taken and is more than temporary, the doctor should be notified.

- Any of these side effects may be amplified when an SSRI is combined with other medications that affect serotonin. In the most extreme cases, such a combination of medications (e.g., an SSRI and a mono amino oxidase inhibitor–MAOI) may result in a potentially serious or even fatal "serotonin syndrome," characterized by fever, confusion, muscle rigidity, and cardiac, liver, or kidney problems.

The small number of people for whom MAOIs are the best treatment need to avoid taking decongestants and consuming certain foods that contain high levels of tyramine, such as many cheeses, wines, and pickles. The interaction of tyramine with MAOIs can bring on a sharp increase in blood pressure that can lead to a stroke. The doctor should furnish a complete list of prohibited foods that the individual should carry at all times. Other forms of antidepressants require no food restrictions. MAOIs also should not be combined with other antidepressants, especially SSRIs, due to the risk of serotonin syndrome.

Antianxiety Medications

Everyone experiences anxiety at one time or another—"butterflies in the stomach" before giving a speech or sweaty palms during a job interview are common symptoms. Other symptoms include irritability, uneasiness, jumpiness, feelings of apprehension, rapid or irregular heartbeat, stomachache, nausea, faintness, and breathing problems.

Anxiety is often manageable and mild, but sometimes it can present serious problems. A high level or prolonged state of anxiety can make the activities of daily life difficult or impossible. People may have generalized anxiety disorder (GAD) or more specific anxiety disorders such as panic, phobias, obsessive-compulsive disorder (OCD), or post-traumatic stress disorder (PTSD).

Both antidepressants and antianxiety medications are used to treat anxiety disorders. The broad-spectrum activity of most antidepressants provides effectiveness in anxiety disorders as well as depression. The first medication specifically approved for use in the treatment of OCD was the

> **✔ Quick Tip**
> **Don't Mix Medications**
>
> Medications of any kind—prescribed, over-the-counter, or herbal supplements—should never be mixed without consulting the doctor; nor should medications ever be borrowed from another person. Other health professionals who may prescribe a drug—such as a dentist or other medical specialist—should be told that the person is taking a specific antidepressant and the dosage. Some drugs, although safe when taken alone, can cause severe and dangerous side effects if taken with other drugs. Alcohol (wine, beer, and hard liquor) or street drugs may reduce the effectiveness of antidepressants and their use should be minimized or, preferably, avoided by anyone taking antidepressants. Some people who have not had a problem with alcohol use may be permitted by their doctor to use a modest amount of alcohol while taking one of the newer antidepressants. The potency of alcohol may be increased by medications since both are metabolized by the liver; one drink may feel like two.

tricyclic antidepressant clomipramine (Anafranil). The SSRIs, fluoxetine (Prozac), fluvoxamine (Luvox), paroxetine (Paxil), and sertraline (Zoloft) have now been approved for use with OCD. Paroxetine has also been approved for social anxiety disorder (social phobia), GAD, and panic disorder; and sertraline is approved for panic disorder and PTSD. Venlafaxine (Effexor) has been approved for GAD.

Antianxiety medications include the benzodiazepines, which can relieve symptoms within a short time. They have relatively few side effects: drowsiness and loss of coordination are most common; fatigue and mental slowing or confusion can also occur. These effects make it dangerous for people taking benzodiazepines to drive or operate some machinery. Other side effects are rare.

Benzodiazepines vary in duration of action in different people; they may be taken two or three times a day, sometimes only once a day, or just on an as-needed basis. Dosage is generally started at a low level and gradually raised until symptoms are diminished or removed. The dosage will vary a great deal depending on the symptoms and the individual's body chemistry.

It is wise to abstain from alcohol when taking benzodiazepines, because the interaction between benzodiazepines and alcohol can lead to serious and possibly life-threatening complications. It is also important to tell the doctor about other medications being taken.

The only medication specifically for anxiety disorders other than the benzodiazepines is buspirone (BuSpar). Unlike the benzodiazepines, buspirone must be taken consistently for at least 2 weeks to achieve an antianxiety effect and therefore cannot be used on an "as-needed" basis.

Medications For Children And Teens

Children and teens have special concerns and needs when taking psychotherapeutic medications. Some effects of medications on the growing body are known, but much remains to be learned. Research in these areas is ongoing. In general, the information throughout this chapter applies to children and teens, but the following are a few special points to keep in mind.

Children And Adolescents

The 1999 MECA Study (Methodology for Epidemiology of Mental Disorders in Children and Adolescents) estimated that almost 21 percent of U.S. children ages 9 to 17 had a diagnosable mental or addictive disorder that caused at least some impairment. When diagnostic criteria were limited to significant functional impairment, the estimate dropped to 11 percent, for a total of 4 million children who suffer from a psychiatric disorder that limits their ability to function.[6]

It is easy to overlook the seriousness of childhood mental disorders. In children, these disorders may present symptoms that are different from or less clear-cut than the same disorders in adults.

Many treatments are available to help these children. The treatments include both medications and psychotherapy—behavioral therapy, treatment of impaired social skills, parental and family therapy, and group therapy. The therapy used is based on the child's diagnosis and individual needs.

When the decision is reached that a child should take medication, active monitoring by all caretakers (parents, teachers, and others who have charge of the child) is essential. Children should be watched and questioned for side effects because many children, especially younger ones, do not volunteer information. They should also be monitored to see that they are actually taking the medication and taking the proper dosage on the correct schedule.

Childhood-onset depression and anxiety are increasingly recognized and treated. Based on clinical experience and medication knowledge, a physician may prescribe to young children a medication that has been approved by the FDA for use in adults or older children. This use of the medication is called off-label. Most medications prescribed for childhood mental disorders, including many of the newer medications that are proving helpful, are prescribed off-label because only a few of them have been systematically studied for safety and efficacy in children. Medications that have not undergone such testing are dispensed with the statement that "safety and efficacy have not been established in pediatric patients."

Table 21.1. Children's Medication Chart

Trade Name	Generic Name	Approved Age
Stimulant Medications		
Adderall	amphetamine	3 and older
Adderall XR	amphetamine (extended release)	6 and older
Concerta	methylphenidate (long acting)	6 and older
Cylert*	pemoline	6 and older
Dexedrine	dextroamphetamine	3 and older
Dextrostat	dextroamphetamine	3 and older
Focalin	dexmethylphenidate	6 and older
Metadate ER	methylphenidate (extended release)	6 and older
Ritalin	methylphenidate	6 and older
Non-stimulant for ADHD		
Strattera	atomoxetine	6 and older

*Because of its potential for serious side effects affecting the liver, Cylert should not ordinarily be considered as first-line drug therapy for ADHD.

Antidepressant and Antianxiety Medications		
Anafranil	clomipramine	10 and older (for OCD)
BuSpar	buspirone	18 and older
Effexor	venlafaxine	18 and older
Luvox (SSRI)	fluvoxamine	8 and older (for OCD)
Paxil (SSRI)	paroxetine	18 and older
Prozac (SSRI)	fluoxetine	18 and older
Serzone (SSRI)	nefazodone	18 and older
Sinequan	doxepin	12 and older
Tofranil	imipramine	6 and older (for bedwetting)
Wellbutrin	bupropion	18 and older
Zoloft (SSRI)	sertraline	6 and older (for OCD)

continued on next page

Table 21.1. Children's Medication Chart, continued from previous page

Trade Name	Generic Name	Approved Age
Antipsychotic Medications		
Clozaril (atypical)	clozapine	18 and older
Haldol	haloperidol	3 and older
Risperdal (atypical)	risperidone	18 and older
Seroquel (atypical)	quetiapine	18 and older
Mellaril	thioridazine	2 and older
Zyprexa (atypical)	olanzapine	18 and older
Orap	pimozide	12 and older (for Tourette's syndrome—Data for age 2 and older indicate similar safety profile)
Mood Stabilizing Medications		
Cibalith-S	lithium citrate	12 and older
Depakote	valproic acid	2 and older (for seizures)
Eskalith	lithium carbonate	12 and older
Lithobid	lithium carbonate	12 and older
Tegretol	carbamazepine	any age (for seizures)

The use of the other medications described in this chapter is more limited with children than with adults. Therefore, a special list of medications for children and adolescents, with the ages approved for their use is given in Table 21.1.

References

1. Fenton WS. Prevalence of spontaneous dyskinesia in schizophrenia. *Journal of Clinical Psychiatry*, 2000; 62 (suppl 4): 10-14.

2. Bowden CL, Calabrese JR, McElroy SL, Gyulai L, Wassef A, Petty F, et al. For the Divalproex Maintenance Study Group. A randomized, placebo-controlled 12-month trial of divalproex and lithium in treatment

> ### 👉 Remember!!
>
> It is important for you to be well informed about medications you may need. You should know what medications you take and the dosage, and learn everything you can about them. When you go to a new doctor, always take with you a list of all of the prescribed medications (including dosage), over-the-counter medications, and vitamin, mineral, and herbal supplements you take. The list should include herbal teas and supplements such as St. John's wort, echinacea, ginkgo, ephedra, and ginseng. Almost any substance that can change behavior can cause harm if used in the wrong amount or frequency of dosing, or in a bad combination. Drugs differ in the speed, duration of action, and in their margin for error.

of outpatients with bipolar I disorder. *Archives of General Psychiatry*, 2000; 57(5): 481-489.

3. Vainionpää LK, Rättyä J, Knip M, Tapanainen JS, Pakarinen AJ, Lanning P, et al. Valproate-induced hyperandrogenism during pubertal maturation in girls with epilepsy. *Annals of Neurology*, 1999; 45(4): 444-450.

4. Soames JC. Valproate treatment and the risk of hyperandrogenism and polycystic ovaries. *Bipolar Disorder*, 2000; 2(1): 37-41.

5. Thase ME, and Sachs GS. Bipolar depression: Pharmacotherapy and related therapeutic strategies. *Biological Psychiatry*, 2000; 48(6): 558-572.

6. Department of Health and Human Services. 1999. Mental *Health: A Report of the Surgeon General*. Rockville, MD: Department of Health and Human Services, Substance Abuse and Mental Health Services Administration, Center for Mental Health Services, National Institute of Mental Health.

7. Altshuler LL, Cohen L, Szuba MP, Burt VK, Gitlin M, and Mintz J. Pharmacologic management of psychiatric illness during pregnancy: Dilemmas and guidelines. *American Journal of Psychiatry*, 1996; 153(5): 592-606.

8. *Physicians' Desk Reference, 54th edition*. Montavale, NJ: Medical Economics Data Production Co. 2000.

Part Four

Preventing Suicide

Chapter 22

Helping Someone Who May Be Suicidal

If you or someone you know suffers from depression or manic depression (also known as bipolar disorder), you understand all too well its symptoms may include feelings of sadness and hopelessness. These feelings can also include thoughts of self-harm or suicide. Whether we have suicidal thoughts ourselves or know a severely depressed person who does, there are ways that we can respond with strength and courage.

Understanding Suicidal Thinking

The most important thing to remember about suicidal thoughts is that they are symptoms of a treatable illness associated with fluctuations in the chemistry of the body and brain. They are not signs of personal weakness or character flaws, nor are they conditions that will just go away by themselves. Depression and the depressive phase of bipolar disorder may cause symptoms such as intense sadness, hopelessness, lethargy, loss of appetite, disruption of sleep, decreased ability to perform ones usual tasks, or loss of interest in once-pleasurable activities. Taken together, these symptoms may lead someone to consider suicide. However, with proper treatment the majority of people do feel better.

About This Chapter: Text in this chapter is from "Suicide Prevention," reprinted with permission from the Depression and Bipolar Support Alliance (DBSA), © 2004. All rights reserved. For additional information, including assistance in finding support group or mental health professional, contact the Depression and Bipolar Support Alliance at 800-826-3632, or visit their website at http://www.dbssalliance.org.

During severe depression, the systems that regulate emotion become disturbed. People in severe depression often think of things that are dark and sad. Physicians refer to this as selective memory—only remembering the bad times or the disappointments in life. This is a symptom of their illness, not who they are, and with proper treatment the person will start to remember good times and develop a more positive outlook.

If You Are Feeling Suicidal

If you have begun to think of suicide, it is important to recognize these thoughts for what they are: expressions of a treatable medical illness. Don't let embarrassment stand in the way of vital communication with your physician, family, or friends. Take immediate action and talk to somebody today. Remember, suicide is a permanent solution to a temporary problem.

When people don't understand the facts about suicide and depressive illnesses, they may respond in ways that can cut off communication and worsen feelings. That's why it is important to find someone you trust and can talk with honesty. It's also why your mental health professional is an important resource in helping you, and your family.

Some Facts About Treatment

There are many different medications and therapies available for the successful treatment of depression. Not all medications work the same on all people, so it may take time for you and your doctor to develop a treatment plan that's right for you. Stick with it, and recognize that your doctor is your partner in this search.

Create A Plan For Life

It is important to have a course of action ready before thoughts of suicide occur. Some people find it helpful to develop a Plan for Life. The Plan for Life lists warning signs you should watch for and actions to take if you feel that you are slipping into suicidal thoughts. Your Plan for Life may include:

• Contact information for your doctor, including back-up phone numbers (emergency services, pager, and mobile phone).

- Contact information for friends and family.

- A description of medical diagnosis, not just your depression but any medical problems you may have. Include information about any medications you are taking.

- Health insurance information.

- Contact information for a local suicide hot line.

- Contact information for your local DBSA support group.

Sample Plan For Life

Educate those you trust about your condition before it becomes a crisis so they can be prepared if they are called upon to help. Provide key support people with your Plan for Life so they can act quickly, if needed. Carry a copy of your Plan for Life with you at all times so you can refer to it or pass it along to someone else who might be helping you in a time of crisis. With all the phone numbers in one place, it will be easier for someone to help.

♣ It's A Fact!!

Many depression-related suicides occur during the first three depressive episodes before a person learns that an episode of suicidal thinking is temporary. As people learn from experience that any given episode will eventually pass, the likelihood that they will actually act on suicidal impulses drops sharply.

What You Can Do To Fight Suicidal Thoughts

- Keep a journal to write down your thoughts. Each day, write about your hopes for the future and the people you value in your life. Read what you've written when you need to remind yourself why your own life is important.

- Go out with friends and family. When we are well, we enjoy spending time with friends and family. When we're depressed, it becomes more difficult, but it is still important. Visiting or allowing visits by family and friends who are caring and can understand may help you feel better.

- Avoid drugs and alcohol. Most deaths by suicide result from sudden, uncontrolled impulses. Since drugs and alcohol contribute to such impulses, it is essential to avoid them. Drugs and alcohol also interfere with the effectiveness of medications prescribed for depression.

- Learn to recognize the earliest warning signs of a suicidal episode. There are often subtle warning signs your body will give you when an episode is developing. As you learn to manage your illness, you will learn how to be sensitive to them. This is a signal to treat yourself with the utmost care, as opposed to becoming angry or disgusted with yourself.

- Talk about suicide. Your ability to explore the feelings, thoughts, and reactions associated with depression can provide valuable perspective and reassurance to your friend or loved one who may be depressed. Talking about suicide does not plant the idea in someone's head. Not everyone who thinks of suicide attempts it. For many, it's a passing thought that lessens over time. For a significant number of people, however, the hopelessness and exaggerated anxiety brought on by un-treated or under-treated depression may create suicidal thoughts that they cannot easily manage on their own. For this reason, take any men-tion of suicide seriously. If someone you know is very close to suicide, direct questions about how, when, and where he or she intends to com-mit suicide can provide valuable information that may help prevent the attempt. Do not promise confidentiality in these circumstances. It is important for you to share this information with the person's doctor.

Recognizing Warning Signs In Others

Sometimes even health care professionals have difficulty determining how close a person may be to attempting suicide. As a friend or family member, you can't know for certain either. If you sense there is a problem, ask the person direct questions and point out behavior patterns that concern you. Remind the person that you care about them and are concerned. Talking about suicide with someone will not plant the idea in his or her head. If necessary, suggest that they make appointment to see their doctor and offer to go with them if you sense they would have difficulty doing it on their own. If you believe that immediate self-harm is possible, take the person to a doctor or hospital emergency room immediately.

- **Feelings of despair and hopelessness.** Often times, people with depres-sion talk about extreme feelings of hopelessness, despair, and self-doubt

♣ It's A Fact!!

Responding To An Emergency Situation

If someone is threatening to commit suicide; if someone has let you know they are close to acting on a suicidal impulse, or if you strongly believe he or she is close to a suicidal act, these steps can help you manage the crisis.

- Take the person seriously. Stay calm, but don't under-react.

- Involve other people. Don't try to handle the crisis alone or jeopardize your own health or safety. Call 911, if necessary. Contact the person's doctor, the police, a crisis intervention team, or others who are trained to help.

- Express concern. Give concrete examples of what leads you to believe the person is close to suicide.

- Listen attentively. Maintain eye contact. Use body language such as moving close to the person or holding his or her hand, if appropriate.

- Ask direct questions. Find out if the person has a specific plan for suicide. Determine, if you can, what method of suicide is being considered.

- Acknowledge the person's feelings. Be understanding, not judgmental or argumentative. Do not relieve the person of responsibility for his or her actions.

- Offer reassurance. Stress that suicide is a permanent solution to a temporary problem, reminding the person that there is help and things will get better.

- Don't promise confidentiality. You may need to speak to the person's doctor in order to protect the person from him or herself.

- Make sure guns and old medications are not available.

- If possible, don't leave the person alone until you are sure they are in the hands of competent professionals. If you have to leave, make sure another friend or family member can stay with the person until they can receive help.

with those closest to them. The more extreme these feelings grow, and the more often they are described as unbearable, the more likely it is that the idea of suicide may enter the person's mind.

- **Taking care of business.** When a person is winding up his or her affairs and making preparations for the family's welfare after he or she is gone, it is a good chance they are considering self-harm or suicide.

- **Rehearsing suicide.** Rehearsing suicide, or seriously discussing specific suicide methods, are also indications of a commitment to follow through. Even if the person's suicidal intention seems to come and go, such preparation makes it that much easier for the individual to give way to a momentary impulse.

- **Drug or alcohol abuse.** A person with worsening depression may abuse drugs or alcohol. These substances can worsen symptoms of depression or mania, decrease the effectiveness of medication, enhance impulsive behavior, and severely cloud judgment.

- **Beginning to feel better.** It may sound strange, but a person with depression may be most likely to attempt suicide just when he or she seems to have passed an episode's low point and be on the way to recovery.

Experts believe there is an association between early recovery and increased likelihood of suicide. As depression begins to lift, a person's energy and planning capabilities may return before the suicidal thoughts disappear, enhancing the chances of an attempt. Studies show that the period six to twelve months after hospitalization is when patients are most likely to consider or reconsider suicide.

✔ **Quick Tip**

If you or someone you know has ongoing thoughts of death or suicide or if a suicide attempt has been made, contact a doctor, go to a hospital emergency room immediately, or call the National Hopeline Network at 800-784-2433.

What You Can Do to Help Someone

Among the many things you can do to help a depressed person who may be considering suicide, most involve simply talking and listening. Do not take on the role of therapist. Often times a person just wants someone to listen. Though this may be difficult, here are some approaches that have worked for others:

- **Express empathy and concern.** Severe depression is usually accompanied by a self-absorbed, uncommunicative, withdrawn state of mind. When you try to help, you may be met by an individual's reluctance to discuss what he or she is feeling. At such times, it is important to acknowledge the reality of the pain and hopelessness he or she is experiencing. Resist the urge to function as a therapist, which can ultimately create more feelings of rejection for the person, who doesn't want to be told what to do. Remain a supportive friend and encourage continued treatment.

- **Describe specific behaviors and events that trouble you.** If you can explain particular ways a person's behavior has changed, this may help to get communication started. Try to help him or her overcome feelings of guilt. Compounding the lack of interest in communication may be guilt or shame over having suicidal thoughts. If there has already been a suicide attempt, guilt over both the attempt and its failure can make the problem worse. It is important to reassure the individual that there is nothing shameful about what they are thinking and feeling. Keep stressing that thoughts of hopelessness, guilt, and even suicide are all symptoms of a treatable medical condition and reinforce the person's good work in keeping with their treatment plan.

- **Work with professionals.** Never promise confidentiality if you believe someone is very close to suicide. Keep the person's doctor or therapist informed of any thoughts of suicide. If possible it is best to encourage the person to discuss it with doctors themselves, but you should be ready to confirm that those discussions have taken place. This may involve making an appointment to visit the doctor together or calling the doctor on your own. Be aware that a doctor will not be able to discuss the person's condition with you. You should only call to inform the doctor of your concern.

Whenever possible you should get permission from the depressed person to call their doctor if you feel there is a problem. Otherwise it could be seen as butting in and may worsen their symptoms or cause added stress. Of course, if you believe there is a serious risk of immediate self-harm, call their doctor. You can work out any feelings of anger the person has towards you later.

- **Stress that the person's life is important to you and to others.** Many people find it awkward to put into words how another person's life is important for their own well-being. Emphasize in specific terms the ways in which the person's suicide would be devastating to you and others. Share personal stories or pictures of past events.

- **Be prepared for anger.** The person may express anger and feel betrayal by your attempt to prevent their suicide or get them into treatment. Be strong. Realize that these reactions are caused by the illness and should pass once the person has received the proper treatment.

- **Always be supportive.** A person who has thought about or attempted suicide will most likely have feelings of guilt and shame. Be supportive and assure the person that their actions were caused by an illness that can be treated. Offer your continued support to help them recover.

- **Take care of yourself.** It is not uncommon for friends and family members to experience stress or symptoms of depression when dealing with a suicidal person. You can only help the person through their own treatment with encouragement and support. You cannot get better for them. Do not focus all of your energy on the one person, ask friends and family to join you in providing support and keep to your normal routine as much as possible. Pay attention to your own feelings and seek help if you need it.

DBSA Support Groups Can Help

With a grassroots network of over 1000 chapters and support groups across the country, no one with depression has to feel alone. While DBSA groups do not offer suicide crisis programs, they do provide a caring environment for people to come together to discuss their challenges and successes in living with depression. They are not group therapy, though many groups have a professional advisor and all groups have appointed facilitators. DBSA groups provide a forum for mutual understanding and self-discovery, help people stay compliant with their treatment plans, and gain support from others who have been there. For information on a DBSA support group in your area, contact DBSA.

Depression and Bipolar Support Alliance (DBSA)
730 N. Franklin Street, Suite 501
Chicago, IL 60610-7224
Toll-Free: 800-826-3632
Phone: 312-642-0049
Fax: 312-642-7243
Website: www.dbsalliance.org

☞ Remember!!

If you suspect that someone is considering suicide, ask them questions about their plans, listen to them, and offer assistance in getting help. Remind the person that thoughts of suicide are symptoms of a treatable medical condition. Never promise to keep secrets when someone's life is in danger. Call 911 if necessary.

Chapter 23

Preventing Gun-Related Teen Suicide

Teen Suicide And Guns

Teenage suicide has truly become a problem of epidemic proportions in America that must be addressed from every angle. While it is certainly most important to address the psychological and emotional issues that lead teenagers to consider committing suicide, it is also crucial to address the access to the means available for suicide. As numerous studies have shown, guns are used in roughly two out of every three suicide attempts by teenagers, and handguns are used in 70% of these.[1] In 1998 alone, 1200 youth in America committed suicide with a gun—the equivalent of one every seven hours.[2]

Using a firearm in a suicide attempt drastically increases the likelihood that the attempt will be fatal. If you compare the lethality of various methods for committing suicide, it is clear that guns kill at a much higher rate than other methods available.[3]

Simply having a gun in the home actually increases the chances of suicide by a factor of 5 for all residents in that house, including teenagers, and the number of teenagers in America who readily have access to firearms is outrageous.[4] According to recent survey data, roughly 43% of all households with

✎ **Weird Words**

Access: Easily available.

Fatal: Causes death.

Impulsive: Acting suddenly without thinking.

children in them have guns[5] and almost 30% of these do not keep their guns locked in a secure location where they cannot be accessed by children and teenagers.[6] Since it often only takes 5–10 minutes from the time a teenager considers committing suicide until the time they actually attempt suicide, easy access to a gun is certainly going to increase the chances that despondent teens will actually kill themselves.

Moreover, if you compare the rate of gun suicide among teenagers in America to that of other industrialized countries throughout the world, it is clear that guns pose an enormous health risk to our youth. In a study published by the Centers for Disease Control and Prevention it was found that youth in America are twice as likely to commit suicide with a gun than youth in all of the 25 other countries studied combined.[7]

The combination of impulsive emotions and the easy access to—and overwhelming lethality of—handguns leads to the inevitable situation where more and more teenagers in America will kill themselves.

References

1. CDC National Center for Injury Prevention and Control Fact Sheet. "Suicide in the United States"; and, Wintemute, GJ, Teret, SP, et al. "The Choice of Weapons in Firearm Suicides." *American Journal of Public Health*. Vol. 78, No. 7. 1988. PP. 824-826.

2. Centers for Disease Control and Prevention. National Center for Health Statistics.

♣ **It's A Fact!!**

Teenage suicide attempts are usually impulsive acts, and the easier it is to carry out, the more often these attempts will be fatal. While only 20% of suicide attempts by teenagers by drug overdose are fatal, 90% of attempts with a gun are fatal.[3]

3. Myron Boor. "Methods of Suicide and Implications for Suicide Prevention." *Journal of Clinical Psychology*. Vol. 37. January 1981. PP. 70-75.

4. Kellerman, AL, Rivera, FP, et al. "Suicide in the Home in Relation to Gun Ownership." *New England Journal of Medicine*. Vol. 314, No. 24. 1986. PP. 1557-1560.

5. Lee, RK, Sacks, JJ. "Latchkey Children and Guns at Home." *Journal of the American Medical Association*. November 7, 1990. Volume 264, No. 17. P. 2210.

6. Peter Hart Research Associates. July 1999.

7. Centers for Disease Control and Prevention. "Rates of Homicide, Suicide and Firearm-Related Death Among Children–26 Industrialized Countries." *Morbidity Mortality Weekly Report*. February 7, 1997. Vol. 46, No. 5. PP. 101-105.

☞ **Remember!!**

If guns were not so readily available, the number of teenage suicides in America would decrease significantly.

Chapter 24

Coping With Stress

What Is Stress?

Stress is what you feel when you react to pressure, either from the outside world (school, work, after-school activities, family, friends) or from inside yourself (wanting to do well in school, wanting to fit in). Stress is a normal reaction for people of all ages. It's caused by your body's instinct to protect itself from emotional or physical pressure or, in extreme situations, from danger.

I've tried dealing with my stress, but I just feel like giving up.

This is a danger sign. Stress can become too much to deal with. It can lead to such awful feelings that you may think about hurting—or even killing—yourself. When you feel like giving up, it may seem like things will never get better. Talk to someone right away. Talking about your feelings is the first step in learning to deal with them and starting to feel better.

About This Chapter: Text in this chapter begins with information that is reproduced with permission from "Stress: Who Has Time For It?" July 2002, www.familydoctor.org/x1931.xml. Copyright © 2002 American Academy of Family Physicians. All Rights Reserved. Text under the heading "Identifying And Handling Stress" is from "Mind-Emotion Commotion: Stress," National Women's Health Information Center, updated February 2004.

Is stress always bad?

No. In fact, a little bit of stress is good. Most of us couldn't push ourselves to do well at things—sports, music, dance, work, school—without feeling the pressure of competition. Without the stress of deadlines, most of us also wouldn't be able to finish projects or get to work or school on time.

If stress is so normal, why do I feel so bad?

With all the things that happen at your age, it's easy to feel overwhelmed. Things that you can't control are often the most frustrating. Maybe your parents are fighting, or your social life is a mess. You can also feel bad when you put pressure on yourself—like pressure to get good grades or to get promoted at your part-time job. A common reaction to stress is to criticize yourself. You may even get so upset that things don't seem fun anymore and life looks pretty grim. When this happens, it's easy to think there's nothing you can do to change things. But you can!

How can I deal with stress?

Although you can't always control the things that are stressing you out, you can control how you react to them. The way you feel about things results from the way you think about things. If you change how you think, you can change the way you feel. Try some of these tips to cope with your stress:

- Make a list of the things that are causing your stress. Think about your friends, family, school and other activities. Accept that you can't control everything on your list.

- Take control of what you can. For example, if you're working too many hours and you don't have time to study enough, ask your boss if you can cut back.

- Give yourself a break. Remember that you can't make everyone in your life happy all the time. And it's okay to make mistakes now and then.

- Don't commit yourself to things you can't do or don't want to do. If you're already too busy, don't promise to decorate for the school dance. If you're tired and don't want to go out, tell your friends you'll go another night.

- Find someone to talk to. Talking to your friends or family can help because it gives you a chance to express your feelings. However, problems in your social life or family can be the hardest to talk about. If you feel like you can't talk to your family or a friend, talk to someone outside the situation. This could be your priest or minister, a school counselor, or your family doctor.

✔ Quick Tip
Signs You Are Stressed Out

- Feeling depressed, edgy, guilty, tired

- Having headaches, stomachaches, trouble sleeping

- Laughing or crying for no reason

- Blaming other people for bad things that happen to you

- Only seeing the down side of a situation

- Feeling like things that you used to enjoy aren't fun or are a burden

- Resenting other people or your responsibilities

Things That Help Fight Stress

- Eating well-balanced meals on a regular basis

- Drinking less caffeine

- Getting enough sleep

- Exercising on a regular basis

Things that don't help you deal with stress

There are safe and unsafe ways to deal with stress. It is dangerous to try to escape your problems by using drugs and alcohol. Both can be very tempting, and your friends may offer them to you. Drugs and alcohol may seem like easy answers, but they're not. Using drugs and alcohol to deal with stress just adds new problems, like addiction, or family and health problems.

Identifying And Handling Stress

Sources Of Stress For Teenagers

- School demands and frustrations

- Negative thoughts and feelings about yourself

- Changes in your body

- Problems with friends

- Unsafe living environment/ neighborhood

- Separation or divorce of parents
- Chronic illness or severe problems in the family
- Death of a loved one
- Moving or changing schools
- Taking on too many activities or having very high expectations for yourself
- Family financial problems

Stress is not always a bad thing. Stress can sharpen your senses, get you excited, and make you focus for the challenges ahead. Being bored is the opposite of stress, and while being bored can be a nice change of pace once in a while, it gets old pretty fast. You need the stimulation of interesting events in your life to keep you active and involved.

Acute stress, or short-term stress that occurs right before a test or a performance, is our body's natural fight-or-flight reaction to events that our body perceives as dangerous. Humans evolved this reaction from the days where we encountered threats such as large animals, and we needed to decide whether to run away or fight for our dinner. Almost everyone feels acute stress at one time or another and it goes away once the event is over.

However, chronic stress, or stress that doesn't let up after a short while, can make you nervous, tired, worried, and distracted. It can even make you sick. Major life events such as divorce or a death in the family, or long periods of time without down-time or rest, can lead to chronic stress.

♣ It's A Fact!!

Stress can make you stupid. Research has shown that parts of the brain may actually shrink as a result of exposure to stressful conditions!

Some Symptoms Of Chronic Stress

- Upset stomach, diarrhea, or indigestion

- Headache, backache

- Insomnia (inability to fall asleep)

- Eating too much or too little

- Feeling hostile, angry, or irritable

- Feeling anxious

- Avoiding other people

- Crying

- Feeling frustrated with things that normally only bother you a little

If you have two or more symptoms on this list, you may have chronic stress.

Fortunately, there are steps you can take to deal with both acute and chronic stress. Before we get to that, however, you need to understand the path of stress and the places where you can take steps to manage stress in your life.

The Stress Model

Stress begins with a life situation that knocks you out of balance. It could be positive, negative, gentle, or strong, but if it happens you need to adapt. The first step in the stress process is your perception of the event. For example, if you fail a test, you could perceive it to be very serious (if it's critical to your grade), or not so seriously (if you've done well on the 5 other tests given in the class). When there is a death in the family, it may be perceived as a devastating loss or as the end of a long, happy, and productive life. Everyone has their own way of looking at stressful situations.

The next step in the stress process is your emotional reaction to the event. Fear, anger, insecurity, or feelings of being overwhelmed, frustrated, or helpless are possible emotional reactions to an event.

Next is the physiological reaction to stress. Stress can cause your respiratory rate, heart rate, and blood pressure to increase, and can cause stomach aches, decreases in your immune system, and problems digesting food.

The final step in the stress process is the consequences. Chronic stress can result in real illnesses and other problems, such as poor performance in school, strained family relationships, fights with friends, etc.

Setting Up Detours

You can set up detours anywhere along the path of stress. Any interruption in the process will short-circuit the consequences. For example, even though a life situation presents itself to you, a detour between that situation and the next stress phase can be set up.

✔ Quick Tip

Controlling Your Anger

Very often, being angry is a natural reaction to a situation. However, handling that anger in a socially appropriate manner is something to be learned and practiced. If you grew up in a family that responds to anger by shouting and yelling, you will probably get angry easily and respond naturally in this way. If you grew up in a family that responds to anger by always talking things through, being polite, and never blowing up, you may still become angry at times, but will learn to handle it by hiding it. There are benefits and drawbacks to both styles.

Expressing your anger can help you to feel relief and avoid further stress, but it may hurt others and put that stress onto them. Worse, it may not help to change the situation which made you angry in the first place. Holding your feelings in and not expressing anger can cause you to feel the effects of stress in other physical and emotional ways if you don't somehow get relief. When you feel yourself getting angry, a first step is to consider the source of the anger. Are your feelings justified, or are they selfish? Will expressing your anger help or hurt the situation? Can you solve the problem in a way that doesn't hurt others physically or emotionally? When you feel yourself getting angry take the following steps.

continued

Detour 1: You can avoid situations that could lead to stress. You don't want to become a hermit and withdraw from life simply because it might be stressful. However, if you know that joining yet another sports team will only add to your already hectic schedule, you might choose to wait and join the team next year if you have more time.

Detour 2: You could simply insist that you will not allow yourself to view this situation as disturbing or threatening in the whole scheme of your life. Keeping things in perspective is an important part of relieving stress in your life because it forces you to recognize that not everything is under your control and that not everything is as important as you may have believed it to be. However, one thing that is under your control is your reaction to what happens to you. You can choose to be stressed by a situation, or choose to view it differently.

continued from previous page

1. Take a deep breath, hold it a minute, then slowly let it out.

2. Take a moment where you don't say anything, but just think about the situation.

3. Ask yourself why you are upset: Are you not getting your way? Does someone not understand you? Has someone else done something to you?

4. Before you react, consider what you will gain by your reaction. Your number one goal should be to get the best results from the situation.

5. Now respond. This might mean walking away rather than making things worse. It might mean talking things over. It might mean expressing your anger in a firm but calm way. It might mean explaining to someone else how they upset you. It might mean letting your anger go because you realize it is unproductive.

If you follow these steps and practice them whenever you can, you will find that, while you might still get angry, you may also get better results and feel less stress.

Source: This information is reprinted with permission from www.Teen Growth.com. © 2004. All rights reserved.

Detour 3: You can focus on the positive aspect of the situation (there's something positive about every situation, even if it is that things can't get any worse). Try to think about the benefits and opportunities created by the situation, rather than the problems. Most people find that even unpleasant events lead to positive growth in some way. If you focus on the potential for positive growth, you can reduce the negative emotional reactions that bring you down.

Detour 4: The same mechanism that turns on the stress response can turn it off. As soon as we decide that a situation is no longer dangerous, changes can occur in our minds and bodies to help us relax and calm down. This relaxation response includes decreased heart and breathing rate and a sense of well being. Teens that develop a relaxation response and other stress management skills feel less helpless and have more choices when responding to stress. Relaxation techniques are excellent ways to keep emotional reactions from turning into physiological ones.

Detour 5: Exercise is an excellent way to relieve the physical tension brought on by stress. Physical activity makes good use of the fight-or-flight arousal in your body and can prevent illnesses and other physical consequences of stress. If you are chronically stressed or if you are getting ill from stress, you might want to talk to your doctor or school counselor about additional ways to make your life more manageable.

☞ **Remember!!**

Extreme stress can cause teens to make impulsive, dangerous decisions. Don't let that happen to you. Learn to identify stress and handle it. Remember that help is available. If the stress you are experiencing seems overwhelming, tell someone about it or call the Nationwide Crisis Hot Line at 800-333-4444.

❖ It's A Fact!!

Negative Roadblocks To Stress

Some people may choose to block their path to stress through alcohol or illegal drugs. This technique may work temporarily, but when the drugs wear off the stress will still be there. There could also be serious consequences for illegal behavior that would be far worse than the consequences of the stress itself, like addiction. Using drugs and alcohol could seriously complicate your life way beyond the stress you have now.

Stress And Illness

Fear, which is a form of stress, affects the body in many different ways. Your pupils will widen to let in more light. You will become more alert. Your adrenal glands will begin to pump more adrenaline and other hormones into your bloodstream. Your heart races, your blood pressure rises, your muscles tense. Your liver starts converting starches to sugars for energy. Digestion slows. Sweat production increases and the hair on your body may feel prickly and actually stand on end. All these physical reactions were designed to save your life. Your body is getting ready to defend itself. But these reactions are no longer useful in modern life and can actually be harmful if you keep yourself in such an alert state for too many hours each day. Too much stress also affects your immune system, weakening it and making you more susceptible to colds, coughs, and infections.

Too Much Or Too Little Stress: Depression

It's perfectly normal to feel down or to have the blues for a while. Everyone does at some point, especially during stressful times or times of boredom. The best ways to cope with these feelings are to get out there and make new friends, participate in sports or your favorite hobbies, and talk to trusted friends and adults about your concerns. Most of the time, your feelings will pass in a couple of days or weeks and you'll be your old self again.

However, sometimes it can all seem to be just too much, for too long. You may be clinically depressed if you've been feeling down for several weeks or more, including any of the following:

- Feeling hopeless
- Feeling worthless
- Losing interest in your favorite activities
- Feeling bored all the time
- Having trouble eating or sleeping

for several weeks or more
- Hating school
- Feeling unloved
- Drinking or using drugs
- Having thoughts of death or suicide

If you've been feeling this way for a long time, it probably won't go away on it's own, so it is very important to talk to a trusted adult about your feelings. There is help available that works.

Chapter 25

The Link Between Abuse And Suicide

Amy's finger was so swollen that she couldn't get her ring off. She didn't think her finger was broken because she could still bend it. It had been a week since her dad had grabbed her hand and then shoved her into the wall, but her finger still hurt a lot. She was so embarrassed that she didn't tell anyone. Amy hated the way her dad called her lots of names—and accused her of all sorts of things she didn't do—especially after he had been drinking. It made her feel awful. She wished he would stop, but didn't feel very hopeful that anything would change.

What Is Abuse?

Abuse in families can take many forms. It may be physical, sexual, emotional, verbal, or a combination of any or all of those. Neglect—when parents don't take care of the basic needs of the children who depend on them—can be a form of abuse.

Family violence can affect anyone, regardless of religion, color, or social standing. It happens in both wealthy and poor families and in single-parent

About This Chapter: This information was provided by TeensHealth, one of the largest resources online for medically reviewed health information written for parents, kids, and teens. For more articles like this one, visit www.TeensHealth.org or www.KidsHealth.org. © 2004 The Nemours Center for Children's Health Media, a division of The Nemours Foundation.

or two-parent households. Sometimes parents abuse each other, which can be hard for a child to witness. Some parents abuse their children by using physical or verbal cruelty as a way of discipline. Both girls and guys can experience abusive physical punishment by a parent—but male children are beaten more often than female children.

- **Physical abuse** is often the most obvious form of abuse. It may be any kind of hitting, shaking, burning, pinching, biting, choking, throwing, whipping, paddling, beating, and other actions that cause physical injury, leave marks, or produce significant physical pain.

- **Sexual abuse** is any type of sexual contact between an adult and child or between a significantly older child and a younger child. If a person is abused by a member of his or her immediate family, this is called incest.

- **Emotional abuse** can be difficult to pin down because there are no physical signs to look for. Sure, people yell at each other, express anger, and call each other names sometimes, and expressing anger can sometimes be healthy. But emotional abuse generally occurs when the yelling and anger go too far or when a parent constantly belittles, threatens, or dismisses a child until the child's self-esteem and feelings of self-worth are damaged. And just like physical abuse can cause physical scars, emotional abuse can bring about emotional damage.

- **Neglect** is probably the hardest type of abuse to define. Neglect occurs when a child doesn't have adequate food, housing, clothes, medical care, or supervision. Emotional neglect happens when a parent doesn't provide enough emotional support or deliberately and consistently pays very little or no attention to a child. But it's not neglect if a parent doesn't give a kid something he or she wants, like a new computer or a cell phone.

✎ **Weird Word**

Adverse Childhood Experiences: Various abusive experiences including emotional, physical, and sexual abuse, parental alcohol and drug abuse problems, or mental health issues.

Abuse doesn't just happen in families, of course. Bullying is a form of abusive behavior that may happen in a peer group—among people of any age. Bullying someone by intimidation, threats, or humiliation can be just as abusive as beating someone up. People who bully others have often been abused themselves. This is also true of people who abuse someone they're dating. But being abused is still no excuse for abusing someone else.

Abuse can also take the form of hate crimes directed at people just because of their race, religion, abilities, gender, or sexual orientation.

Recognizing Abuse

It may sound strange, but people sometimes have trouble recognizing that they are being abused. For example, Amy has been abused, but she doesn't think of it that way. Recognizing abuse may be especially difficult for someone who has lived with it for many years. A person might think that it's just the way things are and that there's nothing that can be done about it. People who are abused might mistakenly think they bring it on themselves by misbehaving or by not living up to someone's expectations.

Someone growing up in a violent or abusive family may not know that there are other ways for family members to treat each other. A person who has only known an abusive relationship may mistakenly think that hitting, beating, pushing, shoving, or angry name-calling are perfectly normal ways to treat someone when you're mad. Seeing parents treat each other in abusive ways may lead a child to think that's a normal relationship. It's important for people who grow up with abuse to know that it is not a normal, or healthy, or acceptable way to treat people.

Why Does It Happen?

There is no one reason why people abuse others, although there are some factors that seem to make it more likely that a person may become abusive. Growing up in an abusive family, for example, can teach someone that abuse is a way of life. Fortunately, though, many people who grow up in abusive families realize that abuse is not acceptable and are able to break patterns of abuse.

♣ It's A Fact!!

Abuse Is A Risk Factor For Suicide

Many research studies have found solid connections between abuse and suicide. Important results include:

- Depressed adults who reported a history of either physical or sexual abuse in childhood were more likely to have made a previous suicide attempt than those who did not report a history of abuse according to a report in the *American Journal of Psychiatry* 2001; 158:1871-1877.

- Adverse childhood experiences are related to attempted suicide in adolescence. In 1998, the Adverse Childhood Experiences Study led by Dr. Vincent Felitti found that there is up to a 5,100 percent increase in the likelihood of a child attempting suicide as an adolescent if they have experienced multiple adverse childhood experiences.

- A study at Duke University Medical Center indicates that sexual assault increases women's lifelong possibility of attempting suicide, especially if the abuse occurred before age 16.

- A history of childhood physical abuse increases the suicide risk among depressed women according to a report in the *American Journal of Psychiatry* 2003;160:933-938.

- Cincinnati Children's Hospital reports that child abuse victims have a suicide rate six to 12 times higher than the general population.

- The Heritage Foundation reports that children who saw their mother abused are six times more likely to commit suicide.

—JBS

Some people become abusive because they are not able to manage their feelings properly. For example, people who are unable to control their anger or people who can't cope with stressful personal situations (like the loss of a job or marital problems) may lash out at others inappropriately. Certain types of personality disorders or mental illness can also interfere with a person's ability to relate to others in healthy ways or cause people to have problems with aggression or self-control. Of course, not everyone with a personality disorder or mental illness becomes abusive.

Substance abuse, such as alcoholism or drug use, can also play a role in abuse by making it difficult for the abuser to control his or her actions.

Of course, just because someone may have a problem, it doesn't automatically mean that person will become abusive. If you're one of the thousands of people living in an abusive situation, though, it can help to understand why some people abuse—and to realize that violence is all about the person doing it, not the fault of the person being abused.

Even if someone close to you has behavioral or other problems that cause him or her to abuse others, these don't make the abuse acceptable, normal, or excusable. Abuse can always be corrected, and everyone can learn how to stop.

What Are The Effects Of Abuse?

If someone is abused, it can affect every aspect of that person's life, especially self-esteem. How much abuse damages a person depends on the circumstances surrounding the abuse, how often and how long the abuse occurs, the age of the person who was abused, and lots of other factors.

Of course, every family has arguments. In fact, it's rare when a family doesn't have some rough times, disagreements, and anger. Punishments and discipline—like removing privileges, grounding, or being sent to your room— are normal in most families. It becomes a problem, though, when the punishment is physically or emotionally damaging. That's called abuse.

Abused teens often have trouble sleeping, eating, and concentrating. They may perform poorly at school because they are angry or frightened or because they don't care or can't concentrate.

Many people who are abused distrust others. They may feel a lot of anger toward other people and themselves, and it can be hard to make friends. Some abused teens become depressed. Some may engage in self-destructive behavior, such as cutting or abusing drugs or alcohol. They may even attempt suicide.

It's normal for people who have been abused by the people they love to not only feel upset but also confused about what happened to them. They may feel guilty and embarrassed and blame themselves, especially if the abuse is sexual. But abuse is never the fault of the person who is being abused, no matter how much the abuser tries to blame it on them.

Abusers often try to manipulate the people they're abusing into either thinking the abuse is their fault or to keep the abuse quiet. An abuser might say things like: "This is a secret between you and me," or "If you ever tell anybody, I'll hurt you or your mom," or "You're going to get in trouble if you tell. No one will believe you and you'll go to jail for lying." This is the abuser's way of making a person feel like nothing can be done so that he or she won't take any action to stop or report the abuse.

People who are abused may have trouble getting help because it means they'd be reporting on someone they love—someone who may be wonderful much of the time and awful to them only some of the time. So abuse often goes unreported.

What Should Someone Who's Being Abused Do?

People who are being abused need to get help. Keeping the abuse a secret doesn't protect a person from being abused—it only makes it more likely that the abuse will continue.

If you or anyone you know is being abused, talk to someone you or your friend can trust—a family member, a friend, a trusted teacher, a doctor, or an adult who works with youth at school or in a place of worship. Many teachers and counselors, for instance, have training in how to recognize and report abuse.

Telephone directories list local child abuse and family violence hot line numbers that you can call for help. There's also Childhelp USA at (800) 4-A-CHILD (800-422-4453).

☞ Remember!!
No one deserves to be abused. Telling someone is the first step in stopping abuse.

Sometimes people who are being abused by someone in their own home need to find a safe place to live temporarily. It is never easy to have to leave home, but it's sometimes necessary to be protected from further abuse. People who need to leave home to stay safe can find local shelters listed in the phone book or they can contact an abuse helpline. Sometimes a person can stay with a relative or friend.

People who are experiencing abuse often feel weird or alone. But they're not. No one deserves to be abused. Getting help and support is an important first step to change the situation. Many teens who have experienced abuse find that painful emotions may linger even after the abuse stops. Working with a therapist is one way for a person to sort through the complicated feelings and reactions that being abused creates, and the process can help to rebuild feelings of safety, confidence, and self-esteem.

Chapter 26

Knowledge Of Suicide: Does It Prevent Or Provoke Other Suicides?

It's happened before. A celebrity overdoses, and fans nationwide make suicide attempts of their own. At least that's the current thinking, but a new study from the Centers for Disease Control and Prevention (CDC) says we could be wrong—that knowledge of, or exposure to, a suicide really protects against copycat attempts.

"Contrary to our expectations, we found that exposure [to suicide] may have beneficial consequences under certain circumstances," says author James Mercy, MD, of the division of violence prevention at the National Center for Injury Prevention and Control.

In a study published in the July 15, 2001 *American Journal of Epidemiology*, Mercy and colleagues compared exposure to suicide among 153 suicide attempters, aged 13–34, in Harris County, Texas, and 513 people randomly selected from the same community. Exposure to suicide included suicides by friends, family, and media icons.

They found that exposure actually appears to protect people from committing suicide—providing the exposure was not recent or emotionally close,

Mercy says. If people are far enough removed from the suicide—both emotionally, and in terms of time—Mercy suggests they gain an objective perspective on the death that allows them to think about the full consequences of suicide.

"The most likely interpretation is that the [suicide] will be seen as inappropriate or incomprehensible, the less close one is to the person [with] the suicidal behavior," he says.

Conversely, being emotionally close to the suicide victim—in combination with glorification of the suicide—could prompt some at-risk individuals to imitate the behavior. For that reason, Mercy says the findings may not so much contradict previous studies as provide a more rounded picture of the relationship between suicide and exposure.

♣ It's A Fact!!
Suicide Contagion Is Real

Between 1984 and 1987, journalists in Vienna covered the deaths of individuals who jumped in front of trains in the subway system. The coverage was extensive and dramatic. In 1987, a campaign alerted reporters to the possible negative effects of such reporting, and suggested alternate strategies for coverage. In the first six months after the campaign began, subway suicides and non-fatal attempts dropped by more than eighty percent. The total number of suicides in Vienna declined as well.

Research finds an increase in suicide by readers or viewers when:

• The number of stories about individual suicides increases.

• A particular death is reported at length or in many stories.

• The story of an individual death by suicide is placed on the front page or at the beginning of a broadcast.

• The headlines about specific suicide deaths are dramatic.

Source: "Reporting On Suicide: Recommendations for the Media," National Institute of Mental Health (NIMH), September 4, 2001.

According to the study, people who were exposed to the suicide of a parent were more likely to attempt to kill themselves. But even in those situations, the association disappeared when researchers took into account prominent risk factors for suicide. These risk factors include depression, alcoholism, and having recently moved from one geographic location to another.

☞ **Remember!!**

Being emotionally close to a suicide victim—in combination with glorification of the suicide—could prompt some at-risk individuals to imitate the behavior.

Suicide attempters in the study had tried what researchers call "nearly lethal" suicides—attempts that are deemed as serious efforts to kill oneself. Mercy says the study did not look at suicide attempts that were more cries for help than serious attempts at killing oneself.

According to the CDC, the number of completed suicides reflects only a small portion of the impact of suicidal behavior. In 1994, an estimated 10.5 million adults (about 6% of the adult population in the U.S.) reported having seriously considered suicide during the previous year, according to the agency. Over 30,000 people die by suicide, and it is the third-leading cause of death among people aged 15–24.

Mercy suggests that people who witness or are exposed to suicide need to reflect on all of the terrible consequences—for family, friends, and others—of the act. "People tend to talk about the positive aspects of the person who committed suicide," Mercy tells WebMD. "A vulnerable person hearing that may choose to imitate the behavior, whereas if they fully understand the negative consequences they are less likely to."

Psychiatrist Alvin Poussaint, MD, says the study results are surprising and indicate a need for more research. Poussaint, professor of psychiatry at Harvard Medical School in Boston, says he wonders if there could be crucial differences between "near-lethal" suicides that were averted by emergency medical care and successful suicides that never made it to the ER. "It's a good study, but you can't say from this that there is no relationship between successful suicides and previous exposure," he says.

Chapter 27

Students Can Educate Their Peers About Suicide

Because of the internal nature of depression and loneliness, thousands of youth who appear to be happy are screaming silently in the deepest emotional pain, but what can we do? We can help by learning about and using a suicide prevention program in our school or community. This chapter highlights three suicide prevention programs which support the National Strategy for Suicide Prevention: Yellow Ribbon Suicide Prevention Program®; Natural Helpers®; and SOS, Signs Of Suicide® High School Suicide Prevention Program.

When teens get involved in suicide prevention they are learning a vital life skill, help seeking behavior, and how to be a link. Lives are being saved!

Yellow Ribbon Suicide Prevention Program®

Yellow Ribbon is

• Awareness

• Education

• Prevention

About This Chapter: Text in this chapter is reprinted with permission from the Yellow Ribbon Suicide Prevention Program, http://www.yellowribbon.org. © 2004 Yellow Ribbon Suicide Prevention Program. All rights reserved.

- Intervention
- Post-intervention
- Collaboration
- Community building
- Replication and sustainability
- Helping save lives
- Helping survivors survive and heal

Chapters, schools, and organizations throughout the United States and 47 countries use this program. The *Be-A-Link®* Gatekeeper Trainings and *It's OK to Ask for Help!®* presentations are available to youth and adults. Curriculums are designed for lay people, professionals, EMS/fire and law enforcement.

> **✔ Quick Tip**
> **National Strategy For Suicide Prevention**
>
> The National Strategy for Suicide Prevention (NSSP) represents the combined work of advocates, clinicians, researchers and survivors around the nation. It lays out a framework for action to prevent suicide and guides development of an array of services and programs that must be developed. It is designed to be a catalyst for social change with the power to transform attitudes, policies, and services. The *NSSP Goals and Objectives for Action* was published by the U.S. Department of Health and Human Services in May of 2001, with leadership from the Surgeon General.
>
> Source: National Strategy for Suicide Prevention, available at http://www.mentalhealth.org/suicideprevention/strategy.asp

FAQs About The Yellow Ribbon Suicide Prevention Program

I want to do something at my school. What can I do?

- Talk, Talk, Talk. The old myth that talking about suicide is risky is totally false. Talking is the first step in trying to prevent it. It is the act which may break through the isolation that a suicidal person feels. One out of every five youths is already thinking about suicide, and one out of ten will make an attempt. (source: San Diego City Schools, additional source: Washington State Department of Health.)

- Introduce the program to your friends by giving them yellow ribbon cards.

- Talk to health teachers about using the program in health curriculum when discussing suicide.

- Talk to your school counselors/peer listeners about distributing the cards in the counseling office.

- Wear a yellow ribbon pin to prompt questions and show you are someone who cares.

- Working with school administrators, have an assembly for the school. To do this, it may help to follow these steps:

  - Show the "No More Tomorrows" 8-minute video to give people a quick overview of the scope of the problem of teen suicide and the Yellow Ribbon program.

  - Introduce all counselors, teachers, coaches, janitors, etc. (every adult at the school) to the program in case a student gives them a card.

  - Have a plan of action, i.e. where to call for help in your community when there is a crisis and make sure everyone knows what to do.

  - Hold an assembly for students with a showing of the video, distribution of Yellow Ribbon Cards and brochures, and a speaker who can talk from the heart about suicide (someone who lost someone or someone who made an attempt).

  - Promote the program with yellow ribbons around campus, an article in the school newspaper, etc.

  - Hold a parent night or community forum immediately after the school presentation and invite parents to hear the same information you gave the students. This is very important. Many parents are unaware that there is a suicide problem at all, let alone a possible problem with their own child. This "not my kid" syndrome is common and is a battle to overcome. At the very least send home a letter to all parents informing them that information was given to their teen about a suicide prevention program and encourage them to discuss it.

- Don't forget to follow up with plenty of cards always available around the school (counseling office, administrative office, gym, etc.).

- Make a presentation again next year to the incoming/freshman class.

I have started a Yellow Ribbon chapter in my community. How can I get the word out?

- Make presentations at schools, churches, community groups, school board meetings, or PTA meetings (show the video "No More Tomorrows" for a quick yet powerful introduction).

- Hold events such as Yellow Ribbon Week and ask your mayor to declare it Yellow Ribbon Week.

- Hold a fundraising or awareness event. Team up with survivor groups (i.e. Survivors of Suicide).

- Inform the media with press releases about your group and events. Create a press kit.

- Find a mental health professional who is an advocate of the Yellow Ribbon program and use him/her as a media spokesperson when an expert is needed to comment.

- Do research in your town to find the annual number of suicides and the budget for suicide prevention programs.

What are Yellow Ribbon Cards and how can I get them?

The Yellow Ribbon Program is based on the premise that suicide is not about death, but rather about ending pain and that it's okay to ask for help. Yellow Ribbon cards are distributed and carried as a simple, effective tool to use to ask for help when feelings of suicide arise. The card has proven to be a lifeline because it is a reminder to young people that they have permission to ask for help, it helps them talk when they may not have the words, and it tells the recipient of the card how to help the suicidal person. To get cards, contact information for Yellow Ribbon is listed at the end of this chapter.

Yellow Ribbon Presentation, Workshop, Inservice, And Training Information

Most teens and their parents do not know that suicidal ideation and thoughts are symptoms of depression. Yellow Ribbon's Be-A-Link™ protocol and education training programs can mean the difference between life and death. Yellow Ribbon offers a comprehensive suicide prevention program for schools and communities. Yellow Ribbon is based on best practices research in suicide prevention. Studies show, and experts agree, that effective suicide prevention must:

- Promote and raise awareness of suicide prevention in a community.

- Provide outreach to those at risk of suicide.

✔ Quick Tip
SOS, Signs Of Suicide®: Suicide Prevention Program

The message of the SOS Program is straightforward: it helps teens to understand the connection between suicide and undiagnosed, untreated mental illness—usually depression—and empowers them to ACT. The acronym—ACT stands for Acknowledge, Care, and Tell—reinforces the program's message of empowerment for teens, it reminds them to:

- **Acknowledge** that their friend has a problem, and that the symptoms are serious.

- **Care**, let that friend know that they are there for them, and want to help.

- **Tell** a trusted adult about their concerns. This simple combination of education and a three-step response can save a teen's life.

Source: SOS Signs of Suicide® is a registered trademark of Screening for Mental Health, Inc. Reprinted with permission from Screening for Mental Health, Inc., http://www.mentalhealthscreening.org. © 2004. All rights reserved. Schools and other organizations that would like to conduct the SOS Suicide Prevention Program can get registration materials and other information by contacting Screen for Mental Health, Inc. at: 781-239-0071, ext. 112 or info@mentalhealthscreening.org.

- Educate people to be gatekeepers including school staff (certified and classified), parents, peers, elders, and the community, so they can recognize suicidal behaviors in youth and adults.

- Respond effectively and knowledgeably in a suicidal crisis.

- Offer support to friends and family of suicide victims. As Yellow Ribbon is a survivor founded and led program, the emphasis is on supporting survivors and working with the new high-risk people in a community following both suicide attempts and completions. YR works with victim advocate groups and survivor support groups throughout the country to assist bringing a greater focus on effective survivor crisis response and support.

♣ It's A Fact!!
Resources Available From Yellow Ribbon

Videos

- "It's OK to Ask 4 Help:" VHS format, 8 minutes in length, to the point and emotionally compelling

- Dale and Dar Emme, full length presentation taped at an actual school: VHS format, 30 minutes, the story of Mike Emme's suicide and the start of the Yellow Ribbon program

- YR School Presentation (40 min)

- Yellow Ribbon Elementary School (This goes with the Elementary school curriculum packet)

- Suicide Prevention Training I with Dr. John McIntosh (20 min)

- Suicide Prevention Training II with Dr. John McIntosh (55 min)

Other Materials

- Yellow Ribbon lapel pins

- Yellow Ribbon Program Manual on Community Development and Suicide Prevention Training

- Yellow Ribbon cards

How Does Yellow Ribbon Suicide Prevention Program® Work?

Community Initiative Development Toolkit

- Teaches 7-Step Yellow Ribbon Community Development Model which facilitates collaboration between the school and community caregivers and stake holders.

- Trains every member of school staff and personnel (certified and classified staff) as well as school board and school administration. No one can predict who a troubled teen (or adult) will turn to for help.

- Educates parents, grandparents, guardians, and other trusted adults to take all talk of suicide seriously and to know how to respond effectively to their child's depression and suicidal ideation.

- Trains the student body within each school (public and private) to understand the causes of suicidal despair, recognize warning signs and risk factors, and how to intervene appropriately with an at-risk friend. Teens are burdened with suicide, some of them daily, with suicidal friends, family, and co-workers. Youth are accustomed to learning life skills and embrace this effective, simple training to know why, how, and when to help a person in crisis.

- Introduces the effective tool that is used by teens and adults alike; the YR *Ask for Help Card*.

- Includes the survivor's perspective which is a powerful tool and one of the most requested parts of the YR trainings.

- Assists educators and administrators to review, update, and develop written policies and procedures for responding to suicidal warning signs, threats, attempts, and completions.

- Assists educators and administrators with developing written policy and procedures for supporting school staff after a suicide completion.

- Assists community to understand and reduce the threat of contagion; cluster (or copycat) suicides.

Natural Helpers

Natural Helpers is an innovative, research-based peer-helping program for students in grades 6–12.

Building Your School's Helping Network

When students have problems, they often look to other students for help before approaching an adult. This helping network of trusted peers can be an invaluable asset in ensuring the emotional and physical health of students at your school. C.H.E.F.'s ® Natural Helpers is designed to build your school's helping network by developing the skills of people who are already seen as natural helpers.

The Program

Natural Helpers is designed to teach participants:

- Effective ways to help their friends

- Positive ways of taking good care of themselves

- Ways to contribute to a safe and supportive school environment

Unique features of Natural Helpers:

- The selection process is designed to increase the likelihood that each of your school's social subgroups will be represented by a natural helper.

- The program is student-driven—it can be tailored to meet the strengths and interests of participants.

- Natural Helpers empowers students to defuse problems before they escalate.

How It Works—Implementation

The first step is to identify your school's natural helpers via an anonymous, school-wide survey. Based on the results of this survey, you will select representatives from each of the subgroups in the school community and invite them to participate in the program.

With C.H.E.F.'s guidance, your school then hosts a retreat for training, often in a camp setting. Students at the retreat develop their helping skills

continued

continued from previous page

and learn when it's appropriate to make referrals to professionals (the training emphasizes that natural helpers are not professionally trained therapists or counselors).

After the retreat, students receive ongoing training, either in a semester class or in a less structured format. Natural Helpers does not require class time.

The Students—Roles and Benefits

Students play a variety of roles as natural helpers:

- Helping friends cope with their problems.

- Recognizing when people have serious problems, such as depression, chemical dependency, or abuse, and referring them to trained professionals.

- Working with members of their helping team to discuss issues and specific problems.

- Providing accurate information to peers.

- Becoming more involved in their school and community.

Participants find that the skills they learn also apply to their relationships with friends, teachers, family, and co-workers. They make new friends and break down some of the barriers that exist in the school community. Natural helpers also experience the special feeling that comes from helping someone else and knowing they've made a difference.

Additional Information

Natural Helpers
Toll-Free: 800-323-9084
Website: http://www.unitedlearning.com/prevention
E-mail: info@unitedlearning.com

Source: Reprinted with permission. © 2004 United Learning. All rights reserved. Natural Helpers was developed by Comprehensive Health Education Foundation (C.H.E.F.). Additional information about Natural Helpers is available at http://www.unitedlearning.com or http://www.chef.org.

- Assists schools and communities with how to incorporate and address the ethnic culture for successful suicide prevention.

Yellow Ribbon presentations, workshops, and seminars include:

- The powerful, moving story of how youth began this program and how it has grown to become a worldwide life-saving organization.

- Address the myths and facts of suicide: Talking about suicide won't cause it to happen.

- What the Yellow Ribbon Suicide Prevention Program is and how is it used.

☞ Remember!!

You can help save lives. There are many excellent resources available to help you start a suicide prevention program in your school or community.

- How to react if someone says, "I'm suicidal"—What to say, to do, and whom to call.

- Teaches a vital life skill and what you can do to help save a life. Youth are accustomed to receiving, and using, life skills to help themselves and others. They are not afraid to learn about suicide prevention and many embrace this powerful program.

- Explains suicide and suicidal tendencies. Suicide is not about human failings, but it is about pain and in most cases caused by the treatable issue of depression.

- Reinforces that suicide in not an option! Teaches that suicide is not romantic—that Romeo and Juliet died from pain.

- Shares how to start the program and/or a Yellow Ribbon Chapter in your community, school, church, or organization.

- For youth assemblies, the simplicity of the program coupled with the teamwork of counselors, teachers, social workers, fire and law enforcement agencies, local mental health workers, and clergy in the community and schools contributes to the incredible effectiveness worldwide.

Yellow Ribbon Suicide Prevention Program® combines experience of survivors, youth, parents, professionals, school, and community emergency personnel with updated content, a user-friendly implementation process, and training materials co-designed by professional suicidologists, mental health professionals, and master level curriculum writers, youth, and survivors.

Additional Information

Yellow Ribbon International Suicide Prevention Program®

P.O. Box 644
Westminster, CO 80036-0644
Phone: 303-429-3530
Fax: 303-426-4496
Website: http://www.yellowribbon.org
E-mail: Ask4help@yellowribbon.org

Part Five

When Someone You Know
Dies From Suicide

Chapter 28

Surviving Suicide Loss

Someone you love has ended their own life—and yours is forever changed.

You are a "survivor of suicide," and as that unwelcome designation implies, your survival—your emotional survival—will depend on how well you learn to cope with your tragedy. The bad news: Surviving this will be the second worst experience of your life. The good news: The worst is already over. What you're enduring is one of the most horrific ordeals possible in human experience. In the weeks and months after a suicide, survivors ride a roller coaster of emotions unlike any other.

Suicide is different. On top of all the grief that people experience after a conventional death, you must walk a gauntlet of guilt, confusion, and emotional turmoil that is in many ways unique to survivors of suicide. "How long will it take to get over this?" you may ask yourself. The truth is that you will never get over it, but don't let that thought discourage you. After all, what kind of people would we be if we truly got over it, as if it were something as trivial as a virus? Your hope lies in getting through it, putting your loss in its proper perspective, and accepting your life as it now lies before you—forever changed. If you can do that, the peace you seek will follow.

About This Chapter: This information is excerpted from *Handbook for Survivors of Suicide*, © 2003 Jeffrey Jackson. Reprinted with permission from the American Association of Suicidology. The complete text of this handbook is available on the American Association of Suicidology website, http://www.suicidology.com.

Suicide Is Different

Death touches all of our lives sooner or later. Sometimes it is expected, as with the passing of an elderly relative; sometimes it comes suddenly in the form of a tragic accident.

But suicide is different. The person you have lost seems to have chosen death, and that simple fact makes a world of difference for those left to grieve. The suicide survivor faces all the same emotions as anyone who mourns a death, but they also face a somewhat unique set of painful feelings on top of their grief.

> ✔ **Quick Tip**
>
> ## Why We Say Suicide Survivor
>
> We apply the term *survivor* to our experience because it accurately reflects the difficulties that face people who have lost a loved one to suicide. Some people prefer the term *suicide griever*, fearing confusion with someone who has attempted suicide themselves. Likewise, some prefer the phrase *completed suicide* to *committed suicide*, feeling the latter implies a criminal act. But there are no rules you need obey. Do and say whatever makes you feel most comfortable.

- **Guilt.** Rarely in other deaths do we encounter any feelings of responsibility. Diseases, accidents, old age—we know instinctively that we cannot cause or control these things. But the suicide survivor—even if they were only on the periphery of the deceased's life—invariably feels that they might have, could have, or should have done something to prevent the suicide. This mistaken assumption is the suicide survivor's greatest enemy.

- **Stigma.** Society still attaches a stigma to suicide, and it is largely misunderstood. While mourners usually receive sympathy and compassion, the suicide survivor may encounter blame, judgment, or exclusion.

- **Anger.** It's not uncommon to feel some form of anger toward a lost loved one, but it's intensified for survivors of suicide. For us, the person we lost is also the murderer of the person we lost, bringing new meaning to the term love-hate relationship.

- **Disconnection.** When we lose a loved one to disease or an accident, it is easier to retain happy memories of them. We know that, if they could choose, they would still be here with us. But it's not as easy for the suicide survivor. Because our loved one seems to have made a choice that is abhorrent to us, we feel disconnected and divorced from their memory. We are in a state of conflict with them, and we are left to resolve that conflict alone.

The Emotional Roller Coaster

The challenge of coping with a loved one's suicide is one of the most trying ordeals anyone ever has to face, but make no mistake—you must confront it. If you attempt to ignore it—sweep it under the carpet of your life—you may only be delaying an even deeper pain. There are people who have suffered breakdowns decades after a suicide, because they refused or were forbidden to ever talk about it.

Time heals, but time alone cannot heal the suicide survivor. You must use that time to heal yourself and lean on the help and support of others. It might take years to truly restore your emotional well being, but you can be assured one thing: it will get easier.

However, some of the difficult emotions you should come to expect include:

- **You may backslide from time to time.** You might have a few days in a row where you feel better and then find your sadness returns suddenly—perhaps even years later. This is natural, so don't be discouraged. You will have ups and downs, but generally, coping with your loss will get easier over time.

- **You will encounter painful reminders unexpectedly.** A song on the radio, the scent of their favorite dish, a photograph—any of these could bring on sudden feelings of sadness or even the sensation that your are reliving the experience of the suicide. When it happens, stay calm. Get away from the reminder if you need to and focus on positive thoughts.

- **Friends and relatives may not offer the support you need.** You will truly learn who your friends are during this crisis. A casual acquaintance may turn out to be your most reliable supporter, while a lifelong friend might turn a deaf ear. Lean on the people who are ready, willing, and able to help you, and rather than suffer the anger try to forgive those who can't.

- **People may make insensitive remarks.** Suicide is generally misunderstood, and people will feel inept at offering you comfort. This is simply human nature, and while it would be wonderful if people rose above it, try not to be too hard on those who can't. If you encounter someone who seems determined to upset you with morbid curiosity, their own self-important theories, or some form of a guilt-trip, simply sidestep them by saying, "I'd rather not talk about it right now," and avoid conversing with them in the future.

- **Your fear of people's judgment may haunt you needlessly.** It's common to project our own feelings of guilt onto others by assuming that they are judging us harshly in their minds. Give people the benefit of the doubt and remind yourself that you are not a mind reader.

- **Others may tire of talking about it long before you do.** Talking through your feelings and fears is essential for recovery from your trauma. Unfortunately, while your closest supporters may be willing to listen and share with you for a few weeks or months, there's likely to come a time when their thoughts move on from the suicide while yours are still racing. This is why support groups are so valuable. Fellow survivors understand what you're feeling in a way that even your closest friends cannot. Your fellow group members will never grow weary of offering supportive words and sympathetic ears.

- **You may feel bad about feeling good.** You'll laugh at a joke, smile at a movie, or enjoy a breath of fresh, spring air, and then it will hit you: "How dare I feel good?" It's common to feel guilty when positive emotions start resurfacing, as if you're somehow trivializing your loss. Don't feel guilty for enjoying the simple human pleasures of daily life. You are entitled to them as much as anyone, if not more. There will be plenty of time for tears. Take whatever happiness life sends your way, no matter how small or brief.

- **Holidays, birthdays, and the anniversary of the suicide are often difficult.** Generally, the first year, with all its "firsts" will be the toughest, but these events may always be difficult times for you. Rest assured that the anticipation of these days is far worse than the day itself. It's only twenty-four hours, and it will pass as quickly as any other day.

- **New milestones may bring feelings of guilt.** As our lives naturally move forward, each new milestone—a wedding, a birth, an accomplishment—may be accompanied by new feelings of guilt and sadness. These events remind us that our lives are moving forward—

  ♣ **It's A Fact!!**
  The American Psychiatric Association ranks the trauma of losing a loved one to suicide as catastrophic—on par with that of a concentration camp experience.

  without our lost loved one. This may even taste of betrayal, as if we are leaving them behind. We must remind ourselves that we have chosen to live. Isn't it fair to say that if there is a divide between us, it is they—not we—who have placed it there?

- **You may entertain thoughts of suicide yourself.** The risk of committing suicide is far greater for those who come from a family in which suicide has been attempted. This may be due to the fact that our loved one's death has made the very idea of suicide far more real in our lives, making it very common for survivors to have suicidal thoughts themselves. However, you must balance your fear of this with the knowledge that suicide is most often preceded by a history of clinical depression. If you share this trait with your loved one, then you may have a reason to seek professional help. However, you now know better than anyone the pain and destruction that suicide causes in the lives of those we love. The very fact that you are reading a book like this one shows that your desire to heal and live far outweighs any desire you have to end your life.

✔ Quick Tip
Write Yourself A Script

Suicide survivors often find themselves faced with uncomfortable questions from outsiders. It will help if you can anticipate some of these and write yourself a script of answers that you can mentally keep at the ready.

For example, when someone probes for details of the suicide that you are not comfortable discussing with them, you might simply say, "I don't really want to talk about it right now," or "I'm sure we can find something happier to discuss."

When new acquaintances learn of your loss, they may ask, "How did they die?" You should have no reservations about saying plainly, "They took their own life," or a straightforward, "They committed suicide."

But if this is a casual acquaintance that you wish to deny this information, you would be equally justified in saying, "They suffered a long illness," which may very much be the truth.

The more you fear these kinds of inquiries, the better a prepared script of answers will serve you.

Battling Guilt

Guilt is the one negative emotion that seems to be universal to all survivors of suicide, and overcoming it is perhaps our greatest obstacle on the path to healing. Guilt is your worst enemy, because it is a false accusation.

You are not responsible for your loved one's suicide in any way, shape, or form. Write it down. Say it to yourself over and over again, (even when it feels false). Tattoo it onto your brain. Because it's the truth.

Why do suicide survivors tend to blame themselves? Psychiatrists theorize that human nature subconsciously resists so strongly the idea that we cannot control all the events of our lives that we would rather fault ourselves for a tragic occurrence than accept our inability to prevent it. Simply put, we don't like admitting to ourselves that we're only human, so we blame ourselves instead.

One of the most unusual aspects of survivor guilt is that it is usually a solo trip—each survivor tends to blame primarily themselves. Try asking another person who is also mourning your lost loved one about any guilt feelings that are haunting them. Chances are you will find that each person—no matter how close or removed they were from the suicide victim—willingly takes the lion's share of blame on themselves. If they were the one closest to the deceased then they theorize, "I should've known exactly what was going on in their mind." If they were distanced from that person, they feel, "If I'd only been closer to them." Well, you can't all be to blame, can you? Isn't it far more logical that none of you are responsible?

> ✔ **Quick Tip**
>
> **A Guilt-Busting Exercise**
>
> Make a list of all the things that you did to help and comfort your lost loved one. You'll probably find the list is longer than you realized.

Well, then who is? The simple truth of the matter is that only one person is responsible for any suicide: the victim. But that's a tough pill to swallow, so instead of ascribing responsibility to our suffering loved one, we nobly sacrifice by taking it on ourselves.

It's understandable to feel such love and empathy toward the person we lost that we are loathe to place blame on them. The key lies in understanding the difference between blame and responsibility. Blame is accusatory and judgmental, but assigning responsibility need only be a simple acknowledgment of fact.

It's unclear how much control, if any, suicide victims have over their actions. And if clinical depression is at the root, then we could easily think of suicides as victims of disease, just like cancer victims. This is why a person who dies by suicide doesn't deserve blame. However, on some level, there was a conscious choice made by that person, even if it was made with a clouded mind. So the responsibility does lie with them. Acknowledging this simple fact does not mean that you did not love them, nor does it mean that you are holding them in contempt. It means that you are looking at a tragic event clearly and accepting it for what it is.

Guilt is anger turned inward. Suicide produces many painful and confusing emotions in survivors, one of which is frustration at being so violently cut off from the victim—from the chance to help them, talk with them, or even simply to say goodbye. This frustration produces anger, and when we turn this anger upon ourselves the result is guilt.

Guilt can also come from an unfounded assumption that others are silently blaming us. Both parents and spouses express fear that the world at large will brand them as failures in their respective roles because of the suicide. While some small-minded people may think or even speak such accusations, most will not, so don't project negative thoughts onto others by judging yourself for them.

"If only I had…" A true tale of two mothers

There were two young women who died by suicide, both about the same age, both after a years-long battle with depression. Each had made several suicide attempts. They would refuse professional help and stop taking their medication just when it seemed to begin helping.

Fearing for her life, the first woman's mother had her committed—against her wishes—to a psychiatric clinic for treatment. While there, despite being on suicide watch, the young girl asphyxiated herself with her bed sheets.

The second woman's mother constantly urged her daughter to seek professional help. However, fearing that she would worsen her daughter's depression, she refused to force her into any kind of institutionalized care. One day, she killed herself with an overdose of medication.

Afterwards, both mothers blamed themselves for not preventing their daughter's suicides. The irony is that each blamed themselves for not doing exactly what the other one did.

The first mother felt that if she hadn't isolated her daughter in that institution, she wouldn't have lost her. The second was sure that if she only had committed her daughter, she would've been saved.

We often fail to realize that, even if we could turn back the clock and do things differently, it wouldn't necessarily change the outcome.

Mistaken Assumptions

The suicide survivor is prone to many self-defeating assumptions, all of which are likely to be mistaken.

"I know why they did it." The motivations behind suicide are complex and often inexplicable. False conclusions about your loved one's suicide may only add to your own pain.

"If I'd only done (X), they'd still be alive." Thinking that you (or anyone else) had could have prevented the suicide, is assuming that we all have far more power over the lives of others than we actually do. Furthermore, many suicide victims persist and succeed in ending their lives despite being rescued before.

"It's their wife's/parents'/doctor's fault." Blaming others is a form of denial. Only by facing the truth of your loss and the responsibility that lies with the victim can you recover from grief.

"I know what people think about me." While suicide survivors are still often stigmatized, our fear of it becomes self-fulfilling when we mistakenly project negative thoughts onto others.

"I will never be able to enjoy life again." Don't deny your mind's natural ability to heal. While your life may be forever changed, it need not be forever painful.

☞ **Remember!!**

Moving forward with your life brings its own dose of guilt. Whether it's returning to the simple routine of daily subsistence or embarking on new journeys in life, survivors often feel as if this is some affront to the person we've lost. "How can I live knowing they're not here?" your mind may taunt you. Your strength lies in knowing that, while your lost loved one has chosen death, you have chosen life—and life is a gift that we honor by living.

Chapter 29

Coping With Grief

If someone close to you has died, you may be feeling many different emotions. You may be sad, worried, or scared. You might be shocked, unprepared, or confused. You might be feeling angry, cheated, relieved, guilty, exhausted, or just plain empty. Your emotions might be stronger or deeper than usual or mixed together in ways you've never experienced before.

You might also notice that your loss is affecting what you're thinking about and how you behave. If you're grieving, you might be having trouble concentrating, sleeping, eating, or feeling interested in the things you usually enjoy. You might be trying to act like you feel okay (even if you don't) because you want to be strong for someone else. And you may wonder if you will ever get over losing someone who means so much to you.

All of these emotions can be natural reactions to the death of someone close. They're part of the process of grieving.

About This Chapter: Text in this chapter includes "Death and Grief," reviewed by D'Arcy Lyness, PhD. This information was provided by TeensHealth, one of the largest resources online for medically reviewed health information written for parents, kids, and teens. For more articles like this one, visit www.TeensHealth.org. or www.KidsHealth.org. © 2004 The Nemours Center for Children's Health Media, a division of The Nemours Foundation. "Helping Yourself Through Grief," is reprinted with permission from American Hospice Foundation. Copyright 2000 American Hospice Foundation. All Rights Reserved. Additional information is available at American Hospice Foundation's website at www.americanhospice.org.

What Is Grief?

Grief is the emotion people feel when they experience a loss. There are many different types of loss, and not all of them are related to death. A person can also grieve over the breakup of an intimate relationship or after a parent moves away from home.

✎ Weird Word

Grief: The normal response of sorrow, sadness, other emotions, and confusion that comes from losing someone or something important to you.

Grief is a natural reaction to the loss of someone important to you. Grief is also the name for the healing process that a person goes through after someone close has died. The grieving process takes time, and the healing usually happens gradually.

Although everyone experiences grief when they lose someone, grieving affects people in different ways. How it affects you partly depends on your situation and relationship with the person who died.

The circumstances under which a person dies can influence grief feelings. For example, if someone has been sick for a long time or is very old, you may have expected that person's death. Although it doesn't necessarily make it any easier to accept (and the feelings of grief will still be there), some people find that knowing someone is going to die gives them time to prepare. And if a loved one suffered a lot before dying, a person might even feel a sense of relief when the death occurs. If the person who has died is very young, though, you may feel a sense of how terribly unfair it seems.

Losing someone suddenly can be extremely traumatic, though, no matter how old that person is. Maybe someone you know died unexpectedly—as a result of violence or a car accident, for example. It can take a long time to overcome a sudden loss because you may feel caught off guard by the event and the intense feelings that are associated with it.

Losing someone because he or she committed suicide can be especially difficult to deal with. People who lose friends or family members to suicide may feel intense despair and sadness because they feel unable to understand what could have led to such an extreme action. They may even feel angry at the person—a completely normal emotion. Or they could feel guilty and wonder if there was something they might have done to prevent the suicide. Sometimes, after a traumatic loss, a person can become depressed and may need extra help to heal.

If you've lost someone in your immediate family, such as a parent, brother, or sister, you may feel cheated out of time you wanted to have with that person. It can also feel hard to express your own grief when other family members are grieving, too. Some people may hold back their own grief or avoid talking about the person who died because they worry that it may make a parent or other family member sad.

Grief can cause some people to feel guilty for no reason. Depending on the circumstances, some people might wonder if something they did—or didn't do—caused the person's death. Others might think if only they had been better people that their loved ones might not have died. These things aren't true, of course—but sometimes feelings and ideas like this are just a way of trying to make sense of something that's difficult to understand.

All of these feelings and reactions are okay—but what can people do to get through them? How long does grief last? Will things ever get back to normal? And how will you go on without the person who has died?

Coping With Grief

The grieving process is very personal and individual—each person goes through his or her grief differently. Some people reach out for support from others and find comfort in good memories. Others become very busy to take their minds off the loss. Some people become depressed and withdraw from their peers or go out of the way to avoid the places or situations that remind them of the person who has died. Just as people feel grief in many different ways, they handle it differently, too.

For some people, it may help to talk about the loss with others. Some do this naturally and easily with friends and family, others talk to a professional therapist. Some people may not feel like talking about it much at all because it's hard to find the words to express such deep and personal emotion or they

✔ Quick Tip

Journaling

A way to create a safe, non-threatening, private place for teens to express feelings is through the use of a journal. Writing and drawing have been proven as very therapeutic tools. Journals also provide a place to monitor their healing progress. It also serves as a connection to their special someone. Consistent writing helps teens get clearer on who they are, and it may reveal to them their own unique way to heal and move forward. Writing allows grieving teens to access the feelings and thoughts that reside in their subconscious minds. Journals also provide teens with a place to revisit their emotions, which is so valuable in the grieving process.

How To Start

There is no right way or wrong way to keep a journal. Keeping a journal is easy. You just need paper or a notebook and a comfortable pen or colored markers, or a computer. Here are some tips to get you started.

- Write when you have uninterrupted time.

- Write for about fifteen to twenty minutes daily.

- Use a comfortable writing tool.

- Choose a comfortable place to write.

- Try to write at the same time everyday.

- Date your entries.

- Don't judge your writing. Don't worry about grammar, spelling, punctuation, or sounding just right. The point is to write about what's on your mind and in your heart.

- Accept your writing and write from within. Don't be a critic.

- Don't try to write a story or a novel.

- Trust your intuitive heart, the words will come.

Journaling (continued)

- Be gentle with yourself.

- As you begin to write close your eyes and take a moment to get centered.

- Begin with a deep breath.

- If you get stuck begin doodling and see where that takes you.

- Experiment, play, be open to where your heart takes you in your writing.

Journal Topics For Grieving Teens

- Write a letter to your special someone who has died.

- Write about a special memory of your special someone.

- Write about what you wish you'd done or not done.

- Write about the things you wish you'd said or not said.

- Write about what you miss most about your special someone.

- Write about a memorial you can design for your special someone and then create it.

Experiencing a loss can be quite frightening for people no matter what their age. They must address their fearful feelings until they come to their own understanding. Listen to their fears and offer reassurance. While grieving, some will regress, others may attempt to overachieve, and others may withdraw or express anger. All teens should be encouraged to grieve in their own way. As a facilitator of the grieving process, remember the best gift you can give a person is the permission to grieve and the help to discover the healing process.

Source: "Opening Your Heart to Your Grieving Teen," reprinted with permission from Katherine Dorn Zotovich, a veteran educator and the author of *Good Grief for Kids* and *My Memory Maker*. © 2001 Journal Keepers Publishing. For additional information, visit www.journalkeepers.com.

wonder whether talking will make them feel the hurt more. This is fine, as long you find other ways to deal with your pain.

A few people may act out their sorrow by engaging in dangerous or self-destructive activities. Doing things like drinking, drugs, or cutting yourself to escape from the reality of a loss may seem to numb the pain, but the feeling is only temporary. The person isn't really dealing with the pain, only masking it, which makes all those feelings build up inside and only prolongs the grief.

If your pain just seems to get worse, or if you feel like hurting yourself or have suicidal thoughts, tell someone you trust about how you feel.

What To Expect

It may feel impossible to recover after losing someone you love. But grief does get gradually better and become less intense as time goes by. To help get you through the pain, it can help to know some of the things you might expect during the grieving process.

The first few days after someone dies can be intense, with people expressing strong emotions, perhaps crying and comforting each other, and gathering to express their support and condolences to the ones most affected by the loss.

Family and friends often participate in rituals that may be part of their religious, cultural, community, or family traditions—such as memorial services, wakes, or funerals. These activities can help people get through the first days after a death and honor the person who died. People might spend time together talking and sharing memories about the person who died. This may continue for days or weeks following the loss as friends and family bring food, send cards, or stop by to visit.

Many times, people show their emotions during this time. But sometimes a person can be so surprised or overwhelmed by the death that he or she doesn't show any emotion right away—even though the loss is very hard. For example, Joey's friends expected he'd be really upset at his mom's funeral, so they were surprised that he was smiling and talking with people as if nothing had happened. When they asked him about it, Joey said that seeing his friends at the funeral cheered him up because it reminded him that some things would still be the same. Joey was able to cry and talk about how he felt when he was alone with his dad after the funeral.

Sometimes, when the rituals associated with grieving end, people might feel like they should be "over it" because everything seems to have gone back to normal. When people who are grieving first go back to their normal activities, it might be hard to put their hearts into everyday things. Many people go back to doing regular things after a few days or a week. But although they may not talk about their loss as much, the grieving process continues.

It's natural to continue to have feelings and questions for a while after someone dies. It's also natural to begin to feel somewhat better. A lot depends on how your loss affects your life. It's okay to feel grief for days, weeks, or even longer, depending on how close you were to the person who died.

No matter how you choose to grieve, there's no one right way to do it. The grieving process is a gradual one that lasts longer for some people than others. There may be times when you worry that you'll never enjoy life the same way again, but this is a natural reaction after a loss.

Caring For Yourself

The loss of someone close to you can be stressful. It can help you to cope if you take care of yourself in certain small but important ways. Here are some that might help:

- **Remember that grief is a normal emotion.** Know that you can (and will) heal from your grief.

- **Participate in rituals.** Memorial services, funerals, and other traditions help people get through the first few days and honor the person who died.

- **Be with others.** Even informal gatherings of family and friends bring a sense of support and help people not to feel so isolated in the first days and weeks of their grief.

- **Talk about it when you can.** Some people find it helpful to tell the story of their loss or talk about their feelings. Sometimes a person doesn't feel like talking, and that's okay too. No one should feel pressured to talk.

- **Express yourself.** Even if you don't feel like talking, find ways to express your emotions and thoughts. Start writing in a journal about the memories you have of the person you lost and how you're feeling since the loss. Or write a song, poem, or tribute about the person who died. You can do this privately or share it with others.

- **Exercise.** Exercise can help your mood. It may be hard to get motivated, so modify your usual routine if you need to.

- **Eat right.** You may feel like skipping meals or you may not feel hungry—but your body still needs nutritious foods.

- **Join a support group.** If you think you may be interested in attending a support group, ask an adult or school counselor about how to become involved. The thing to remember is that you don't have to be alone with your feelings or your pain.

- **Let your emotions be expressed and released.** Don't stop yourself from having a good cry if you feel one coming on. Don't worry if listening to particular songs or doing other activities is painful because it brings back memories of the person that you lost; this is common. After a while, it becomes less painful.

- **Create a memorial or tribute.** Plant a tree or garden, or memorialize the person in some fitting way, such as running in a charity run or walk (a breast cancer race, for example) in honor of the lost loved one.

Getting Help For Intense Grief

If your grief isn't letting up for a while after the death of your loved one, you may want to reach out for help. If grief has turned into depression, it's very important to tell someone. How do you know if your grief has been going on too long? Here are some signs:

- You've been grieving for 4 months or more and you aren't feeling any better.

- You feel depressed.

- Your grief is so intense that you feel you can't go on with your normal activities.

♣ **It's A Fact!!**

Helping Yourself Through Grief

Grief is experienced whenever you lose something important to you. Grief is so powerful that people sometimes look for ways to go around it rather than experience it. This approach will not work. The best thing you can do for yourself is to work through grief and express your feelings. The following are specific ways to help yourself work through grief.

Basic Health Concerns

Grief is exhausting and it is important to continue your daily health routines.

1. Try to eat regular, nourishing meals. If it is too difficult to eat three regular meals, try 4 or 5 small ones. Have nourishing food available to nibble on rather than chips and candy.

2. Rest is important. Try to develop regular bedtime routines. If you are having a hard time getting to sleep, try a glass of warm milk or some soft, easy listening music to soothe your thoughts.

3. Continue your exercise program and develop a manageable routine.

4. Meditation, perhaps in the form of prayer or yoga, can help you get the rest you need.

5. Make sure your family doctor knows what has happened so he or she can help monitor your health.

Outside Support

Grief does not have to be as isolating as it seems.

1. Look for a support group, lecture, or seminar that pertains to your situation.

2. Continue attending church services and stay in contact with this "family," if that has been a source of support to you.

This information from American Hospice Foundation continues on the next few pages.

Helping Yourself Through Grief (continued)

3. Let your friends and other family members know what your emotional or physical needs are. The more they know what to do to help you, the more available they will be.

Feelings

1. Read books or articles of the process of grief so you can identify what you are feeling and have some ideas on how to help yourself.

2. Allow your feelings to be expressed appropriately.

3. Crying is good. You feel lighter after you have had a good cry. Consider sharing your tears with other loved ones. We laugh together, why not cry together as well?

4. Find friends or family members to share your feelings with.

5. Be careful not to use alcohol, drugs, or tranquilizers. These will only mask the pain and could lead to problems.

6. Keeping a journal is a good way to identify feelings and also to see progress.

7. Holidays and anniversaries need special planning. They are impossible to ignore. Look for a workshop on dealing with the holidays and make plans with your family and friends.

Be Kind To Yourself

1. If you desire some alone time, take it as often as you need to.

2. Give yourself rewards along the way as something to look forward to.

3. Look for small ways to pamper yourself, such as bubble baths, a new cologne, soft pajamas, or a new hair cut.

Helping Yourself Through Grief (continued)

4. A short trip can be a good break from grief, but be aware that upon your return, the pain of grief will be waiting for you. However, you will have had a rest and the knowledge that you can enjoy some things in life again.

5. Look for some new interests, perhaps a new hobby or resuming an old one.

6. Carry a special letter, poem, or quote with you to read when the going gets tough.

7. Try to enjoy the good days and don't feel guilty for doing so.

8. Reach out to help someone else.

9. Learn to have patience with yourself. Remember, grief takes time.

10. Know that you will get better and there will be a time when you can look forward to getting up in the morning and be glad you are alive.

Help For Your Marriage And Relationships

1. Good communication is necessary. People cannot read your mind. They may not know that this particular day is difficult or they may not know how to help you.

2. Talk about what is helpful to you and what is not helpful to you.

3. Be sensitive to the needs of your partner. Grief is different for each person.

4. By reviewing past losses together, you can understand how your partner may react to the recent one.

5. Avoid competition in who is hurting most. Each person will have difficult issues to cope with. Grief is hard for everybody.

Helping Yourself Through Grief (continued)

6.   Consult each other regarding birthdays, holidays, and anniversaries. It is a mistake to hope the holiday will slip by unnoticed. Make plans and discuss them.

7.   Try not to expect too much from your partner. People do not operate at 100 percent during the grieving period. The dishes may not get done or the yard may not be mown as regularly as before. Many chores can wait. Hire someone to help you catch up.

8.   Read and educate yourself about the grief process. Go to the library and get an armload of books. Read ones in which you feel the author "is speaking to you" and return the others. Grief books do not need to be read cover to cover. Look for a book with a detailed table of contents that will enable you to select certain parts as you need them.

9.   Consider the "gender" differences. Men and women grieve differently. Usually women are more comfortable expressing their emotions. Men often get busy, burying themselves at work or taking on projects at home.

10. Avoid pressuring your partner about decisions that can wait. Of course, some decisions cannot be postponed, and those you will have to deal with. However, many can be put off for a day or a week or even longer.

11. Take a short trip to "re-group." If a child has died, it is very important to re-acquaint yourself with the new family structure. Getting away from the telephone and memories for a few days can help you do this.

12. Seek professional guidance, especially if you feel your loss is interfering with your marriage or relationships.

Source: Reprinted with permission from American Hospice Foundation. Copyright 2000 American Hospice Foundation. All Rights Reserved.

- Your grief is affecting your ability to concentrate, sleep, eat, or socialize as you normally do.

- You feel you can't go on living after the loss or you think about suicide, dying, or hurting yourself.

☞ Remember!!

It's natural for loss to cause people to think about death to some degree. But if a loss has caused you to think about suicide or hurting yourself in some way, or if you feel that you can't go on living after your loss, it's important that you tell someone right away.

Counseling with a professional therapist can help because it allows you to talk about your loss and express strong feelings. Many counselors specialize in working with teens who are struggling with loss and depression. If you'd like to talk to a therapist and you're not sure where to begin, ask an adult or school counselor. Your doctor may also be able to recommend someone.

Will I Ever Get Over This?

Well-meaning friends and family might tell a grieving person they need to "move on" after a loss. Unfortunately, that type of advice can sometimes make people hesitate to talk about their loss, or make people think they're grieving wrong or too long, or that they're not normal. Every person takes his or her own time to heal after a loss. The way someone grieves a particular loss and the time it takes is very individual.

It's important for grieving people to not drop out of life, though. If you don't like the idea of moving on, maybe the idea of "keeping on" seems like a better fit. Sometimes it helps to remind yourself to just keep on doing the best you can for now. If you feel sad, let yourself have your feelings and try not to run away from your emotions. But also keep on doing things you normally would such as being with friends, caring for your pet, working out, or doing your schoolwork.

Going forward and healing from grief doesn't mean forgetting about the person you lost. Getting back to enjoying your life doesn't mean you no longer miss the person. And how long it takes until you start to feel better isn't a measure of how much you loved the person. With time, the loving support of family and friends, and your own positive actions, you can find ways to cope with even the deepest loss.

Chapter 30

Helping Your Bereaved Friend

You have a good friend who has just experienced the death of a loved one. Perhaps you know instinctively what to do, but maybe you do not. Perhaps you have never lost a person you love. Maybe you haven't even been to a funeral. This is not unusual. Many people do not have occasion to attend a funeral until late in adulthood. Maybe your friend is of a different culture and you are not sure what rituals or customs would be correct. Use the following as a guide in preparing for the day when a friend has lost a loved one.

Preparing Yourself

You can do some things now to prepare yourself for a future event:

- **Review a personal grief experience.** Think back to your childhood and to a time you experienced the death of a loved one or even a pet. Remember what it was like for you. Who died? How did you feel? What was helpful? And what was not helpful? The more you understand your personal experience with death and grief, the more comfortable you can be in reaching out to a friend.

- **Become familiar with the process of grief.** There are many books in libraries and bookstores that are written about grief and loss. Find one and read it to understand better what your friend may be experiencing.

- **Use the correct language.** If someone has died, say the word "died" instead of euphemisms, such as "passed."

- **Pace yourself.** Helping a bereaved friend is hard work, and your friend will need you for months to come. Think realistically about how much time you can give without denying your own family or important time together. In the beginning, your friend will need you more, with less assistance required as he or she becomes more independent.

When Death Occurs

There is so much to do after a death, but ordinary, practical help is needed first.

Practical Help

- **Make phone calls** and answer the telephone, keeping a record of messages. Make sure the house is presentable, and help to clean it, if necessary. Keep track of food and other gifts for thank you notes, and note which bowls belong to whom for later return.

- **Help with the children.** Children have special needs and may be ignored during this time. Talk to them about what they are feeling and thinking.

- **Run errands.** There are usually dozens of errands that need to be done. Ask for a list or help prepare one. Perform the ones you can and delegate the others.

- **Pick up out-of-town friends and relatives.** Offer to make trips to the airport or bus station to pick up those who are arriving to attend the funeral. Help find convenient and affordable lodging, or make arrangements with neighbors or friends to offer spare bedrooms.

- **Encourage your friend to take time out to rest.** Grief is exhausting, but if your bereaved friend is running on adrenaline, he or she may not be aware of the body's need to take a break.

- **Help with funeral arrangements.** At the time of death, families are tempted to spend huge amounts of money for the funeral, but their decisions may not be well thought through. Offer to go with your friend to the funeral home, but have a discussion about price beforehand. Spending thousands of dollars is not necessary for a nice funeral. Help your friend make the funeral more personal by incorporating the deceased's personality into a service of celebration of that person's life. If there are children present, suggest a special funeral service that would be shorter and more informal than the adult service.

Emotional Help

- **Think about how much time you can give.** Before committing yourself, determine how much time you can give without creating problems in your own family. Visits over a longer period of time are more important than many visits during the first week, when other friends and relatives are still available. With the departure of these people, the bereaved may feel isolated. Now is the time for you to start your visits, which may vary in length.

- **Learn good communication skills.** It is easy to do all of the talking, especially if you are anxious. Try not to fill every pause with chatter unless you have something important to say. Communication isn't always with words; use your eyes, as well. How does your friend look? Is she restless? Has her posture changed?

- **Be a good listener.** Listening is the most important gift you can offer a grieving person. Every time your bereaved friend tells his or her story, the reality of what has happened will sink in. The loss must become real in order for your friend to move through the process of grief. As a listener, encourage your friend to talk and express feelings.

- **Help your friend organize his or her day.** People tend to feel overwhelmed when a loved has died because there is so much to do. Help organize urgent tasks, and those that can wait until a later time. Develop and post a list that can be checked off when tasks are completed.

- **Help with thank-you notes.**
  With an outpouring of support from family, friends,
  and co-workers, this
  task may seem monu-
  mental. Your friend
  will have certain people
  to whom he or she will
  want to write personal notes.
  However, there are many
  thank-you notes that can be signed
  on behalf of your friend. That intimidating pile of cards can decrease
  quickly with your help.

> **✔ Quick Tip**
>
> Having a family member or close friend commit suicide increases a person's personal risk of suicide. If your friend is depressed, or talks about being with the person who died, tell their family, a teacher, or school counselor. Call 911 if your friend threatens to commit suicide.

- **Watch the children and their emotional needs.** Grief is so encompassing that children may be forgotten or ignored. See to their needs.

- **Share memories.** Sharing memories is so healing. Bereaved people love to hear stories about their loved ones.

- **Watch for depression.** It is normal for bereaved people to experience some depression, and reminiscing usually helps break it up. However, if you feel concerned about the degree of depression your friend may be exhibiting, suggest seeking professional help.

- **Identify local resources.** Find further resources for your friend, such as support groups, books, or therapists who specialize in grief. You can locate resources by calling your local hospice or mental health center.

- **Take care of yourself.** Helping the bereaved is hard work. Don't forget to take care of yourself. Find someone you can talk to. Check with your family and remain aware of their needs. Take time for yourself to do something special, such as taking long walks, reading a book, watching a favorite TV program, enjoying a quiet bath, or listening to some of your favorite music. Take care of yourself. Your friend will need you for a long time.

Avoid Vacuous Platitudes

People sometimes worry that they will say the wrong thing. The following are some things to avoid:

"I know how you feel." One can never know how another may feel. You could, instead, ask your friend to tell you how he or she feels.

"It's part of God's plan." This phrase can make people angry and they often respond with, "What plan? Nobody told me about any plan."

"Look at what you have to be thankful for." They know they have things to be thankful for, but right now they are not important.

"Call if you need anything." They aren't going to call. It is much better to offer something concrete, such as: "I have two free hours and I want to come over and vacuum your house or work on your lawn."

"He's in a better place now." The bereaved may or may not believe this. Keep your beliefs to yourself unless asked.

"This is behind you now; it's time to get on with your life." Sometimes the bereaved are resistant to getting on with because they feel this means "forgetting" their loved one. In addition, moving on is easier said than done. Grief has a mind of its own and works at its own pace.

Statements that begin with "You should" or "You will." These statements are too directive. Instead you could begin your comments with: "Have you thought about. . ." or "You might. . ."

Making decisions for your friend. You can help your friend make decisions by exploring the pros and cons of what or what not to do. If you make a decision and it ends up being a bad one, your friend may be very angry with you. Moreover, you may be reinforcing dependence on you.

Discouraging expressions of grief. It is best to "encourage" your friend to express grief. If your friend begins to cry, do not change the subject, rather give a hug, make a pot of coffee, or find the tissue.

Promoting your own values and beliefs. Listen to your friend talk about his or her values and beliefs. It's okay to share yours as long as you are not trying to convince your friend that your way is better.

Encouraging dependence. The bereaved may tend to lean on you too much. It is better to gently encourage independence with your support and guidance.

 Remember!!

Online Sources Of Additional Information About Grief

The Compassionate Friends
Website: http://www.compassionatefriends.org

GriefNet
Website: http://www.griefnet.org

Growth House, Inc.
Website: http://www.growthhouse.org

Transformations
Website: http://www.transformations.com

Chapter 31

How Suicide Affects Families

Suicide forcibly derails the lives of parents and children, partners and siblings, hurtling them into unfamiliar and sometimes perilous territory. But the study of suicide has for the most part been devoted to those who choose to end their lives, not to those left behind. Only recently have researchers begun to investigate, in a systematic fashion, the effects of suicide on family members.

"Survivors were always seen as a source of information about suicides, but few studies looked into the problems that survivors were having," said Herbert Hendin, the medical director of the American Foundation for Suicide Prevention, which joined with the National Institute of Mental Health in May 2003 in convening experts to assess the state of research on suicide survivors, the first meeting of its kind. The report from the conference was released in late September 2003.

Studies Suggest That The Psychological Legacy Of A Suicide May Differ From That Of Other Deaths

"Suicide flies in the face of people's beliefs about how life is and how it operates," said John Jordan, the author of a 2001 review of research on suicide survivors. He is also the director of the Family Loss Project, a group based near Boston that conducts research and offers treatment to the bereaved.

About This Book: Text in this chapter is from "How Suicide Affects Family," by Erica Goode, October 30, 2003. Copyright © 2003 The International Herald Tribune.

"Survivors spend a great deal of time trying to figure things out," Jordan said. "What was the person's frame of mind? How could they have done this? Who is responsible for it? What does it mean?"

Some people pass through a normal grief process and heal quickly, but studies suggest that suicide survivors often experience more guilt, rejection, shame, and isolation than those who grieve other deaths. If they have spent years dealing with a relative bent on self-destruction, they may also feel relief.

✔ **Quick Tip**

Suicide survivors may experience extreme grief and stress that can strain their relationships with family and friends. If you have experienced a family member dying by suicide, a suicide survivor's support group can help you through this difficult time.

Some studies have found that family members bereaved by suicide feel worse about themselves and are viewed more negatively by others. In a 1993 study, wives who had lost their husbands to suicide were seen as more psychologically disturbed, less likable, and more blameworthy than wives whose husbands had died from heart attacks or in accidents.

Suicide survivors have an elevated risk of suicide, and according to some studies, are more vulnerable to depression, a risk factor for suicide. In a 1996 study, David Brent, a child and adolescent psychiatrist at the University of Pittsburgh, and his colleagues found higher levels of depression in the siblings of adolescent suicide victims six months after the death, and in the mothers of the victims one year afterward, compared with a control group. At three years, siblings were no more depressed than a control group, but mothers were still having difficulty.

Attempts to follow the tracks of such a death through children's lives have come up with conflicting results.

A few early studies, involving children receiving psychiatric treatment, found troubled youngsters who grew into troubled adolescents. Other studies, based on interviews with adults bereaved in childhood, also suggested that serious emotional difficulties were not uncommon.

More recent studies, with broader samples and more rigorous methodology, have found that, at least in the first years after a suicide, many children show surprising resilience.

In a 1999 study of bereaved children, for example, Julie Cerel of the University of Rochester in New York found the rates of depression, traumatic stress, and suicidal behavior to be no higher in those who had lost a parent to suicide than in those whose parent had died from other causes. Yet a parent's suicide, Cerel found, led to more feelings of anxiety, anger, and shame, and greater difficulty accepting the death. It was also linked with more behavioral problems in the two years after the suicide.

Such studies are far from conclusive, experts say, in part because there are so few of them. Most involve only small numbers of children.

Suicide is a rare event, and researchers often have difficulty gathering subjects. Most of the studies focus on the first months or years after a suicide and cannot say much about what happens later on.

♣ It's A Fact!!

Studies over the last several decades have shown that suicides cluster in families. Researchers who conduct "psychological autopsies," by interviewing family members and friends of suicide victims and examining written records, have found higher rates of suicide among the victims' relatives than among people who died from other causes. Also, adults and adolescents who have attempted suicide have more family members who have tried to end their lives.

"We don't know what the longer-term issues will be as children get to the age of higher risk," said Cynthia Pfeffer, a professor of psychiatry and director of the child bereavement program at Weill Medical College of Cornell University, who has studied the impact of suicide for many years.

Experts say that how the surviving parent copes has a significant effect on how a child ultimately fares.

Steven Bailley, a clinical psychologist and researcher in Houston who leads groups for survivors, said that in some cases the imprint left by a suicide may be so subtle that even the best research will fail to capture it. "Do you trust people? What happens in your intimate relationships? It's so hard to measure," he said.

Bailley speaks from personal experience: His mother killed herself when he was 16. "Everything changed in that moment," he said. "It takes everything that came before and everything that comes afterward and puts it in a different light."

One study, based on Sweden's death registry, found that suicide was twice as common among the first-degree relatives of suicide victims born between 1949 and 1969 as it was in the families of comparison subjects. The study, by Bo Runeson and Marie Asberg, was published in the August 2003 issue of *The American Journal of Psychiatry*.

Experts estimate that a first-degree relative's risk is two to six times as great as that of someone with no family history of suicide. "We know that it's heritable," said John Mann, a professor of psychiatry and radiology at Columbia.

Yet the experts are quick to add that family members are by no means doomed to follow a similar path. Though they are at higher risk, that risk is still very low. And simply knowing that the risk is there can, as Brent put it, be "a wake-up call," providing the impetus for change.

Why suicide selectively sprinkles family trees is still unknown. One possibility is that such a death lowers social barriers, in a sense giving permission for other family members to consider suicide an option.

🖝 Remember!!

Knowing that you are at higher risk for suicide if a family member died by suicide allows you to change that by choosing to get help for long-lived depression, grief, or hopelessness. You can choose to live.

But genes are also at work. More suicides are found among the biological relatives of suicide victims who were adopted in childhood than in their adoptive families, one study found. Identical twins, who share the same genes, other studies show, are significantly more likely than fraternal twins to commit suicide if their twin has done so.

Such findings hint of something written in strands of DNA that, combined with environmental pressures, impels some people toward suicide. Yet what that genetic message says is an open scientific question.

Chapter 32

Handling Post-Traumatic Stress Disorder After Suicide

Each year many children and adolescents sustain injuries from violence, lose friends or family members, or are adversely affected by witnessing a violent or catastrophic event. Each situation is unique, whether it centers upon a plane crash where many people are killed, a suicide, automobile accidents involving friends or family members, or natural disasters where deaths occur and homes are lost—but these events have similarities as well, and cause similar reactions in children and adolescents. Even in the course of everyday life, exposure to violence in the home or on the streets can lead to emotional harm. Research has shown that both adults and children who experience catastrophic events show a wide range of reactions.[1,2] Some suffer only worries and bad memories that fade with emotional support and the passage of time. Others are more deeply affected and experience long-term problems.

About This Chapter: This chapter includes excerpts from "Helping Children and Adolescents Cope with Violence and Disaster," National Institute of Mental Health, NIH Publication No. 01-3518, updated September 21, 2001. Also included is text from "Coping with PTSD and Recommended Lifestyle Changes for PTSD Patients," by Joe Ruzek, Ph.D. National Center for Post-Traumatic Stress Disorder, updated May 14, 2003.

Research on post-traumatic stress disorder (PTSD) shows that some soldiers, survivors of crimes, torture, and other violence, and survivors of natural and man-made catastrophes, including suicide, suffer long-term effects from their experiences. Children and teens who have witnessed violence in their families, schools, or communities are also vulnerable to serious long-term problems. Their emotional reactions, including fear, depression, withdrawal, or anger, can occur immediately or some time after the tragic event. Children and adolescents who have experienced a catastrophic event often need support from parents and teachers to avoid long-term emotional harm. Most will recover in a short time, but the few who develop PTSD or other persistent problems need treatment.

✎ Weird Words

Adversely Affected: Harmed emotionally.

Catastrophic Event: A disaster which results in death and/or widespread damage.

Trauma: In psychiatric terms, trauma refers to an experience that is emotionally painful, distressful, or shocking, which often results in lasting mental and physical effects.

How Adolescents React To Trauma

Reactions to trauma may appear immediately after the traumatic event or days and even weeks later. Loss of trust in adults and fear of the event occurring again are responses seen in many children and adolescents who have been exposed to traumatic events. Other reactions vary according to age.[4-7]

Adolescents 12 to 17 years old may exhibit responses similar to those of adults, including flashbacks, nightmares, emotional numbing, avoidance of any reminders of the traumatic event, depression, substance abuse, problems with peers, and anti-social behavior. Also common are withdrawal and isolation, physical complaints, suicidal thoughts, school avoidance, academic decline, sleep disturbances, and confusion. The adolescent may feel extreme guilt over his or her failure to prevent injury or loss of life, and may harbor revenge fantasies that interfere with recovery from the trauma.

Some youth are more vulnerable to trauma than others, for reasons scientists don't fully understand. It has been shown that the impact of a traumatic event is likely to be greatest in the child or adolescent who previously has been the victim of child abuse or some other form of trauma, or who already had a mental health problem.[8-11] And the teen who lacks family support is more at risk for a poor recovery.[12]

Coping With Post-Traumatic Stress Disorder (PTSD)

Because PTSD symptoms seldom disappear completely, it is usually a continuing challenge for survivors of trauma to cope with PTSD symptoms and the problems they cause. Survivors often learn through treatment how to cope more effectively. Recovery from PTSD is an ongoing, daily, gradual process. It doesn't happen through sudden insight or cure. Healing doesn't mean that a survivor will forget a suicide experience or have no emotional pain when remembering it. Some level of continuing reaction to memories is normal and reflects a normal body and mind. Recovery may lead to fewer reactions and reactions that are less intense. It may also lead to a greater ability to manage trauma-related emotions and to greater confidence in one's ability to cope.

When a trauma survivor takes direct action to cope with problems, he or she often gains a sense of personal power and control. Active coping means recognizing and accepting the impact of traumatic experiences and then taking concrete action to improve things.

Positive Coping Actions

Positive coping actions are those that help to reduce anxiety and lessen other distressing reactions. Positive coping actions also improve the situation in a way that does not harm the survivor further and in a way that lasts into the future. Positive coping methods include:

- **Learning about trauma and PTSD.** It is useful for trauma survivors to learn more about PTSD and how it affects them. By learning that PTSD is common and that their problems are shared by hundreds of thousands of others, survivors recognize that they are not alone, weak, or crazy. When a survivor seeks treatment and learns to recognize and understand what upsets him or her, he or she is in a better position to cope with the symptoms of PTSD.

- **Talking to another person for support.** When survivors are able to talk about their problems with others, something helpful often results. Of course, survivors must choose their support people carefully and clearly ask for what they need. With support from others, survivors may feel less alone, feel supported or understood, or receive concrete help with a problem situation. Often, it is best to talk to professional counselors about issues related to the traumatic experience itself; they are more likely than friends or family to understand trauma and its effects. It is also helpful to seek support from a support group. Being in a group with others who have PTSD may help reduce one's sense of isolation, rebuild trust in others, and provide an important opportunity to contribute to the recovery of other survivors of trauma.

- **Talking to your doctor about trauma and PTSD.** Part of taking care of yourself means mobilizing the helping resources around you. Your doctor can take care of your physical health better if he or she knows about your PTSD, and doctors can often refer you to more specialized and expert help.

- **Practicing relaxation methods.** These can include muscular relaxation exercises, breathing exercises, meditation, swimming, stretching, yoga, prayer, listening to quiet music, spending time in nature, and so on. While relaxation techniques can be helpful, they can sometimes increase distress by focusing attention on disturbing physical sensations or by reducing contact with the external environment. Be aware that while uncomfortable physical sensations may become more apparent when you are relaxed, in the long run, continuing with relaxation in a way that is tolerable (i.e., interspersed with music, walking, or other activities) helps reduce negative reactions to thoughts, feelings, and perceptions.

♣ It's A Fact!!
What Is Post-Traumatic Stress Disorder?

Some children and adolescents will have prolonged problems after a traumatic event. These potentially chronic conditions include depression and prolonged grief. Another serious and potentially long-lasting problem is post-traumatic stress disorder (PTSD). This condition is diagnosed when the following symptoms have been present for longer than one month:

- Re-experiencing the event through play, in trauma-specific nightmares or flashbacks, or distress over events that resemble or symbolize the trauma.

- Routine avoidance of reminders of the event or a general lack of responsiveness (e.g., diminished interests or a sense of having a foreshortened future).

- Increased sleep disturbances, irritability, poor concentration, startle reaction, and regressive behavior.

PTSD may arise weeks or months after the traumatic event. PTSD may resolve without treatment, but some form of therapy by a mental health professional is often required in order for healing to occur. Fortunately, it is more common for traumatized individuals to have some of the symptoms of PTSD than to develop the full-blown disorder.[14]

People differ in their vulnerability to PTSD, and the source of this difference is not known in its entirety. Researchers have identified factors that interact to influence vulnerability to developing PTSD. These factors include:

- characteristics of the trauma exposure itself (e.g., proximity to trauma, severity, and duration),

- characteristics of the individual (e.g., prior trauma exposures, family history, prior psychiatric illness, gender—women are at greatest risk for many of the most common assault traumas), and

- post-trauma factors (e.g., availability of social support, emergence of avoidance/numbing, hyperarousal, and re-experiencing symptoms).

Research has shown that PTSD clearly alters a number of fundamental brain mechanisms. Abnormal levels of brain chemicals that affect coping behavior, learning, and memory have been detected among people with the disorder. In addition, recent imaging studies have discovered altered metabolism and blood flow in the brain as well as structural brain changes in people with PTSD.[15-19]

- **Increasing positive distracting activities.** Positive recreational or work activities help distract a person from his or her memories and reactions. Artistic endeavors have also been a way for many trauma survivors to express their feelings in a positive, creative way. This can improve your mood, limit the harm caused by PTSD, and help you rebuild your life. It is important to emphasize that distraction alone is unlikely to facilitate recovery; active, direct coping with traumatic events and their impact is also important.

- **Calling a counselor for help.** Sometimes PTSD symptoms worsen and ordinary efforts at coping don't seem to work. Survivors may feel fearful or depressed. At these times, it is important to reach out and telephone a counselor, who can help turn things around.

- **Taking prescribed medications to tackle PTSD.** One tool that many with PTSD have found helpful is medication treatment. By taking medications, some survivors of trauma are able to improve their sleep, anxiety, irritability, anger, and control urges to drink or use drugs.

Negative Coping Actions

Negative coping actions help to perpetuate problems. They may reduce distress immediately but short-circuit more permanent change. Some actions that may be immediately effective may also cause later problems, like smoking or drug use. These habits can become difficult to change. Negative coping methods can include isolation, use of drugs or alcohol, workaholism, violent behavior, angry intimidation of others, unhealthy eating, and different types of self-destructive behavior (e.g., attempting suicide). Before learning more effective and healthy coping methods, most people with PTSD try to cope with their distress and other reactions in ways that lead to more problems. The following are negative coping actions:

- **Use of alcohol or drugs.** This may help wash away memories, increase social confidence, or induce sleep, but it causes more problems than it cures. Using alcohol or drugs can create a dependence on alcohol, harm one's judgment, hurt one's mental abilities, cause problems in relationships with family and friends, and sometimes place a person at risk for suicide, violence, or accidents.

✔ Quick Tip
Treatment Of PSTD

People with PTSD are treated with specialized forms of psychotherapy and sometimes with medications or a combination of the two. One of the forms of psychotherapy shown to be effective is cognitive behavioral therapy, or CBT. In CBT, the patient is taught methods of overcoming anxiety or depression and modifying undesirable behaviors such as avoidance of reminders of the traumatic event. The therapist helps the patient examine and re-evaluate beliefs that are interfering with healing, such as the belief that the traumatic event will happen again. Children who undergo CBT are taught to avoid catastrophizing. For example, they are reassured that dark clouds do not necessarily mean another hurricane, that the fact that someone is angry doesn't necessarily mean that another shooting is imminent, etc.

Art therapy can help people to remember the traumatic event safely and express their feelings about it. Other forms of psychotherapy that have been found to help persons with PTSD include group and exposure therapy. A reasonable period of time for treatment of PTSD is 6 to 12 weeks with occasional follow-up sessions, but treatment may be longer depending on a patient's particular circumstances. Research has shown that support from family and friends can be an important part of recovery.

There is accumulating empirical evidence that trauma/grief-focused psychotherapy and selected pharmacologic interventions can be effective in alleviating PTSD symptoms and in addressing co-occurring depression.[20-23] However, more medication treatment research is needed.

A mental health professional with special expertise in the area of child and adolescent trauma is the best person to help a young person with PTSD.

- **Social isolation.** By reducing contact with the outside world, a trauma survivor may avoid many situations that cause him or her to feel afraid, irritable, or angry. However, isolation will also cause major problems. It will result in the loss of social support, friendships, and intimacy. It may breed further depression and fear. Less participation in positive activities leads to fewer opportunities for positive emotions and achievements.

- **Anger.** Like isolation, anger can get rid of many upsetting situations by keeping people away. However, it also keeps away positive connections and help, and it can gradually drive away the important people in a person's life. It may lead to job problems, marital or relationship problems, and the loss of friendships.

- **Continuous avoidance.** If you avoid thinking about the trauma or if you avoid seeking help, you may keep distress at bay, but this behavior also prevents you from making progress in how you cope with trauma and its consequences.

Recommended Lifestyle Changes—Taking Control

Those with PTSD need to take active steps to deal with their PTSD symptoms. Often, these steps involve making a series of thoughtful changes in one's lifestyle to reduce symptoms and improve quality of life. Positive lifestyle changes include:

- **Calling about treatment and joining a PTSD support group.** It may be difficult to take the first step and join a PTSD treatment group. Survivors say to themselves, "What will happen there? Nobody can help me anyway." In addition, people with PTSD find it hard to meet new people and trust them enough to open up. However, it can also be a great relief to feel that you have taken positive action. You may also be able to eventually develop a friendship with another survivor.

- **Increasing contact with other survivors of trauma.** Other survivors of trauma are probably the best source of understanding and support. By joining a survivors organization (e.g., teens may want to join a student organization) or by otherwise increasing contact with other survivors, it is possible to reverse the process of isolation and distrust of others.

- **Reinvesting in personal relationships with family and friends.** Most survivors of trauma have some kind of a relationship with a brother or sister, a mother or father, or an old friend or school or work acquaintance. If you make the effort to reestablish or increase contact with that person, it can help you reconnect with others.

- **Changing neighborhoods.** Survivors with PTSD usually feel that the world is a very dangerous place and that it is likely that they will be harmed again. It is not a good idea for people with PTSD to live in a high-crime area because it only makes those feelings worse and confirms their beliefs. If it is possible to move to a safer neighborhood, it is likely that fewer things will set off traumatic memories. This will allow the person to reconsider his or her personal beliefs about danger.

- **Refraining from alcohol and drug abuse.** Many trauma survivors turn to alcohol and drugs to help them cope with PTSD. Although these substances may distract a person from his or her painful feelings and, therefore, may appear to help deal with symptoms, relying on alcohol and drugs always makes things worse in the end. These substances often hinder PTSD treatment and recovery. Rather than trying to beat an addiction by yourself, it is often easier to deal with addictions by joining a treatment program where you can be around others who are working on similar issues.

- **Starting an exercise program.** It is important to see a doctor before starting to exercise. However, if the physician gives the okay, exercise in moderation can benefit those with PTSD. Walking, jogging, swimming, weight lifting, and other forms of exercise may reduce physical tension. They may distract the person from painful memories or worries and give him or her a break from difficult emotions. Perhaps most important, exercise can improve self-esteem and create feelings of personal control.

- **Starting to volunteer in the community.** It is important to feel as though you are contributing to your community. When you are not working, you may not feel you have anything to offer others. One way survivors can reconnect with their communities is to volunteer. You can help with youth programs, medical services, literacy programs, community sporting activities, etc.

References

1. Yehuda R, McFarlane AC, Shalev AY. Predicting the development of posttraumatic stress disorder from the acute response to a traumatic event. *Biological Psychiatry*, 1998; 44(12): 1305-13.

2. Smith EM, North CS. Posttraumatic stress disorder in natural disasters and technological accidents. In: Wilson JP, Raphael B, eds. *International handbook of traumatic stress syndromes*. New York: Plenum Press, 1993; 405-19.

3. March JS, Amaya-Jackson L, Terry R, Costanzo P. Posttraumatic symptomatology in children and adolescents after an industrial fire. *Journal of the American Academy of Child and Adolescent Psychiatry*, 1997; 36(8): 1080-8.

4. Osofsky JD. The effects of exposure to violence on young children. *American Psychologist*, 1995; 50(9): 782-8.

5. Pynoos RS, Steinberg AM, Goenjian AK. Traumatic stress in childhood and adolescence: recent developments and current controversies. In: Van der Kolk BA, McFarlane AC, Weisaeth L, eds. *Traumatic stress: the effects of overwhelming experience on mind, body, and society*. New York: Guilford Press, 1996; 331-58.

6. Marans S, Adelman A. Experiencing violence in a developmental context. In: Osofsky JD, et al., eds. *Children in a violent society*. New York: Guilford Press, 1997; 202-22.

7. Vogel JM, Vernberg EM. Psychological responses of children to natural and human-made disasters: I. Children's psychological responses to disasters. *Journal of Clinical Child Psychology*, 1993; 22(4): 464-84.

8. Garbarino J, Kostelny K, Dubrow N. What children can tell us about living in danger. *American Psychologist*, 1991; 46(4): 376-83.

9. Duncan RD, Saunders BE, Kilpatrick DG, Hanson RF, Resnick HS. Childhood physical assault as a risk factor for PTSD, depression, and substance abuse: findings from a national survey. *American Journal of Orthopsychiatry*, 1996; 66(3): 437-48.

10. Boney-McCoy S, Finkelhor D. Prior victimization: a risk factor for child sexual abuse and for PTSD-related symptomatology among sexually abused youth. *Child Abuse and Neglect*, 1995; 19(12): 1401-21.

11. Roth SH, Newman E, Pelcovitz D, Van der Kolk BA, Mandel FS. Complex PTSD in victims exposed to sexual and physical abuse: results from the DSM-IV Field Trial for Posttraumatic Stress Disorder. *Journal of Traumatic Stress*, 1997; 10(4): 539-55.

12. Morrison JA. Protective factors associated with children's emotional responses to chronic community violence exposure. *Trauma, Violence, and Abuse: A Review Journal*, 2000; 1(4); 299-320.

13. Smith EM, North CS, Spitznagel EL. Post-traumatic stress in survivors of three disasters. *Journal of Social Behavior and Personality*, 1993; 8(5): 353-68.

14. Breslau N, Kessler RC, Chilcoat HD, Schultz LR, Davis GC, Andreski P. Trauma and posttraumatic stress disorder in the community: the 1996 Detroit Area Survey of Trauma. *Archives of General Psychiatry*, 1998; 55(7): 626-32.

15. Bremner JD, Randall P, Scott TM, Bronen RA, Seibyl JP, Southwick SM, Delaney RC, McCarthy G, Charney DS, Innis RB. MRI-based measurement of hippocampal volume in combat-related posttraumatic stress disorder. *American Journal of Psychiatry*, 1995; 152(7): 973-81.

16. Stein MB, Hanna C, Koverola C, Torchia M, McClarty B. Structural brain changes in PTSD: does trauma alter neuroanatomy? In: Yehuda R, McFarlane AC, eds. *Psychobiology of posttraumatic stress disorder.* Annals of the New York Academy of Sciences, vol. 821. New York: The New York Academy of Sciences, 1997; 76-82.

17. Rauch SL, Shin LM. Functional neuroimaging studies in posttraumatic stress disorder. In: Yehuda R, McFarlane AC, eds. *Psychobiology of posttraumatic stress disorder.* Annals of the New York Academy of Sciences, vol. 821. New York: The New York Academy of Sciences, 1997; 83-98.

18. De Bellis MD, Baum AS, Birmaher B, Keshavan MS, Eccard CH, Boring AM, Jenkins FJ, Ryan ND. Developmental traumatology part I: biological stress systems. *Biological Psychiatry*, 1999; 45(10): 1259-70.

19. De Bellis MD, Keshavan MS, Clark DB, Casey BJ, Giedd JN, Boring AM, Frustaci K, Ryan ND. Developmental traumatology part II: brain development. *Biological Psychiatry*, 1999; 45(10): 1271-84.

20. Yule W, Canterbury R. The treatment of post traumatic stress disorder in children and adolescents. *International Review of Psychiatry*, 1994; 6(2-3): 141-51.

21. Goenjian AK, Karayan I, Pynoos RS, Minassian D, Najarian LM, Steinberg AM, Fairbanks LA. Outcome of psychotherapy among early adolescents after trauma. *American Journal of Psychiatry*, 1997; 154(4): 536-42.

22. March JS, Amaya-Jackson L, Pynoos RS. Pediatric posttraumatic stress disorder. In: Weiner JM, ed. *Textbook of child and adolescent psychiatry*, 2nd edition. Washington, DC: American Psychiatric Press, 1997; 507-24.

23. Murphy L, Pynoos RS, James CB. The trauma/grief-focused group psychotherapy module of an elementary school-based violence prevention/intervention program. In: Osofsky JD, et al., eds. *Children in a violent society*. New York: Guilford Press, 1997; 223-55.

☞ Remember!!

If you experience post-traumatic stress disorder after someone dies by suicide, take direct positive action to cope with the problems by seeing a doctor, establishing support through friendships and by joining a support group, and taking care of yourself physically and mentally.

Part Six

If You Need More Information

Chapter 33

Additional Information About Suicide

Suggested Additional Reading

A Special Scar: The Experience of People Bereaved by Suicide
By Alison Wertheimer
Published by Brunner-Routledge, 2001
ISBN: 0415220270

An Empty Chair: Living in the Wake of a Sibling's Suicide
By Sara Swan Miller
Published by Writers Club Press, June 1, 2000
ISBN: 0595095232

Do They Have Bad Days in Heaven? Surviving the Suicide Loss of a Sibling
By Michelle Linn-Gust
Published by Chellehead Works; 2nd edition, July 9, 2001
ISBN: 0972331808

About This Chapter: The list of resources and organizations in this chapter was compiled from many sources deemed accurate. The books listed represent a sampling of available material; this list is not complete. The organizations are intended to serve as a starting point for further research. Inclusion does not constitute endorsement. All contact information was verified in June 2004.

How I Stayed Alive When My Brain Was Trying To Kill Me:
One Person's Guide to Suicide Prevention
By Susan Rose Blauner
Published by Quill; 1st Quill edition, July 2003
ISBN: 0060936215

Mental Health Information for Teens
Edited by Karen Bellenir
Published by Omnigraphics, Inc., 2001
ISBN: 0780804422

Night Falls Fast: Understanding Suicide
By Kay R. Jamison, Kay Redfield Jamison
Published by Vintage Books USA, October 2000
ISBN: 0375701478

No Time to Say Goodbye: Surviving the Suicide of a Loved One
By Carla Fine
Published by Main Street Books, November 1999
ISBN: 0385485514

Step Back from the Exit: 45 Reasons to Say No to Suicide
By Jillayne Arena
Published by Zebulon Press, April 1996
ISBN: 0964734001

Suicide Survivors' Handbook
By Trudy Carlson
Published by Benline Press, 2000
ISBN: 0964244381

Suicide: The Forever Decision...for Those Thinking About Suicide,
and for Those Who Know, Love, or Counsel Them
By Paul G. Quinnett
Published by Crossroad Publishing Company; Expanded edition, January 1997
ISBN: 0824513525

Organizations With Mental Health And Suicide Prevention Information

Al-Anon/Alateen Hot Line
1600 Corporate Landing Pky.
Virginia Beach, VA 23454-5617
Toll-Free: 800-344-2666
Phone: 757-563-1600
Fax: 757-563-1655
Website: http://www.al-anon.alateen.org
E-mail: wso@al-anon.org

American Psychiatric Association
1000 Wilson Blvd.
Suite 1825
Arlington, VA 22209-3901
Phone: 703-907-7300
Website: http://www.psych.org
E-mail: apa@psych.org

American Psychological Association
750 First St., N.E.
Washington, DC 20002-4242
Toll-Free: 800-374-2721
Phone: 202-336-5500
TDD/TTY: 202-336-6123
Website: http://www.apa.org

American Academy of Child and Adolescent Psychiatry
3615 Wisconsin Ave., N.W.
Washington, DC 20016-3007
Phone: 202-966-7300
Fax: 202-966-2891
Website: http://www.aacap.org

Anxiety Disorders Association of America
8730 Georgia Ave., Suite 600
Silver Spring, MD 20910
Phone: 240-485-1001
Fax: 240-485-1035
Website: http://www.adaa.org

Association for the Advancement of Behavior Therapy
305 Seventh Ave., 16th Floor
New York, NY 10001-6008
Phone: 212-647-1890
Fax: 212-647-1865
Website: http://www.aabt.org

American Association of Suicidology
4201 Connecticut Ave., N.W.
Suite 408
Washington, DC 20008
Phone: 202-237-2280
Website: www.suicidology.org
E-mail: info@suicidology.org

Center for Mental Health Services (CMHS)

Emergency Services and Disaster Relief Branch
P.O. Box 42557
Washington, DC 20015
Toll-Free: 800-789-2647
Toll-Free TDD: 866-889-2647
Phone: 301-443-1805
Fax: 301-984-8796
TDD: 301-443-9006
Website: http://
www.mentalhealth.org/cmhs/
emergencyservices/index.htm

Compassionate Friends

P.O. Box 3696
Oak Brook, IL 60522-3696
Toll-Free: 877-969-0010
Fax: 630-990-0246
Website: http://
www.compassionatefriends.org
E-mail: nationaloffice
@compassionatefriends.org

CrisisLink

5275 Lee Hwy., Suite 301
Arlington, VA 22207
24-hour hot line: 703-527-4077 (in Northern VA)
Toll-Free: 800-SUICIDE (784-2433)
Phone: 703-527-6603 (Business Calls Only)
Fax: 703-516-6767
Website: http://www.crisislink.org
E-mail: info@crisislink.org

Depression and Bipolar Support Alliance

730 N. Franklin St.
Suite 501
Chicago, IL 60610-7224
Toll-Free: 800-826-3632
Phone: 312-642-0049
Fax: 312-642-7243
Website: http://
www.dbsalliance.org
E-mail: questions@dbsalliance.org

Federal Emergency Management Agency

Information for children and adolescents
500 C Street, S.W.
Washington, DC 20472
Toll-Free Publications: 800-480-2520
Phone: 202-566-1600
Website: http://www.fema.gov/kids

Feeling Blue Suicide Prevention Committee

A Non-Profit Community Service Organization
P.O. Box 7193
St. Davids, PA 19087
Phone: 610-715-0076
Website: http://
www.feelingblue.org

Hopeline

2001 N. Beauregard St., 12th floor
Alexandria, VA 22311
Phone: 703-837-3364
Fax: 703-684-7438
Website: http://www.hopeline.com
E-mail: info@hopeline.com

International Society for Traumatic Stress Studies (ISTSS)

60 Revere Dr., Suite 500
Northbrook, IL 60062
Phone: 847-480-9028
Fax: 847-480-9282
Website: http://www.istss.org
E-mail: istss@istss.org

Jason Foundation

116 Maple Row Blvd., Suite C
Henderson, TN 37075
Toll-Free: 888-881-2323
Phone: 615-264-2323
Fax: 615-264-0188
Website: http://
www.jasonfoundation.com

Jed Foundation

583 Broadway, Suite 8B
New York, NY 10012
Phone: 212-343-0016
Fax: 212-343-1141
Website: http://
www.jedfoundation.org/index.php
E-mail: emailus@jedfoundation.org

National Alliance for the Mentally Ill

2107 Wilson Blvd., Suite 300
Colonial Place Three
Arlington, VA 22201-3042
Toll-Free: 800-950-NAMI (6264)
Phone: 703-524-7600
Fax: 703-524-9094
TDD: 703-516-7227
Website: http://www.nami.org

National Anxiety Foundation

3135 Custer Drive
Lexington, KY 40517-4001
Website: http://www.lexington-on-line.com/naf.html

National Center for PTSD

215 N. Main St.
White River Junction, VT 05009
Phone: 802-296-6300
Website: http://www.ncptsd.org
E-mail: ncptsd@ncptsd.org

National Center for Victims of Crime

2111 Wilson Blvd., Suite 300
Arlington, VA 22201
Phone: 703-276-2880
Website: http://www.ncvc.org
E-mail: mail@ncvc.org

National Institute of Mental Health Publications List

5600 Fishers Lane, Room 7C-02
Rockville, MD 20857
Toll-Free: 866-615-6464
Phone: 301-443-4513
Fax: 301-443-4279
TTY: 301-443-8431
Website: http://
infocenter.nimh.nih.gov
E-mail: nimhinfo@nih.gov

National Institute of Mental Health (NIMH)

Information Resources and Inquiries Branch
6001 Executive Blvd.
Rm. 8184, MSC 9663
Bethesda, MD 20892-9663
Toll-Free: 866-615-6464
Phone: 301-443-4513
Fax: 301-443-4279
TTY: 301-443-8431
Website: http://www.nimh.nih.gov
E-mail: nimhinfo@nih.gov

National Mental Health Association

2001 N. Beauregard St., 12th Floor
Alexandria, VA 22311
Toll-Free: 800-969-6642
Toll-Free TTY: 800-433-5968
Phone: 703-684-7722
Fax: 703-684-5968
Website: http://www.nmha.org

National Organization for People of Color Against Suicide

4715 Sargent Rd. N.E.
Washington, DC 20017
Toll-Free: 866-899-5317
Phone: 202-549-6039
Website: http://www.nopcas.com
E-mail: nopcas@onebox.com

National Organization for Victim Assistance (NOVA)

1730 Park Rd., N.W.
Washington, DC 20010
Toll-Free: 800-879-6682
Phone: 202-232-6682
Fax: 202-462-2255
Website: http://www.try-nova.org
E-mail: nova@try-nova.org

Office for Victims of Crime Resource Center

National Criminal Justice Reference Service
P.O. Box 6000
Rockville, MD 20850
Toll-Free: 800-851-3420
Toll-Free TTY: 877-712-9279
Phone: 301-519-5500
Fax: 301-519-5212
Website: http://www.ncjrs.org
E-mail: askncjrs@ncjrs.org

Organization for Attempters and Survivors of Suicide and Interfaith Services (OASSIS)
101 King Farm Blvd., #D401
Rockville, MD 20850
Phone: 240-632-0335
Fax: 240-632-0336
Website: http://www.oassis.org

Samaritans of NY
P.O. Box 1259
Madison Square Station
New York, NY 10159
Suicide Prevention Hot Line: 212-673-3000
Website: http://www.samaritansnyc.org/samhome.html

SAVE—Suicide Awareness Voices of Education
7317 Cahill Rd., Suite 207
Minneapolis, MN 55439-2080
Phone: 952-946-7998
Website: http://www.save.org
E-mail: save@save.org

Suicide Prevention Resource Center
55 Chapel Street
Newton, MA 02458-1060
Toll-Free: 877-GET-SPRC (438-7772)
TTY: 617-964-5448
Website: http://www.sprc.org
E-mail: info@sprc.org

Trevor Project
8950 W. Olympic Blvd., Suite 197
Beverly Hills, CA 90211
Phone: 310-271-8845
Fax: 310-271-8846
Website: http://www.thetrevorproject.org/home.html
E-mail: Support@TheTrevorProject.org

U.S. Department of Education
400 Maryland Ave., S.W.
Washington, DC 20202
Toll-Free: 800-872-5327
Toll-Free TTY: 800-437-0833
Fax: 202-401-0689
Website: http://www.ed.gov
E-mail: customerservice@inet.ed.gov

U.S. Department of Justice
950 Pennsylvania Ave., N.W.
Washington, DC 20530-0001
Phone: 202-353-1555
Website: http://www.usdoj.gov
E-mail: AskDOJ@usdoj.gov

Yellow Ribbon
P.O. Box 644
Westminster, CO 80036-0644
Phone: 303-429-3530
Fax: 303-426-4496
Website: http://www.yellowribbon.org
E-mail: ask4help@yellowribbon.org

Chapter 34

Suicide, Depression, And Mental Health Hot Lines

Hot lines offer a confidential, anonymous way to speak with a counselor. Talking with a caring, independent person can be helpful if you have a problem, or if you are concerned about a friend or family member. You don't have to be in crisis to call. It is better to deal with problems before they become a crisis. Remember that help is as close as your phone.

Suicide And Depression Hot Lines (Listed Alphabetically)

Access Line
Toll-Free: 888-7-WE HELP (93-4357)

Covenant House Nine-Line
Toll-Free: 800-999-9999

Distress/Suicide Help Line (Canadian)
Toll-Free: 800-232-7288

Hope Line Network
Toll-Free: 800-SUICIDE (784-2433)

National Adolescent Suicide Hot Line
Toll-Free: 800-621-4000

National Suicide Hot Line
Toll-Free: 888-248-2587

Nationwide Crisis Hot Line
Toll-Free: 800-333-4444

Trevor Help Line
To aid in suicide prevention in gay and questioning youth.

Toll-Free: 800-850-8078

Youth Crisis Hot Line
Toll-Free: 800-448-4663

Mental Health Hot Lines And Help Lines (Listed Alphabetically)

Alcohol and Drug Help Line
Provides referrals to local facilities where adolescents and adults can seek help. Brief intervention.

Toll-Free: 800-821-4357

Al-Anon/Alateen Hot Line
Toll-Free: 800-344-2666

American Anorexia/Bulimia Association
Toll-Free: 800-522-2230

Childhelp USA National Child Abuse Hot Line
Toll-Free: 800-422-4453

Eating Disorder Awareness and Prevention
Toll-Free: 800-931-2237

Emergency Shelter For Battered Women (And Their Children)
Toll-Free: 888-291-6228 (24-hour hot line)

Friends Of Battered Women And Their Children
Toll-Free: 800-603-4357

Gay And Lesbian Youth Talk Line
Toll-Free: 800-773-5540

Grief Recovery Institute
Phone: 818-907-9600 (U.S.)
Phone: 519-586-8825 (Canada)

Help Line USA
Phone: 561-659-6900

Kid Help
Children and adolescents in crisis will receive immediate help. Referrals to shelters, mental health services, sexual abuse treatment, substance abuse, family counseling, residential care, adoption/foster care, etc.

Toll-Free: 800-543-7283

National Alliance For The Mentally Ill (And Their Families)
Toll-Free: 800-950-6264

National Association Of Anorexia Nervosa And Related Disorders
Not toll-free, but will call you back if you can't afford the call.

Phone: 847-831-3438

National Domestic Violence Hot Line
Toll-Free: 800-799-7233
Toll-Free TTY: 800-787-3224

National Foundation for Depressive Illness, Inc.
Toll-Free: 800-239-1265

National Mental Health Association
Toll-Free: 800-969-6642

National Organization for Victim Assistance
Toll-Free: 800-879-6682

National Youth Crisis Hot Line
Toll-Free: 800-HIT-HOME (448-4663)

OC Foundation (Obsessive-Compulsive Disorder)
Phone: 203-401-2070

Rape, Abuse, And Incest National Network
Toll-Free: 800-656-4673

SAFE (Self-Abuse Finally Ends)
Toll-Free: 800-DONT-CUT (800-366-8288)

United Way Help Line
Toll-Free: 800-233-HELP (800-233-4357)

Youth Crisis Hot Line
Toll-Free: 800-448-4663

Chapter 35

Support Groups For Suicide Survivors

The organizations listed provide a starting place for locating a support group. A brief listing of resources is included about each organization. The list is alphabetical by the organization's name.

American Association of Suicidology
4201 Connecticut Ave., N.W., Suite 408
Washington, DC 20008
Phone: 202-237-2280
Website: www.suicidology.org; E-mail: info@suicidology.org

AAS provides an online listing by state of suicide survivors support groups. Go to http://www.suicidology.org/associations/1045/files/Support_Groups .cfm on the Internet or call to locate support groups available near you.

Compassionate Friends
P.O. Box 3696
Oak Brook, IL 60522-3696
Toll-Free: 877-969-0010; Fax: 630-990-0246
Website: http://www.compassionatefriends.org
E-mail: nationaloffice@compassionatefriends.org

About This Chapter: The list of organizations in this chapter was compiled from many sources deemed accurate. Inclusion does not constitute endorsement. All contact information was verified in June 2004.

Offers support groups and resources for parents who have had a child die and children who have had a sibling die.

Depression and Bipolar Support Alliance
730 N. Franklin Street, Suite 501
Chicago, IL 60610-7224
Toll-Free: 800-826-3632
Phone: 312-642-0049; Fax: 312-642-7243
Website: http://www.dbsalliance.org
E-mail: questions@dbsalliance.org

DBSA support groups are available for people with depression or bipolar disorder with separate groups available for friends and family members. They have face-to-face support group meetings and online support group meetings. The online meetings meet weekly and follow the general format of face-to-face DBSA support groups. To contact a support group in your state go to http://www.dbsalliance.org/info/findsupport.html or call DBSA for assistance.

Hopeline
2001 N. Beauregard St., 12th floor
Alexandria, VA 22311
Phone: 703-837-3364
Fax: 703-684-7438
Website: http://www.hopeline.com
E-mail: info@hopeline.com

Provides conferences for volunteer and crisis workers where ideas are shared and new information distributed about crisis intervention.

National Alliance for the Mentally Ill (NAMI)
Colonial Place Three
2107 Wilson Blvd., Suite 300
Arlington, VA 22201-3042
Toll-Free: 800-950-NAMI (6264)
Phone: 703-524-7600; TDD: 703-516-7227
Fax: 703-524-9094
Website: http://www.nami.org

Provides online discussion groups and information about support group training and facilitating.

Organization for Attempters and Survivors of Suicide and Interfaith Services (OASSIS)

101 King Farm Blvd., #D401
Rockville, MD 20850
Phone: 240-632-0335; Fax: 240-632-0336
Website: http://www.oassis.org

OASSIS offers conferences for survivors of suicide. Contact them for information about upcoming events.

Samaritans of NY

P.O. Box 1259
Madison Square Station
New York, NY 10159
Suicide Prevention Hot Line: 212-673-3000
Website: http://www.samaritansnyc.org/samhome.html

The Samaritans offer suicide survivor support group meetings in New York city. Call the hot line to leave your name, address, and phone number to receive information about specific meetings.

SAVE—Suicide Awareness Voices of Education

7317 Cahill Road, Suite 207
Minneapolis, MN 55439-2080
Phone: 952-946-7998
Website: http://www.save.org; E-mail: save@save.org

Provides information about what a suicide survivors' support group is and suggestions for running a support group.

Suicide Prevention Resource Center

55 Chapel Street
Newton, MA 02458-1060
Toll-Free: 877-GET-SPRC (438-7772); TTY: 617-964-5448
Website: http://www.sprc.org; E-mail: info@sprc.org

Offers Internet links to suicide survivor support groups and resources for survivors of suicide.

Survivors of Suicide
P.O. Box 4325
La Mesa, CA 91944-4325
Phone: 619-482-0297
Website: http://www.sossd.org
E-mail: sossandiago@yahoo.com

Provides support groups in the San Diego, CA area, offers resources on the website, and provides phone numbers of individuals who will talk with survivors of suicide.

Yellow Ribbon
P.O. Box 644
Westminster, CO 80036-0644
Phone: 303-429-3530
Fax: 303-426-4496
Website: http://www.yellowribbon.org
E-mail: ask4help@yellowribbon.org

Yellow Ribbon has an online directory of support group information available at http://www.yellowribbon.org/SurvivorSupportGroups.html.

Index

Index

Page numbers that appear in *Italics* refer to illustrations. Page numbers that have a small 'n' after the page number refer to information shown as Notes at the beginning of each chapter. Page numbers that appear in **Bold** refer to information contained in boxes on that page (except Notes information at the beginning of each chapter).